Published by Friends Bulletin Corporation
United States of America
www.WesternFriend.org
editor@westernfriend.org

Friends Bulletin Corporation is the publisher of *Western Friend*, the official publication of Pacific, North Pacific, and Intermountain Yearly Meetings of the Religious Society of Friends.
Opinions expressed in this book are of the author, not necessarily of the Yearly Meetings.

Cover design by Meredith Jacobson
Sight&Sense, www.sightandsense.com

TO BE BROKEN AND TENDER:

A QUAKER THEOLOGY FOR TODAY

Margery Post Abbott

All or portions of the following have been included in this volume and are used with permission:

"A Tender Broken Meeting," *Friends Bulletin*, Vol. 72, No. 7, September 2001.

"Friends, A Broken, Tender People?" *Friends Journal*, Vol. 52, No. 10, October 2006.

"A Tender Broken Meeting," Keynote address to Intermountain Yearly Meeting, Friends World Committee for Consultation Wider Quaker Fellowship pamphlet, 2001.

"What Does it Mean to Call Oneself a Friend?" Friends World Committee for Consultation Wider Quaker Fellowship pamphlet, 1999.

"What Does It Mean to Call Oneself a Friend?" *The Carillion*, Vol. 1, No. 8, November 2003.

"Whose DNA is it Anyway?" *Friends Journal*, Vol. 53, No. 2, February 2007.

"A Friend of God," in *Enlivened By the Mystery: Quakers and God* (Western Friend, 2009).

"A Concise Sermon on the Mount," by Peggy Senger Parsons (unpublished).

›

Contents

ACKNOWLEDGMENTS

This book has been long in the birthing and gone through several iterations as I have sought ways to speak of my faith as a liberal, unprogrammed Friend. The original impetus to write came from John Punshon when I had lunch with him one day at Earlham School of Religion, and his support of all my work over the years has been invaluable.

Many members of my Meeting community have heard and commented on this work as it evolved and this material has been the basis of workshops as well as plenary presentations in the U.S, and in Britain. The basic outline of the book became clear when I gave the keynote talk as Friend-in-Residence at Intermountain Yearly Meeting.

In addition to thanks for the hard work of Kathy Hyzy, editor of *Western Friend* publications and Jessica Bucciarelli who helped with editing and proofreading, I am indebted to the members of my Support Committee, who were appointed by Multnomah Monthly Meeting, and the more informally named members of my Writers' Group. These groups, which evolved over time, include Ron Marson, Kate Holleran, Kirby Urner, Susan Riggs, Tina Tau McMahon, Timothy Travis, Carole Spencer, MaryKate Morse, Carol Urner, Judy Maurer and Rachel Hardesty. Ben Dandelion and Jane Elder Wulff have been most helpful in reading and commenting on the manuscript at different stages. And above all, thanks to my husband, Carl, who has been most patient with me and my various efforts to bring this manuscript to fruition over the years.

INTRODUCTION

These days, when I want to describe someone I would like as a mentor, or a healthy, vibrant Quaker Meeting, I tend to use the words "broken and tender." A broken, tender community contains many individuals who have found that place in themselves where they can be still: a place where love has broken apart the bounds of the ego. Such people are transparent: compassion is visible in their movements and intent. They are formed by the Meeting even as they shape it. With even a few such people present, community is more tender in its care for one another and more passionate in its concern for the well-being of the world.

A broken, tender person or Meeting is far from flawless. People still bump up against each other roughly and do foolish things. People still hurt each other even when the intention is not there. But there is space for seeing to the heart of the matter and coming to know what was meant. There is space for mending what was broken and coming to forgiveness.

This book articulates the way I see God at work in the hearts of individuals so that they are tender to the pain of the world and the selfish power of the ego is broken apart. Here, I also name some of the ways Friends' practice and faith help form strong individuals able to challenge the destructive values and institutions of the world around them.

This narrative is informed by my own story of being broken open by God's love and tenderly re-formed within such a community. As I learned more about the faith I was raised in and have claimed as an adult, I found extra layers of meaning underlying various of our practices and testimonies which have been important in my growth both personally and as part of a Meeting. Part of my calling is to share what I have learned with others.

A Transforming Way

Many of us experience a point in our lives when it is time to take stock, to review where we are going, and to move forward on a path which reflects our values and our hopes. This hiatus may be voluntary, or it may come without warning. Upon my father's death in 1991, I found myself suddenly confronted with the reality of the Eternal Presence in the world. Until then, I defined my faith in terms of action: what Friends call the testimonies of peace, simplicity, equality, community and integrity. Mysticism was an abstract concept. Theology seemed irrelevant.

Early Friends rejected academic theology and church-imposed creeds. They saw both as dry and devoid of life. While George Fox, the founder of Quakerism, and others wrote much that can be called "theology," their sole purpose was to point others to the living reality of Christ present. Yet the letters of Margaret Fell, Isaac Penington and others offered spiritual guidance and encouragement to individuals, theological and practical instruction to Meetings, and warnings to persecutors of the danger to their souls. These Friends also wrote many tracts defending their faith in a time when blasphemy, and even worshiping outside the established church were grounds for imprisonment and fines. Thus, when I speak of "theology" I follow their practice of referring to what they personally knew of God, not some academic exercise or what I've heard from other people. But I also hope that what I write will help others to find their way and to articulate what unites Friends as a body, as well as what gives life to us as individuals.

The intensity of that mystical opening in 1991 sent me into the Quaker journals which spoke of such encounters with Christ Jesus. Theology – the way we speak of the nature of God and all that is holy — began to make sense and allowed me to integrate this new inner life with a life of activism. It gave my head and heart a place to meet and helped me articulate my experience of spiritual growth and discernment. As I named the Eternal at work in me, contrasts sharpened and my soul and brain became less at odds. The Light exposed traps which had too long held me in a place of fear, and highlighted the ways in which worship reshapes social justice actions. One thread running quietly through the book is Friends' commitment to peace and the multiple ways this might shape us even in our failures to live into it. The peace testimony asks for nonviolence at many levels, as well as removing the seeds of war. In it I find a commitment to engage without rancor people whose beliefs seem in sharp contrast to mine. I have lived this out among Quakers who are deeply divided across the theological and political spectrum. I have had to deal with my own prejudices and fears in order to be faithful to this testimony. My work benefits from the pressure of evangelical Friends to articulate and examine my own beliefs.

I have questions about what underlies the work of bridging divides, directly or indirectly: How does a person of faith who is not at all certain about Christianity (especially as that term gets battered about in 21st-century America) speak about that hope which grounds her work and life? Is everything up for grabs? How does community inform individual spirituality and growth? Is Christianity hopelessly bankrupt, the tool of those who want to press just one version of morality? As the world grows smaller, how can Christians, Muslims, Hindus, Buddhists and all the myriad of others learn to cooperate so that all might enjoy this earth?

As a Friend, I am part of a faith community which nourishes my longing for answers to these questions and supports me when I am raw from the rubbing. I am part of a faith community which links back well over 300 years, then back thousands more, yet has fragmented itself again and again and forgotten much of its way. I am part of a faith community that as it links forward in hope for unseeable generations needs to lift the weight of prejudice and disdain for other members of that community today. I am part of a faith community which seeks to stand with all who are oppressed, speak for justice and integrity, and follow the path of nonviolence.

My answers to such queries are inexorably linked to a faith grounded in Christ which simultaneously affirms that Truth is present in many forms. This Truth is not uniquely bound to any creed but can be recognized by actions made visible in any life filled with the mercy, justice and humility which flow from Life and Love offering hope to the world.

A Bit of Historical Context

George Fox, Margaret Fell, James Nayler, Edward Burrough, Elizabeth Houghton, William Penn, Robert Barclay, Mary Dyer. These early Friends are only a few of the individuals who shook English society and roused the fury of the established church. They suffered imprisonment and even death because of their direct knowledge that Christ was come to lead his people himself. The immediacy of this experience shaped their actions and words. The Sermon on the Mount was not an abstraction. It described the way of being which seemed natural to individuals who knew the Seed formed within, and sank down into holy reliance on the Light of Christ as the measure of life.

These people were audacious enough to call themselves "Friends": Friends of Truth, the Truth, the Way, the Life that is Jesus. They were called "Quakers" by others deriding their shaking as they worshiped. Both names stuck. They rejected the conventional wisdom of the Christian church that humanity is waiting for some distant time when Jesus will reappear and the kingdom of God will be realized. They said that Christ's Light is here now to guide all who are open to the Truth.

The Truth of God also searches the human heart and shows all that is contrary to this absolute love – much of what is considered the convention in human cultures – and prunes it away. This Light of Christ leads away from materialism, from flattery, from stepping on others to gain prestige or advantage, from pride, from hatred, from frittering away life, from destroying the earth, from violence. The Light of Christ leads to respect for each person, a way of life which takes away even the occasion for war, complete honesty, a way of being attentive to divine leading and the sacredness which is part of all creation so that all things take their rightful place, and a transparency so complete that divine love is visible in all relationships.

This community, now called the Religious Society of Friends, is widely scattered around the world. Some individuals among us still live out of that power and certainty, acting with quiet conviction in a way which ripples through society, but as a body, we have lost the clarity of vision which once unified us and made us a threat to the established order. Our failures are the failings of our humanity, not of the vision or the way. Many of the questions which push us apart are questions which all humanity faces: Is the Way, the Truth and the Life available to all humanity or only those who profess Christ Jesus as their personal Savior? When is the use of violence acceptable? What constitutes loving relationships?

My faith calls me to encourage all people to wait and to attend on the still, small voice which transforms the heart. In the silence of our soul and in gathered worship, we encounter the Seed, the Holy Light that guides and admonishes us. Through this Light, we learn to take up the cross to self-will and enter into the suffering of the world with compassion. Our lives can show others something of what it means to live in what I think of as the City of God, which honors at its center the waters of Life and the tree for the healing of the nations. Ever again we are called into times of waiting when we step back from the pressures of the world so that we might attend to God's way, becoming broken and tender in the process.

If we can live as a broken, tender community which calls us forth away from fear, we can be transparent to the Light in a way which makes visible to the world the spaciousness of God's love for all people. We can count ourselves among those who make visible the City of God.

This Volume

I wish I could say this book provides the ultimate Quaker answer to achieving all this, or solid answers to these questions. Rather, it is a picture of my struggle to be open to the Way. I have seen glimpses of that original power in others' lives and moments when it flows certain in my veins. I have been given a measure of Light and offer it in its incompleteness. The answers I come to for myself are sometimes like koans – those paradoxical Buddhist sayings — for I find that Jesus is the Way, the Truth and the Life, but that Way is present in all true faiths, even those without organized churches. I am a pacifist, but can accept that with proper constraints, the state must at times step in forcefully to stop violence. While I am more patient than many in my Meeting with those who object to same-gender marriage, I affirm the rightness of loving, respectful relationships between equals no matter their gender. I believe in the sacredness of life: executions clearly harm the souls of those who carry them out as well ending a life. I am not so clear when life begins — when does the transition happen between being a few cells with the potential for life and having a soul – but am not ready to leave that decision to the state.

In order to express some of the complexity of the changes I experienced, at times my writing is meditative and invites the reader to share in a sense of God present among us. At times I wrestle with the historical theology of Quakerism and concepts which prod me off any sense of self-satisfaction or settling for an easy way. At yet other times the pragmatic dimension of my work among Friends is visible as I reflect on practices which connect me to the larger whole. The study guide included at the end of this volume is intended as a way for individuals or small groups to engage more deeply with the theology and concepts presented in each chapter.

I find my spiritual home among Quakers who are accepting of a wide range of beliefs and who worship in unprogrammed Meetings (I use "liberal Quakers" as a shorthand for this.) Friends have our own language for much of what we do as well as our own understanding of the Gospel, traced from the early years of Quakerism. I aim at making this language transparent without losing its flavor or getting distracted by definitions, and so I have included a brief glossary. I have capitalized words like "Life," "Spirit" and "Way" when I use them to refer to divine rather than human aspects. All biblical quotations are New Revised Standard Version unless otherwise noted. The "we" of this book is often those of us in liberal, unprogrammed Quaker Meetings, but it can broaden to include anyone who feels connected with the words I write. I use it to invite you into the conversation.

To Be Broken and Tender

Waiting and Attending

WAITING and ATTENDING

Friends are called to expectant waiting, to anticipate the Eternal Presence, to know or to hope to know God as immediate and real. Whether in blinding visions or gentle, intuitive nudges on the heart, we can hear the Spirit and let her guide our feet as we listen, attend and witness to the availability of the Spirit to all people. How hard that can be! How easy that can be! How varied the experience is among all who share this globe.

My own experience was that of *waiting and attending*: for many years I waited passively and without awareness, and for many more years in the more active form I call *attending*, attending on those around me and inwardly attentive for the Unknown. After Love changed my entire awareness in an experience which echoes *the consuming fire* which some early Friends describe, my life was turned in unexpected directions. Waiting and listening perhaps became even more important. Today, patience gradually grows in me and takes new forms. I have learned what it is like to listen with the inner ear and see with the inner eye in order to better *sift through the fears* which once controlled my life and oft times still dance through my consciousness. Remembering that I am held in Love, no matter what, takes regular reminders, both from myself and others.

Having been opened to a new realm of life and awareness of an entirely fresh dimension which seemed to encompass both the universe and my inner life, I found myself having to sift through the fears which had always been present but never faced.

Modern Friends have sat with me as I struggled into new life – into the process of healing and transformation which some might name *salvation*. Other Friends teach me with their lives as well as their words. Our faith is not passive. It is one of engagement, with God, with each other, and with the world.

My soul waits for The Lord,
more than those who watch for the morning,
more than those who watch for the morning.
– Psalm 130:6

Mind and watch to that which quickens and enlivens the soul towards God, and
watch against that which flats and deadens it; for they are both near.
– Isaac Penington, 1671[1]

Come into the true silence and stilling of the fleshly part ... There thou comest to
hear the voice behind thee, ... and directing thee ... and saying to thee, "This is the
way, walk in it." – Isaac Penington, ca. 1670[2]

WAITING AND **1** ATTENDING

O ne day in prayer I saw a mound of clay being worked by two hands,
one the hand of a child, the other the hand of an adult. Then I saw
the infinite faces of Jesus. Some faces were familiar— one, the face in the
children's book of my youth, another the rough-hewn face of a vigorous
Jewish man— the infinite images of Jesus we hold singly and together.
Then I saw a darkness, and in that darkness a door opened up into
incredible beauty and light beyond comprehension.

The closeness of love and friendship—a dimension of holiness made
visible in Jesus—defines my life. Comfort is as simple as a hand on my
knee as I cry. Friendship is as complex as listening to my delights, my
frustrations, and my fury with a willingness to say when I am off track.
Love is full of passion. Love is a deliberate action arising out what I
know of God. Dreams give a place for words and a shape to the ongoing
experiment which is my life.

It has not always been this way. Forty years of waiting preceded
my experience of this vision, and the depths of the opening and
transformation it represents. Years of living into the image of my

taciturn Dad, a mix of athleticism, technological expertise, gentleness, without ever considering I might be loved for myself. That waiting was an unconscious seeking which gradually opened me and made space within me for God's work to be visible. This time made space for me to accept unconditional, infinite love when it broke into my awareness at a moment of grieving my father's death. Only awareness of being loved was enough to change me at the core so I might become more tender to the condition of those I encounter and to myself. In this process I came to know divine Love as powerful comfort and as a huge, not always pleasant, impetus for transformation.

How do I summarize those years of waiting in a few words? I can only hint at the ways I now make sense of my inner journey in the years before a mystical opening and call to ministry totally disoriented my rational mind, breaking open my entire being to a new way of living.

Silence as Absence

The silence of Quaker Meeting for Worship has always been a part of my life. In the 1950s and 60s, as a child I sat each Sunday in the large Meeting room in Philadelphia, watching the sun filter through the blinds, listening to the words offered in worship. I twitched impatiently, inventing games and various methods to make the time go more quickly. At times, I resisted leaving home on Sunday mornings – most notoriously by locking myself in the bathroom – because I disliked First Day School. But between Sundays and the Friends' school I attended on weekdays, I learned much about the Bible and Quaker history as I absorbed the culture around me.

Despite caring parents and energetic teachers, I never gained words to speak of my inner state, or of the Spirit. My father was a lifelong Friend, yet I don't recall ever hearing him, or Mom, speak in Meeting for Worship.

Was my silence learned from family? From culture? As an adult, I see the cultural influences of the period, and in particular the socially-conscious, highly-educated dimension of East Coast culture of the mid-20th Century, which weighed against speaking of feelings or spirituality. Or was silence part of my own temperament? I do not know, but the result was clear. I loved time spent alone and read thick volumes – even the encyclopedia. I knew the flag and capitol of every nation on earth. Doing complicated algebra problems was fun and an important connection with Dad, a mechanical engineer. But my inner sense that I had nothing worth saying, reinforced by a habit of going over things again and again in my head, left me uneasy in company.

Because of my silence I reached young adulthood with few real friends, despite knowing many people. After college I literally fled the East Coast, marrying right out of college and moving halfway across the country. But I still felt the pull to worship among Friends, as did my husband Carl, who had grown up Methodist. We were active in a Chicago Meeting while I ran a biochemistry research lab and Carl worked on his PhD in urban history.

Sitting in the silence was essential to my well-being, even if I did not know why. I might spend the hour going over what needed doing or worrying about things I had done wrong, but being there was important. Something worked deep inside me in ways I did not understand.

Preparation

In my thirties, I was actively drawn into the life of sustaining a Friends' Meeting when Carl and I moved to Portland, Oregon. Within a year I was clerk of a committee and started to learn how being a clerk differed from leadership in secular organizations. Friends pushed me into new roles and different ways of seeing my faith. It took a long time, but they exposed me to new ways of listening and put me in the way of the Spirit.

Still, I did not know how to listen to the guidance of the Inward Teacher. Such prompting seemed only for the saints, or for those gifted in a way I was not. I could hear the external call to live according to the testimonies of Friends: the call to equality, the call to peace, the call to simplicity, the call to integrity. I lived them as best I could.

Meanwhile, I built a career working for the port authority in Portland. Having stepped away from completing a PhD in biochemistry, my own insecurities continued to push me to act in ways which won the approval of others. I was afraid of challenging the status quo. Just as I had always sought to show that a woman could follow in her father's footsteps, excelling in science and sports, I now focused on proving that a woman could work in the seaport business as well as a man. I lost track of the larger picture, and the activism that had been so central

to my twenties— peace marches against the Vietnam War, founding
a chapter of the National Organization for Women (NOW), heading
the Civic League in the only integrated neighborhood in Norfolk,
Virginia, and working to pass the Equal Rights Amendment—faded
into the background. I became used to running meetings both in secular
organizations and in the Quaker manner of listening and drawing others
out, although I embarrassed myself numerous times with my shyness.
At work I met with a diverse array of people who had conflicting ideas
about the Portland waterfront and tried to find ways through the tangle
which might benefit the whole. These all turned out to be foundational
lessons that helped to break me open to God.

Attending

Attending is a word intriguing in its multiple meanings. Paying attention
is the first sense which comes to mind: I watch when crossing the street
so as not to get run over. And I've always been good at attending events
when I said I would. But I think more relevant for me is the sense of
attending to others, of being in service.

Having grown up with silent worship, it seemed natural to me to sit
quietly— even if I did not always use the time well. In the silence, I felt
something which nourished me. I felt sustenance and a perspective
for going about my daily business. I felt both prodded and comforted.
Messages spoken could irritate or inspire. What I felt was never quite
the same from week to week. I had no words to express what I felt in the
silence, and at times went for months or years without setting foot in a
Meetinghouse. But always, I was drawn back to Meeting. And once there, I
started to pay attention in a fuller way.

My path to an inward knowing of prayer as "paying attention" – to God
as well as to others – was one which needed many guides. When two
members of my Meeting in Portland, Meg Jump and Barbara Janoe,
encouraged me to accompany them as they visited among Friends, I
accepted the invitation. Barbara took me with her when she led a retreat
at a small Meeting a five hour drive from Portland. There I had my first
experience of "Quaker Dialogues," a method of learning about the inward
experience of others and sharing one's own experience of God. Not very
aware of my own reactions, and not having even considered keeping a
journal, I can only surmise that this "Dialogue" worked on me over the

months and years as I continued to sit in the silent worship on Sundays.

The Roots of A Leading

Growth into tenderness to the Spirit took a long time in me, and required immersion in other people's dreams before I could name my own. In 1985 Cilde Grover, an evangelical Friend from Portland, attended the World Gathering of Young Friends and returned with a burning awareness that it was possible to break through the wariness and hostility dividing evangelicals and liberals. Annis Bleeke, a liberal Friend about forty years old, went to the 1985 Triennial Meeting of the Friends World Committee for Consultation (FWCC) in Mexico and independently realized a similar desire to create new connections in place of antagonism. These two women traveled together in the Pacific Northwest, speaking about the fire these gatherings lit in them. Some of this fire was expressed in the Epistle written by the Young Friends Gathering, which declared in part:

> We have come together from every continent, separated by language, race, culture, ways we worship God, and beliefs about Christ and God … We have been challenged, shaken up, at times even enraged, intimidated, and offended by these differences in each other. We have grown from this struggle and have felt the Holy Spirit … Our differences are our richness, but also our problem…. After much struggle we have discovered that we can proclaim this: there is a living God at the centre of all, who is available to each of us as a Present Teacher at the very heart of our lives.[4]

Both a proclamation and a challenge, this letter to Friends worldwide describes the tension and mixed feelings these international gatherings stir up, the way such gatherings work on the heart and the hope they breathe. Cilde, who was comfortable describing Jesus as her personal savior and was used to programmed meeting and messages from Quaker pastors, and Annis, who was used to worshiping out of the silence with Friends uneasy about even naming Jesus, jointly found themselves led to break through the theological and cultural barriers which push Friends so far apart. Soon, they asked me to be part of a group of women—later named Multwood, as half were from Multnomah Monthly Meeting and half from Reedwood Friends Church—who would read books together and talk about their faith. I joined this group readily out of friendship with Annis, but with few expectations beyond discomfort.

Multwood's roots in those two congregations span much of the spectrum of faith found among American Friends today. Reedwood Friends Church is over a century old and is part of a Yearly Meeting formed by 19th-century Quaker migrants who established the town of Newberg, Oregon, and adopted a pastoral style of worship more in tune with other Protestants affected by the Wesleyan Holiness Movement. By contrast, my Meeting, Multnomah, exists because of efforts by Friends who moved west after World War II. These Friends wanted to create an unprogrammed Meeting in Portland where they could gather in expectant silence without any specific expectations about belief.

Cilde's and Annis's leading gradually grew in me as well, as I struggled with my own perceptions about who Friends are. Just moving to the Pacific Northwest where Friends' churches outnumber unprogrammed Meetings by five to one was a shock, as I had never even *heard* of a Quaker church growing up. Engaging with these "other" Friends forced me to become more conscious of my own suspicion and distrust of evangelical Christians and my presumption that they would condemn all who did not accept Jesus as Savior. That fear of judgment was sharp and played on the raw spot of inadequacy inside me.

In addition to our monthly Multwood discussions, Cilde and Annis convinced me to work with Friends World Committee for Consultation (FWCC), as a way to build connections among disparate groups of Quakers worldwide, and soon I was organizing regional FWCC gatherings. These gatherings kept in front of me the question, "Who are Quakers?" The preaching and singing in the Friends' churches seemed alien to my sensibilities honed in Meetings where people gathered in silence. Christianity and the Bible were part of my Meeting in Philadelphia, but I was never pushed to hold particular beliefs.

In living rooms around Portland, Multwood women made cautious inquiry about each other's way of worship and tested reactions to words which seemed alien. Our host acted as facilitator for the evening. Mary Kate Morse, the professor among us, often suggested books on spiritual formation to read and discuss, but we rarely spoke of our individual faith for the first several years. We were tentative in reaching out as we sought to be tender with each other and with ourselves until we reached a point of trust where we could be more honest and open about our personal faith and doubts. Women have moved in and out of the group as lives changed, but we continue to meet decades later.

In those early days of Multwood, I soon noticed my inability to articulate my own faith beyond describing what we are not: no pastor, no set order of service or sermon, no sacraments, no creed. If pushed further, I would refer someone to a history book in the Meeting library. My knowledge of Friends was about past events rather than theology. This further complicated my experience of the tensions among Friends. I persevered in my work across Yearly Meetings, but as an organizer and behind-the-scenes worker, not as a spokesperson or visionary.

Watching, listening and waiting kept working on my heart. Despite the disappointments and failures of some other efforts to bring Friends together, the conviction that we share much that is essential grew. It was not yet a leading, but it worked the ground for later flowering. Questions formed. Assumptions were shaken and destroyed. I could no longer claim my heritage as "true Quakerism." Growing respect and caring broke open my tendency to easy answers and dismissive lumping of "them" as off-base.

Becoming Still, Turning In

In the mid-1980s, as Multwood was slowly growing, I was drawn deeper into the life of my Meeting. Multnomah was in the midst of an intense and volatile process which eventually led to our recognition of same-sex relationships in the same way we married heterosexual couples. In 1987, when the consideration of marriage was at its most acrimonious, Carl and I were out of town while he took an academic sabbatical. We missed several very angry Business Meetings, and were not associated with one group or another within the Meeting. It became clear, both to me and to the Meeting nominating committee, that on our return I should become clerk of the Meeting.

In practice, being clerk required both study and personal preparation. Workshops on the practical dimensions helped. My love of reading came into play as I sought advice across the centuries, often urging reflection as well as engagement with a contentious Meeting. I sought to know what it meant to listen to what was not said as I became more conscious of body language to help me sense beyond the words.

One factor in developing an inward awareness of the movement of the Spirit was the outwardly simple task of closing Meeting for Worship. I do not normally wear a watch, and there is no clock in the Meeting room. People have a tendency to offer vocal ministry towards the end of the hour, sometimes spilling over. I could cheat a bit on the time – often someone near me had a watch I could see. But I tried to hear if worship was truly over. I became much more aware of the underlying unity and connections among the people gathered. At times I could sense when someone I could not see had something to say. A seed inside me began to awaken and become a part of my conscious being.

I started to learn to attend, and know that there will be a Guide for us, "livingly pointing out" the way of truth, peace and love, as Isaac Penington once said. Looking back, I can see that this is when I first started to hear that still, small voice of God within, directing me on the path of all that is holy. Both the Multwood women and my Meeting were teaching me about the signposts we can offer one another and the quiet ways we can help one another through the dark, fog, and exhaustion which sometimes confuse the path or weigh us down.

Turmoil

Though I could not see it then, a sharp transformation in my heart began almost a year before my father died. I was attending a retreat with all the other Friends from the Pacific Northwest who were preparing to attend the 1991 World Gathering of Friends. I had learned that Dad had cancer and probably did not have long to live. In the rawness of my pain, I could not bear to be in the group even though several good friends were there. Instead, I skipped meals and walked the dirt roads amid the tall trees. Even when friends tracked me down, my heart was so tender I could not let them know why I was so broken.

My Dad's cancer and the month I spent in Kenya are all tumbled together inside me. Both upset all my sense of the order of things and blasted at my best attempts to control my life. Dad was from a long-lived family: finding a melanoma in his seventies was not on my agenda. It was a total violation of my image of myself and my family. It cracked the pride which had always quietly been there been there and brought me face to face with mortality in a way that left me shouting at the heavens. And, of course, trying to do it all alone. Despite the growing circle around me, despite Multwood, I could not speak of my fears and pain. About the same time, I had learned of the World Conference. I knew I was to go, despite having no formal reason to be there. And my application was accepted.

Living with a Kenyan family for part of that time, then being immersed in the Conference, are a book in themselves. I will share only one fragment of that experience. I was assigned to write the daily bulletin, a job expected to take an hour or so a day. I had a room with two expensive computers, including one with a good battery, and a Xerox machine. But the ferocious thunderstorms of western Kenya undid all our planning and technology. The power outages were so constant that even the battery failed and I had to resort to a typewriter, then post a few copies at strategic spots on campus. It wasn't the personal copy for each attender that we "Europeans" expected. In the meantime, frantic searches for back-ups and parts meant the job took all afternoon most days and became a burden rather than a comforting escape from all the strangers surrounding me.

During the time my father was ill, as I had for much of my life, I played tennis weekly. These games took on some of the character of meditation and kept seeming to be a metaphor for my condition. I was hitting beautiful shots – aces and put-aways – interspersed with whop-de-do losers. All the while I couldn't keep my shoelaces tied.

The next step in my journey was unexpected and intense, probably because of how tightly I was closed off from my own emotions and spiritual life. Jeremiah speaks of Yahweh's covenant with humankind, "I will put my law within them, and I will write it on their hearts; . . ." a promise central to Friends' ways. A few prophets are given direct, clear words as Jeremiah was. My daily experience of divine guidance today is that of gentle nudging, as seems to be the case with most people I meet. But there have been a few occasions when God worked on my heart with a directness and clarity that was shattering. It was the initial shattering — the consuming fire — which set me so strongly on the path of seeking words for my faith, and the desire to communicate what I have come to know.

This opened me so, that it cut me to the heart. Then I … cried bitterly … in my spirit to the Lord: "We are all thieves, we are all thieves. We have taken the Scriptures in words, and know nothing of them in ourselves."
– Margaret Fell, 1652[5]

From this time forward I make you hear new things, hidden things that you have not known. – Isaiah 48:6

THE CONSUMING FIRE

In 1652 Margaret Fell had a sharp revelation that caused her to cry in her spirit, "We are all thieves; we are all thieves. We have taken the Scriptures in words, and know nothing of them in ourselves."[6] These words told of the searing power of the Light burning through Fell's soul. These words marked her transition from a reliance on outward guidance of the church to awareness of Christ Within and her own obligation to listen and follow that Guide. Two years later she could write an epistle to all Friends with assurance about the work of that Inward Guide, which "opens the Mystery of God, … [and] who is a Consuming Fire to all that is not of him."[7] The quickness with which she stepped into leadership and spoke with the authority evident in this letter bespeaks her preparation for this opening: her thorough knowledge of the Bible, her privileged position in society, and the long period of seeking which preceded her encounter with George Fox.

My transformation began as sharply as Fell's, but took longer in its realization. Only looking back can I see it as the result of a long search. In 1991, in my early forties, in many ways I felt lost. After nearly five years of interacting with evangelical Friends, I wasn't at all clear about who Quakers were. I was clear about attending the Fifth World Conference of Friends in Kenya that summer, even though I was not a Yearly Meeting representative. I was disoriented by my father's cancer. My work as a planning consultant was erratic: good jobs alternated with time spent marketing myself. I became more and more vulnerable and in despair; a precondition to being opened and broken.

That December, I flew from the West Coast to Philadelphia to be with my father in his last days. The Sunday after Dad died, when Carl had not yet arrived for the memorial and no one in the family would accompany me, I headed off alone to an unfamiliar Meeting. I sat in worship in my Sunday best and with my usual stiff upper lip — in my family, we don't cry, and certainly not in public. As soon as someone rose to offer vocal ministry, something inside me cracked and the tears flowed. They flowed the entire hour. I must have been a sight – with no handkerchief to boot! In that hour, my life-long sense of worthlessness was consumed in all encompassing love as I sat, enfolded in God's arms.

Mickey Edgerton, a friend who had relocated from Seattle, was there at worship, sitting in the old facing bench and feeling (as she later told me) apologetic for what she perceived as a "popcorn" Meeting: the vocal ministry was frequent and seemed disconnected to her ears. Yet every message "spoke to my condition" and opened up my heart in some way. A woman's song spoke of hope. In the rambling of an old man was a reassurance that I could speak to the condition of others without being eloquent. Throughout the hour I experienced invisible arms around me, holding me and guiding me.

Mickey took me home with her, offering more space for my tears, an attentive ear attuned to the inward motion of the Spirit, and words which helped me recognize the grounding present amidst all the upheaval. By that evening, I wrote two letters. One, out of a fresh tenderness to the spirit in others, was to a close friend, apologizing for the ways I had treated her poorly. The other spelled out a call to ministry. At the time I thought this call only meant I had to offer a few words out of the silence during Meeting for Worship. I had no hint of the books and workshops which would emerge from this experience. This initial call also included the need for a clearness committee to help me with discernment, and a need to seek professional counseling to address the personal pain bottled deep inside.

Friends believe every person is called to be a minister: attuned to the Inward Guide and able to allow the Light to be visible in their lives. But the thought of *me* being called to ministry was a shock, even simply a call to the vocal ministry – to stand and speak during worship when words rise up inside me.

Some of my evangelical friends teased me and said this was my conversion experience. "Transformation" or "mystical opening" or sometimes "*metanoia*" – the Greek word for turning – are easier words for me. Most often I name it a "call to ministry." My friends' word, "conversion," in this context implies acceptance of Jesus as Lord. Uncomfortable with this, in my usual fashion I headed to a biblical dictionary where I was pleased to find experiences in the Bible labeled as "conversion" illustrating a call to a new relationship with God or a new ministry. So perhaps my friends are right after all, but not as they expected.

One use of the word "conversion" can be seen in George Fox's frequent description of conversion "from death to life" or "from darkness to light."[8] "Even through that darkness was I brought, which covered-over all the world, and which chained down all, and shut up all in the death," Fox said in 1647, conveying his place as one of many who are thus bound up in pain or fear. Then he stated the hope for everyone: "And the same eternal power of God, which brought me through these things, was that which afterwards shook the nations, priests, professors, and people."[9]

This opening of the soul to the Divine Comforter is at the heart of Friends' encounter with the Light, whether it be by sudden, mystical experience, by a steady sense of the Spirit beginning in childhood, or by a gradual growth into awareness of the gentle nudges on the soul often named as intuition.

Perhaps I could say I was "convinced" if we still used the old Quaker meaning more clearly expressed by "conviction of sin" rather than the more modern sense of rationally deciding to join Friends. This is what Margaret Fell came to know when she first heard George Fox speak: that she had sinned — she had been separated from God – *and* now was no longer held captive by sin. Knowing Christ formed in her heart, and the living Spirit guiding her, she warned others to "be silent, and to wait low in the Silence … And be sure, that that which you judge in another, be cast out in your selves."

"The consuming fire" is a traditional way of speaking of this divine encounter. As I learned, the Inward Light is unconditional love, yet at the same time, it is a searing of the soul. The Light pierces with total honesty into our behaviors, words and attitudes. This is not an easy thing to experience! In the refiner's fire, metal is purified so that it can be made useful, as a tool or as a sword. The fire of the Light likewise burns away the dross of life – the foolish or harmful things we have done – to re-form us closer to the image of God.

Many Baptisms

In many churches, baptism follows a conversion experience. I have never experienced water baptism. Reportedly, my Presbyterian grandmother never forgave my mother for not having her four Quaker children christened or baptized; she was convinced this condemned us eternally. I don't know if this story is true, but this is the memory I carry.

"Quakers don't do the sacraments" is a familiar phrase. More accurately, Quakers consider the sacraments to be inward and spiritual and believe that the outward signs can too easily become a symbol which hides rather than reveals the spiritual reality. I accepted this statement with an emphasis on "don't do" for most of my life. The sacraments held no particular meaning for me.

One confirmation of God's sense of humor is that I now see why my spiritual ancestors insisted on the inward experience of baptism. In fact, Quakers often spoke of "baptism of the Spirit," "baptism in the heart," "baptism by fire" or, occasionally, "many baptisms." Romans 6:3 states, "Do you not know that all of us who have been baptized into Christ Jesus were baptized into his death?" and was a reference they knew well. This inward baptism that they knew was a direct experience of the Holy Spirit – an experience of cleansing, forgiveness and renewal, of death of the old being and of new life. It could happen more than once in one's life and often seemed to be unexpected. Reading their words, I feel echoes in my own experience: "So *that's* what they meant!"

By this measure, something within has died and something new has sprung up in its place. I certainly experienced a dying of my presumptions that knowing the world rationally was enough and that I was in control of my life. More than that, the gut feeling I held so tightly – that I was unworthy of love along with an accompanying denigration of self — died in the overwhelming reality of God's love. In place of unworthiness I came to realize a sense of divine love flowing through me when I responded to those gentle nudges on the heart. In place of the totally rational view of the world came a fuller use of all my senses and the new inner eye and ear which were now part of my consciousness.

And Friends, Take heed of that Spirit that still will seek to excuse himself, and to diminish and hide that which is not well, … this is the Spirit of the world, and is out of Truth, … – Elizabeth Hendricks, 1672[10]

[Jesus said] *"Do not judge, so that you may not be judged. For with the judgment you make you will be judged, and the measure you give is the measure you will get."* – Matthew 7:1-5

SIFTING THROUGH FEARS

One Sunday during worship, a young woman spoke how that same morning she woke to a wing brushing her cheek. A small bird was thrashing about, banging against the glass near her head as it sought to exit her window. She took a towel to guide it out, but the bird slipped between the two sections of the window in its panic. Watching its frightened actions, she broke the window so it might find release. Still it did not fly free. She reached in yet again with a towel to gently set it free, and it took off into the open air.

I carry with me a similar image of a caged bird resisting release. How often do we panic when the Inward Guide offers us freedom? How often do we fight back when the hand of God seeks to move us from the place where we are stuck and damaged? Why do we so fear that which will save us? Impatience and fear are tangled. The holy delight too often is masked.

This same fear colors my relationships. Childhood patterns of finding ways to be invisible lasted long into adulthood. I was slow to sense how stiff my body gets when someone questions me or to be open even to myself when I am angry. Self-knowledge and honesty are central to the spiritual life. Psychologists tell us a lot about "projection." Jesus tells us to look first to the "log" in our own eye before we attempt to remove the mote in our neighbor's. Unless we know the byways of our own inner landscape, how can we recognize the path marked by the Spirit?

The recognition of our own motes and logs is not sufficient in itself. Awareness of the Inward Guide is a first step. The sifting – the discernment – is part of the ongoing mechanism of transformation. Yes, there is a day I can mark on the calendar and say that on this day my life changed. But it would have been nothing but a memory without the years of learning to discern which aspects of my life were permeated by bark beetles and where healthy new shoots might grow.

Sifting

When I experienced the leading to take up a ministry of speaking and writing, I was nearly paralyzed by fear, and fear is the central component of what Isaac Penington calls "the enemy" who "kindles great distress." Fear does not easily let go its hold. Thus, one crucial step is to recognize fear and taste its character. I've come to recognize many flavors of fear. Fear can be sharp and alive, a basic reflex which tells us that danger is at hand. Knowing real danger and responding to it with calm action are crucial. Confidence in God, clear awareness of strengths and weaknesses, and practice in ways of dealing with danger, can allow us to react without panic and take leadership when appropriate.

In contrast, some fear is old, so old I can almost smell the dust and mold. Fears of ugly words and of an angry older brother, which were real in childhood, have no weight when examined in the light of adult experience. Yet for too long I treated these fears as if they were still protecting me from some immediate threat. To lay these aside took attention and awareness, but was not particularly hard once I got the knack of it.

So often I imagine how others see me, magnifying my own insecurities and negative opinions. Or I put thoughts in someone's head which have no basis in reality. I judge them even as I assume they are judging me. I give them power over me. As I shift my focus to the Giver of Life and away from my imagination, my smile is easier and my words firmer. I step out of a self-imposed invisibility. As a result, I have had to work to rebuild relationships – asking what was meant rather than assuming a desire to harm then fuming quietly; suspending judgment, and offering more of myself rather than expecting the other to be the only one vulnerable. Once more I need to attend to the person in front of me. Relationships cannot be forced or based on one person having power over another. Respect, caring and mutual empowerment thrive in the movement of the Spirit.

Still other fears live and are exaggerated only in my own mind. There might be reason to be nervous, but I am skilled at imagining disastrous scenarios. I either make myself so nervous and upset that I generate the scene I most feared, or I freeze and refuse to participate at all. To set these fears in proper proportion requires trust. This occurs each time I must speak from my heart. It is frightening at various levels, but not truly dangerous. I risk having others disagree with me, or that they will dismiss me as irrelevant or foolish. This has been the hardest set of fears for me to deal with.

More and more often I recognize and laugh at the tapes which replay in my head. But speaking of my faith in public requires I let go, speak what the Spirit requires of me, and trust that I have not run ahead of the Guide. When I can focus on what is needed, then my fears take their rightful place and drop away.

One day, while feeling quite discouraged, I began to doodle the word: AWFUL! That was how I was experiencing the world – things were awful. Yet writing the word over and over, it became a form of prayer. My being shifted and suddenly I saw the AWE which was embedded in my heart. Here I began to glimpse why the Psalmists sing of fear of the Lord: a rightful fear before the mystery and power of the Eternal.

Each one of us must find where our fears lie and seek to discern when they are valid and when they should be set aside. At times the indicators of the path are like marks in the dirt defining the mountain trail. I have a tendency, however, to kick some dust over those small arrows in the dirt when I don't like the look of the path to which they point. Much wisdom in many traditions besides our own indicates that each time we do this – resist the leading – the harder it is to find the path in the future. And that, ultimately, the habit of kicking up dust will become so thoroughly well-ingrained that we no longer even see the arrows. Despite my ambivalence, I keep encountering further markers for the journey.

Examples of following the path are plentiful in my life: picking up the phone to call a friend when I am feeling an intense desire to hide; responding to Carl's suggestion that maybe work I had done for a class should become a book; opening a book apparently at random and finding just the words I need; acting on the sense that I was to travel among Friends – actions large and small.

Fear is by no means the only block to healing or obstacle to attending to the voice of the Spirit. For some it may be anger, or a need to control, or desire for wealth, but the underlying tests for discerning the leadings of the Light are the same. The variations are substantial and, as in my case, professional help as well as community support can be invaluable. Holding one's life up to the Light of hope and using of discernment can change everyday actions and make space for radical reorientation, as happened to a man I met when giving a talk. During the Vietnam War, his family and the pastor at a Protestant church he attended all expected him to enlist. Yet he found this action to be at odds with all his pastor had preached over the years. The refusal to enlist or cooperate with the draft changed the course of his entire life, he told us gratefully.

For me, this reorientation was from virtual silence (my report cards from school always complained, "Marge never says anything") to becoming a public speaker. The fears which kept me from speaking were not simple to name, much less break. I had to develop a regular practice of reading devotional books, praying and keeping a journal. Three f/Friends met with me faithfully and were patient with my faltering attempts to articulate even basic ideas. As I attempted to give talks to my Meeting about what I was learning, I found it essential to write out every word and had to be constantly told to "speak up." Through all this, I had to learn, then keep asking myself the various questions Friends have traditionally used for discernment (see box).

Being attuned to the Spirit also allows a different response to the wounds we inflict and receive throughout our lives. I have never been able to avoid periodically hurting the people most close to me, not to mention strangers, whether through inattentiveness, preoccupation with other things, or any of a million other reasons. When I am paying attention to the Inward Monitor I am less apt to do such harm. When I am focused on my own needs, and do harm, attention to the Light makes me more aware and prompts me to make amends. I don't always respond, but the potential to do less damage is there. Similarly, when I am listening to the Inward Guide, I am less apt to take offense when others inadvertently hurt me. This entire process seems akin to what the Buddhists call "non-attachment" – not holding on to my own sense of being the center of the universe so I might be more present to others in a less self-interested

TESTS FOR DISCERNMENT ====

Am I responding to the guidance of the Inward Light or to the demands of my ego?

Am I patient and willing for my words and actions to be tested?

How do my actions accord with the guidance of my faith tradition and scripture?

Do others I respect agree?

What are the results of my words and actions? Are compassion, mercy, joy, generosity, kindness and self-control evident?

Do I feel a sense of inward peace and rightness deep in my gut or do I remain uneasy?

way. Being changed and healed in the process is ongoing and I expect it to take the rest of my life or longer. Being actively engaged in this transformation is knowing Life.

We can become practiced at recognizing the quirks of our own inner life and learn to sort what is destructive from the movement of grace in the soul, although Penington warned us how "the enemy kindles a great distress in the mind, by stirring up an earnest desire, and a sense of seeming necessity to know." I know this habit of over-reliance on the rational and its accompanying desire to control everything I possibly can. But oh, how this can lead me off base when not tempered. Penington's advice after warning about letting rationality run rampant was to suggest "But what if it be better for thee at present to be darkened about these things, than as yet to know?"[11] The thought of remaining in limbo and not satisfying my mind's urge to *know* is disconcerting. Years of practice at discernment better allow my mind to rest uneasily in the place of unknowing. I find I must often attempt to stand in a place of not knowing what comes next when only the next small action is visible. And I know that my heart has a deep desire to know the contours of the universe, a desire which led me to God. In such ways following the motion of the Spirit may cause us to stand in a place of paradox.

*Now in Jerusalem by the Sheep Gate there is a pool, called in Hebrew
Bethzatha, which has five porticos. In these lay many invalids – blind,
lame, and paralyzed. One man was there who had been ill for thirty-
eight years. When Jesus saw him lying there and knew that he had been
there a long time, he said to him, "Do you want to be made well?" The
sick man answered him, "Sir, I have no one to put me into the pool when
the water is stirred up; and while I am making my way, someone else
steps down ahead of me." Jesus said to him, "Stand up, take your mat
and walk." At once the man was made well, and he took up his mat and
began to walk.* – John 5: 2-9

*I [William Penn] close this Scripture doctrine of waiting with that
passage in John about the pool of Bethesda:*

*There is at Jerusalem, a pool ... which is called Bethesda, having five
porches. In these lay a great multitude of invalids, of blind, lame and
paralyzed, waiting for the moving of the water. For an angel went down
at a certain time into the pool, and troubled the water. Whoever then first
stepped in was made whole of whatever disease he had. (John 5:2-4)*

*This represents exactly the subject of waiting. For, as there was then
an outward and legal Jerusalem, so there is now a gospel and spiritual
Jerusalem. This is the church of God, consisting of the faithful. The pool
in that old Jerusalem represented that fountain which is now set open in
this new Jerusalem. That pool was for those that were under infirmities
of body. This new fountain is for all that are invalid in soul. There was
an angel then that moved the water, to make it beneficial. It is the angel
of God's presence now that blesses this fountain with success. They that
went in before and did not watch the angel found no benefit in stepping
in. Those that now do not wait for the moving of God's angel, but
rush before God, as the horse to the battle, are sure to miscarry, their
expectation.* – William Penn, 1669[12]

SALVATION

William Penn's words about waiting stir contradictory feelings in me. I am eager to hear of healing in the waters of the pool. I am distressed to think I have to wait until the angel stirs the water before healing is possible and even more so, to think that only the first person to step into the pool may be healed. In times of waiting, I am impatient. I want to jump into the waters and be made whole.

What is this waiting? Why should I be patient when I am desperately in need of healing? Penn admonished us to wait for the moving of God's angel, otherwise we are sure to go astray. But in his telling of the story, patience is not passive. Those who wish to be healed pick up their beds and come close to the pool of Bethesda, ready to step in it as soon as the angel comes. Thus, waiting is active and involves getting ready to respond.

I don't have many good role models for how to show my willingness to be healed; instead I think of my Dad, who once hardly made a sound after closing the car door on his thumb, then took himself off to the doctor. In a funny way, the time I threw Sandra Cronk's book *The Dark Night Journey* across the room was such a display. This action gave me a story to tell, which then opened the conversation of "why," and allowed me space to express pain and my anger at seeing myself in its pages.

When I turn, if ever so slightly, towards the Guide I finally am willing to reach out or listen to difficult words. The movement towards the pool sends sharp pains through my spiritual and emotional limbs. Even worse than the pain is the fear. To sit by the pool is to wonder if the angel will come. Can I make myself step into the waters? Why can it be so hard to reach out for the salve on the soul – for salvation?

Salvation?

Revisiting the pool of Bethesda and reading the biblical text with all its differences from William Penn's interpretation, I note that Jesus came and asked, "Do you want to be made well?" The man waiting by the pool had lots of excuses. Jesus then said, "Stand up, take your mat and walk." Jesus bypassed all the tradition about the angels and waiting to be the first person to step into the pool. His message was simply: believe and do it! So is this passage a straightforward admonition to believe in Christ and be saved? Perhaps it is a declaration of self-will: if we only have the strength of mind to decide to walk, we can.

My response to the word "salvation" is one either of questioning or dismissal. I associate the word with a litany I probably heard at Grandmother's Presbyterian church: "Believe in Christ Jesus and you will have eternal salvation." I don't know what that means. Use of this phrase almost always involves admonitions to "repent" – repent your evil ways, repent your sins. Harsh judgmentalism too often accompanies this litany. I don't believe that simply saying the words is enough or that if I, or others, don't say the magic words, we are damned. Enlightenment[13] is a word I sometimes use instead, yet enlightenment seems too intellectual. My soul needs something more.

Words about healing abound through religious as well as psychological writings. In psychological questions we look to what we can do with the help of another person, the counselor. In the context of faith, our actions can be informed and given power by the Spirit, a process aided by individuals attuned to the Eternal. In the Gospels, Jesus speaks of salvation from sin using the same Greek word he uses when he is curing illness or healing wounds.[14] Thus the healing at the pool of Bethesda can be seen as physical or spiritual. In this context, salvation from sin is about being restored to mental and spiritual health – about knowing perfect love. Coupled with the definition of "sin" as "missing the mark" or "turning away from God," the concept of salvation starts to take on meaning for me. I can be healed and made whole.

Transformation

What I do know about "salvation" is that it is not like physical healing – it does not simply make a neat scar or mend a bone so that we can walk again the way we always have. Once I felt God's arms around me, nothing was the same. Whatever mending was to occur, its purpose was not simply to make me better able to continue my life in the same routine.

I like the way Patricia Loring, a Friend from Baltimore Yearly Meeting who lived for a while in Oregon, speaks of salvation and transformation in her book, *Listening Spirituality*:

> Quakers cherish the palpable sense of divine presence and have their share of visions. Yet, ultimately, the goal of the spiritual life within Quakerism has not been visions, ecstatic experience or even a sense of union. Rather Friends have seen salvation or the goal of the inward life in transformation of the will to conformity with God's purposes. Visionary experience or experience of the power and presence of God are in aid and support of the transformation of the will, rather than vice versa.

> We let whatever willingness we have for that transformation to take place underlie our prayer. If we are not, to some degree, willing we will probably not continue in our prayer much past a particular crisis or desire. If we are open to the possibility of deeper life with God, we trust that our willingness may be transformed to deeply integrated intentionality of our whole being toward God.[15]

In the experience of the Source, I knew I was to step into a ministry of words, an action at once discomfiting and very right, very much a part of what early Friends called "taking up the cross." Slowly I came to see what it means to say that when words or actions arise out of the Spirit, they echo in other souls. That such words and actions open the heart and reduce fear. That words can have the power to heal and to encourage growth.

Responding to the work of the Spirit in the soul can be extremely painful: an act of cauterizing the wound. Depending on the severity of the wound and the behavior of the wounded person, the process can be lengthy. If someone refuses to take the steps prescribed, the wound can even grow worse. In John 3:14, Jesus refers to the story of Moses leading the people out of Egypt. When life became difficult in the desert, the people balked and wanted to return to Egypt. They feared the difficult path to freedom. I know the pull of the old slavery: the familiarity and comfort of a bowl of ice cream, even when my stomach is bulging, the mindlessness of a stupid TV show, the ease of not speaking even when words are at the surface. There are so many innocuous ways to nurture fear and to smother the impulses which make me feel vulnerable.

So how to go forward when the way seems too rough? Can I believe that if I rely on the divine Lover and wait in faith, a way will open even in the most difficult circumstances? With early Friends I do believe that there is an Eternal Presence which accompanies us in all suffering and protects the soul from evil – if we allow — but not necessarily the body. Is my soul's well-being more central than that of my body?

And to what am I going forward? If I am not being healed simply to be what I was, then what? The standard Christian answer—which early Friends would affirm, although they might instead speak of Christ being formed in us—is to become more like Jesus. So what's that? I most assuredly am not a first-century, Palestinian male. I don't do miracles. Early Friends spoke of Christ as the "new Adam" and also said that we are to be brought into the state that "Adam was before the Fall," part of the New Creation. As best I can understand, they are speaking of a different condition of the soul – a way of obedience.

Giving up control to Yahweh/God is frightening because it leads into the unknown. It brings peace to the soul in an inexplicable way. I have no pretense of being like Jesus, but I do know the rightness which settles deep in my belly when I am faithful to the gentle nudges on my heart and my actions are consistent with his words.

New Life

The desert Southwest, particularly the Navajo lands of the Four Corners area, which I visit when I can, has become a template for my new life. The vast spaces speak of the infinite nature of God. The apparently flat land, upon closer inspection, is laced with arroyos — steep drop-offs into small canyons where water races across the landscape and animals wander out of sight. Mesas – those steep, apparently inaccessible tablelands – are reached by trails which seem to dead end in blank rock-faces, then wind up through invisible cracks in the rocks. As I clamber up through the rock, the sky appears as a narrow streak above me until suddenly I step up into another land where hawks might fly below my feet as I scan the desert skies on the brink of the tabletop. These images of unseen things, of unexpected opportunity and hidden potential, conceptualize the new inward world which has been opened to me.

So must our defenses be broken for our spirits to take on new life. Soon after the initial inbreaking of Light in my soul, I wrote letters to people I see all the time, letters which revealed what my spoken words could not. Sent on impulse — perhaps divine, perhaps desperation — they gave others the opening to ask questions and treat me differently. These letters forced me into visibility. They made me step off the cliff and hope the winds of God would catch me.

Giving Care

Healing and transformation are active processes. As much as we might want them to be, they are not under our control. Something holy is involved in the cure of spiritual and emotional wounds. John Calvi, a New England Friend who does such work, speaks of the commitment to joy, which is essential when healing from trauma because "the monsters are gigantic and they take your breath away if you're not glad to be here, not glad to be doing the work."[16]

The act of healing often benefits by the presence of those who can clearly see the damage and can recognize the actions consistent with finding a cure. Friends' clearness process can provide eyes and ears which recognize when transformation is moving towards wholeness and when actions are damaging to the soul.

The gentle, strong, listening presence which helped me find my way came in the form of individuals in the Meeting who sat with me as a Clearness Committee (see box), as well as in the expertise of a trained professional. While anyone with a well-tuned ear can help, training in trauma work is invaluable. Yet much is gained from the person who will walk alongside someone wounded making use of well-honed listening skills, humility (a willingness to let God use them), and wisdom. A story is told, however, by a respected Friend about a time when she drifted inconspicuously off to sleep while someone poured out his heart. As she left, he thanked her honestly for listening so well. I love this story as it lifts the burden from me to always be perfect in some way beyond my limits and it makes clear the holy space which can form in unlikely situations.

My Clearness/Support Committee – Annis, Lorraine and Nancy – met with me regularly for more than two years initially as I struggled to find words. Later, as it became evident that my call was broader than I first thought, they were invaluable as I sought to find the shape of my call to ministry. Without consciously thinking about it, I asked three women who were miles apart in their personal theology and background, something which turned out to be a great gift. With this tripod of belief holding me up I could find my own balance point without being pulled strongly in any predetermined direction. Their different theologies and personalities made space for me to focus on what was being asked of me.

Annis and I could commiserate about how hard it is to come up with good questions and about how alien all this disclosure felt, while Nancy delighted in all kinds of spirituality. She would push me to speak about what it is like to simply "be" and to be a child of God. Lorraine's hearty laugh often broke the tension. At times Nancy's impatience with the slowness of the pace would burst forth or I would get overwhelmed with the quickness of Nancy and Lorraine's interactions. Then, Annis would make us all stop and remember why we were there. All three of them loved to talk and sitting with me was an intense form of spiritual discipline for them as they had to make space for the slow formation of my words.

CLEARNESS COMMITTEES

* A focus person asking for the committee to help him/her hear what God is asking them to do in a particular area of life.
* Two to four trusted individuals (but not necessarily close friends) willing to listen.
* Someone to convene the group and keep it focused and perhaps someone to take notes.
* Gathering, beginning in silent worship.
* A clear definition out of the silence of the question weighing on that person's heart.
* Gentle questions offered out of the silence by the listeners.
* Responses from the heart by the focus person.
* A commitment by all present to attend to the movement of the Spirit and a recognition that this is a time for the focus person to find their own way in accord with the Light, not an opportunity for others to offer lots of advice or stories about how they solved similar problems.
* Awareness of the confidentiality of the process.
* Reflection from the listeners of what they are hearing.
* Affirmation (or not) of a right direction by the focus person.
* Further Meetings if appropriate.

Together, these three women provided a solid base, a net to catch the pieces as I felt my pride and my sense of ability to control life being broken again and again. They were there for lunch or for the odd late-night phone call when I needed them and Lorraine could be counted on for assurance that "we are all big girls here" as she counseled me not to sugar-coat my words. And they were a physical reminder of the inability to hide from God, even as they affirmed the new self forming within me.

Douglas Steere, a 20th century Quaker writer, teacher and ecumenist, once wrote about listening another into life. We can listen to another with a divine ear and tenderness which can make visible the divinity in their soul. "Human listening then becomes what it is: a previously thin point in the membrane where the human and divine action can be felt to mingle with the least opaque cloud of concealment."[17]

Steere also told us that the absolute, loving acceptance of the listener does not preclude an element of judgment (but not judgmentalism!). By the person's very being, the prayer-like quality of listening and the acknowledged presence of the Giver of Life, both listener and speaker are formed anew.

Encountering the Seed

∿ ENCOUNTERING THE SEED ∿

Friends are called to honor and to engage the Seed of God within all people. Learning to recognize that Seed is part of our worship and daily practice. What is its taste and feel? Can I acknowledge that Seed within my own soul? These are essential questions of faith. Some of us may find them easy to answer; others are unsure or have few words which suffice. In the encounter with the Seed, the Light of God became alive to me and *broke down the walls* within my heart.

Increasingly, I am able speak to what I know directly of *the nature of God* in my life, and of *the nature of Christ*. Part of my calling is to share as best I can how my spiritual ancestors knew this Seed and what they have taught me. I find I must take Christianity seriously if I claim to be an inheritor of their faith. I worked hard to come to this position both through healing and substantial probing of what it means to honor the divine Seed in others. Only in facing the depth of my prejudice against those Friends who are evangelical Christians was I able to listen to them, recognize the Seed in them, and accept that they hold at least as much claim to being Friends as I do. This process turns many things upside down in me and pushes me into looking afresh at my own sense of myself and the faith I profess.

Most of us in the uprogrammed Meetings readily speak of *that of God in every person* as a central tenet of our faith. Its great strength is in the way it speaks to so many, but the vagueness of the term often leaves me frustrated. Exploration of the full text of George Fox's letter most often cited as the source of this phrase has opened up a depth of meaning for me.

The light that is in us all is another central phrase used to described Quakerism which when probed yields unexpected meaning. Early Friends knew an encounter with Christ Jesus as immediate as that of first century Christians and believed this encounter was available to all people even if they had never heard of Jesus. Today, unprogrammed Friends also see our faith as universal, but many of us would not name this as Christ incarnated within. My experience holds in tension the awareness that it is Christ who speaks to our condition and that this same Spirit, present before the universe was, is available to all people in all times and places. This is integral to how the Holy has touched my life. I know Christianity as a particular manifestation of universal Truth and Love and am shaped by both the universal and the particular. The immediacy and guidance of the Spirit reshapes lives and is the impetus for our work in the world.

God, Christ, that of God in each person, the Light, universal Love are all dimensions of the same eternal, unnameable force which works in the human heart. This work is both healing and challenging, so that we might grow towards wholeness – towards *spiritual maturity*. The movement towards living in a fullness of Love and Truth can be jerky and erratic, yet inexorable, as hearts are broken open and made tender to the Spirit. As this tenderness grows, *being present to others* is an increasingly joy-filled dimension of life.

So by this faith you come to know the partition wall broken down, that hath been betwixt you and God. – George Fox, 1676[18]

For [Christ Jesus] is our peace; in his flesh he has made both groups into one and has broken down the dividing wall, that is, the hostility between us. – Ephesians 2:14-16

BREAKING DOWN THE WALLS

One day as my private, self-contained being began to open up, instead of sitting at my computer to write in my journal I started to doodle. The doodles were of stone walls and occasional stones being moved off the wall. Later, a strong image of a massive castle came to me — one of those early medieval ones, made of stone and earth with walls several feet thick and no windows, only tiny slits where archers can defend what is within. Then the heavy wooden doors opened down on thick chains to create a bridge across the moat. Unexpectedly, all kinds of filth and waste poured out – like a massive cleansing of the castle, this fortress which had been kept locked tight much too long. An interior cleansing let in light and air.

This image says much about why I resonate when George Fox speaks of being "broken" as a positive happening. When my inner defenses broke, the air became sweeter to me – literally – and my eyes saw things they had never viewed before. I knew why Fox exclaimed that "all creation had a new smell."[19] My heart was filled with song. I went to sleep with music in my inner ear and woke to other tunes. A wide crack had appeared in the wall betwixt God and me. I began to trust other people in a new way, and trust myself.

At the core of the debris which washed away was my conviction that I was worthless and unlovable, a fear which had formed stone walls so thick that not I could not imagine who I truly might be. There seem to be infinite ways people respond to this sense of inner corruption and

self-hatred. Building walls is only one option. Another is the attempt to
be so much like others that we become invisible within the community.
Alternately, we might charge forth, weapons drawn, to take on the world,
daring anyone to see what lies beneath the armor and label all who
disagree with us as our enemies. When we encounter the Infinite Love,
all guises are broken open and the beauty within is given room to grow.
As Thich Nhat Hanh, the Vietnamese Zen Buddhist pacifist, tells us,
what seems to be garbage is truly compost for the soul.

A year or so later, I became aware of another image. The castle was gone
and its stones had been used to build a bridge, a low-lying structure
which people could cross easily. Most of the time the river it spanned
flowed freely under it. However, when massive storms struck, the bridge
was strong enough to serve as a dam to hold back the flood waters so
they would not wash away everything which had been built along the
river. This image of accessibility combined with appropriate protection
from danger has stood me well for a long time as I've made new friends
in unlikely places, led retreats and taken on various leadership positions.

In the Pacific Northwest, where Friends are so different from one
another, the barriers are sometimes very high. At least one Friend in
my Meeting insists that no group with a pastor can call themselves
"Friends." In the pastoral Meetings, a few argue vigorously against
"unequal yoking," that is, any cooperation with non-Christians. Even
within the immediate context of my unprogrammed Meeting, some
have left because we are "too Christian," and others because we are not
Christian enough. Individuals have taken it on themselves to criticize
vocal ministry which used language they found offensive. These barriers,
which so easily grow when we ignore, or even condone them, stand
"betwixt us and God." These barriers of fear – and sometimes hatred
– are strong enough that it is not possible today to assert that you will
recognize Friends by "how they love one another."

In practical terms, learning to speak to and respect both the Friends
who are fundamentalist Christians and those who are uneasy about use
of the word "God" is one of the challenges for Quakers in this century.
Without such clarity among ourselves, how can we witness to the whole
world about the universal Light which leads to true peace? Being open
to apparently incompatible people has changed me. In such interactions

I've encountered space both to receive and to offer nourishment and challenge. I recall with delight a session I attended at the fourth or fifth Pacific Northwest Women's Theological Conference, which brought together evangelical and liberal Quaker women in roughly equal numbers. There, two women, one from each yearly meeting, named all the things about the other which drove her nuts. This was done with such obvious respect for the other and with such humor that belly laughs were the order of the day even as we recognized the truth of what was said.

Facing the challenge of "the other" does not mean that waves of invective or fear do not arise. It does mean that Grace grounds the inward and outward work of reconciliation, establishes new foundations for those bridges, and opens the potential space for a ease and gentleness to replace fear.

My awareness of the breaching of the castle walls — the internal shattering – is intimately intertwined with how I know the Breath of Life: all encompassing, all forgiving, fierce and demanding, is God's love for each of us. This love pushes and shapes us, compelling us to let go while, at the same time, inviting us to choose freely to engage. It calls us to share with unstinting compassion. Divine love may be felt as a sharp impetus or a gradual easing, a striking awareness or simplicity in knowing. God encountered enclosed castles and creates a bridge out of the stones, tunneling slowly, shattering into life all that is fragile and broken.

Doth the kingdom of God consist in righteousness, peace, and joy in God's Spirit? This is all in this seed, and is partaken of and enjoyed, as this seed springs up, … and who is gathered into it, born of it, and one with it, partakes of the divine nature. – Isaac Penington (n.d.) [20]

This is the message we have heard from him and proclaim to you, that God is light and in him there is no darkness at all. – I John 1:5

THE NATURE OF GOD

A significant number of us in the unprogrammed Friends Meetings (and some in evangelical Meetings) have bumped up against — or been inundated with — concepts of God which either offend us, have been used to punish or threaten us, or which strain the imagination or reason. A lot of notions about God get lumped under the rubric of "Christianity." I count myself among those whose spirit needed respite from the Bible as a young woman. The uneasy tensions between Quaker teachings and what I heard when I, in best hat and gloves, accompanied my Presbyterian Grandmother to church were set aside rather than resolved.

Yet years later, I found all my limited concepts of God shaken apart through encounter with the Source. The stories of the Hebrew Testament and of Jesus I learned as a child now became the stories of individuals and a people trying to make sense of the Unknowable, not some kind of rule book. What had been abstract became alive. Having long ago learned intellectually that there is "that of God" — the Seed — in each person, I began to reach for words to convey what this feels and tastes like.

Images of God

As a young teenager I exploded in fury at the concepts and paintings of God as a white-haired man, sitting on a throne or a cloud, and directing the course of each event on earth. I dismissed this all-powerful, all-knowing figure who seemed arbitrary and whose primary purpose was to judge every action and thought. I mentally dismissed from my cosmos a God who could only be approached politely, wearing white gloves, but the impulse to be perfect in everyone's eyes remained with me.

Around the same time I also rejected Jesus. My accumulated image of Jesus was epitomized by the romantic pictures of a man in a spotless white robe holding a lamb. I did not find him comforting: he did not seem to have the strength to help anyone in real pain or danger. Now I know that these are merely images left over from the Victorian era, but I didn't need a weak pat on the head from a gentle Jesus. I needed someone who could protect me.

I turned instead to the infinite power and beauty of the universe made visible in the night sky. "God" – whatever that was – was beyond all knowing. Seeking to know the secrets of the universe, I became a scientist. George Fox wandered the countryside filled with agonizing questions. I turned to test tubes and mathematics, to the point of starting on a PhD in biochemistry, bent on exploring the secrets of the human brain. Like Fox, I wanted to know "experimentally" – with my hands, eyes, and mind – and actively, what drives the human soul and the mystery of the universe.

For a long time I was not ready to hear or engage the full message that Friends can offer or its power, thinking such knowledge was only available through science.[21] It has been a surprising gift to find new words and images to express how the Mystery can arise out of dreams, visions and other means my rational mind struggles with, as well as out of the natural world.

Elizabeth Bathurst, though she lived over 300 years ago and died young, speaks very much to my condition when she affirmed the multiple ways the Spirit engages us, and comforts us according to our needs. While she would have only used words from the Bible, and I draw from wider sources, I do not think we are far apart. For the Bible offers images of God as the eagle teaching the young to fly, the mother hen herding her chicks, and the woman nursing her child at her breast.[24] Many other such feminine biblical images of God are ignored and omitted from lists of names of God, lists too often tilted towards military or regal concepts. I want to reclaim a fuller vocabulary for all that is holy.

Names of God

Simply saying "Yahweh" — Adonai — evokes the breath of life and expresses this central aspect of the Divine Presence. The winds of God, the breath of God: these hold me and give lift to my wings that I might soar. Being the hawk, soaring on the breath of God, is something I know inwardly. There is a gentle breath which lifts, protects, enfolds me so I can simply soar in the soft sunlight. And there is a breath of fury and power which buffets me and drives me to refuge in inner trees or caves, a power beyond my capability to control or withstand. I must learn to move with it and sometimes anticipate its shifts. Even as I feel I might be crushed in its changing pressures, I learn to trust that it will hold me with no visible support and will not harm me. This divine breath gently nudges my heart and makes the way clear through the words of a friend, or a strong, unexpected sense of what comes next. When I am able to drop my attempts at control and truly pray, answers arise.

Early Friends encourage me to be open to an unexpected range of names for God. Margaret Fell often referred to God as "Power." Like other early Friends, she used "Truth" almost interchangeably with "Christ." Other names for the Eternal Friends have used over the generations include: the Word, the Pure Principle, the Law, Grace, the New Covenant, a Rod, a Staff, a Shepherd's Crook, the Word nigh in the heart and in the mouth, the sure Word of prophecy, a Shield, a Boulder, a strong Tower, the Armor of Righteousness. Elizabeth Bathurst, in her book on Quaker theology, wrote that these are all "one in nature, though diversely expressed."[22]

Each name gives us a sense of the different ways God operates in the soul. Bathurst noted how the Light acts "sometimes to lighten [the soul's] darkness, at other times to lead it in the way of holiness: one while it instructs, another while it corrects." The functions of the Light shift according to our needs: "Sometimes it counsels, other times it consoles, and as its counsel is heeded and the soul guided by it, it preserves and defends in all exigencies."[23]

The Character/Characteristics of God

If we have such varied images of the divine center of the universe, then how do we have any idea whether we are talking about the same thing? Is there such a thing as one God (named variously) that is at least potentially known by all people in all times? My heritage tells me that there is. My heart does also. Yet I know how we know the Pure Principle is influenced by our times, our culture, our personalities. The nuclear age, psychiatry and evolution are among the realities which shape us, just as the propensity to be outgoing or introverted flavors our reactions to life.

One gift of spending time with evangelical Friends is to better see these influences in my own life. For many years I considered God to be solely an abstract force in the universe. If pushed, I might speak of Spirit or love. In this I am like a significant number of unprogrammed Friends. The sense that all that is Holy is within ourselves, or perhaps open and vast as the night sky, is rich and affirming. Trying to describe this, some Friends such as Kenneth Boulding draw heavily on evolutionary thought and other science. Knowing the Light as within opens us to the potential that we, as humans, can comprehend and act on that infinite love in our daily lives. Seeing that of God in every heart affirms that we have to take responsibility for acting justly and compassionately. To harm another is to damage something sacred.

In contrast, many Friends worldwide—particularly evangelical Friends— would assert that the Lord created the earth, sustains it, and is active in history. God is revealed in creation, they assert, and His creative work provides the basis for order, beauty, purpose and rationality, an understanding which is sometimes in tension with the concept that Jehovah gave humanity dominion over all the earth. The Lord God created humanity and offers forgiveness to the world for our sins through the death and resurrection of his son, Jesus Christ. The broader evangelical culture presses for acceptance of Jesus and can make Friends' testimonies seem as obstacles to this narrow definition of salvation. Along with a God who is all-knowing and all-wise, holy, all powerful, and eternal, evangelical Friends experience Jesus as a personal comforter and guide.[25]

A major challenge of today's world is to acknowledge and respect such apparently divergent views. Truly listening to one another opens the possibility that we may be changed and in this change come to know the truth in words which initially seem alien, harsh or even threatening. I have been graced with coming to know the Sacred in multiple ways and to see how different words might express a single inward experience.

George Fox spoke of thankfulness for comfort to the soul as well as his infinite wonder in the presence of all that is sacred. He knew God as Guide, Inward Monitor and Mystery. My consciousness of God is in the power, awe, and infinity of the night sky. I experience God as unconditional, intimate Love, yet a love which is both Guide and Monitor. Both dimensions shape me. The characteristics of God embrace both the intensely personal and the eternal and are found in the Bible though not dependent on it. Any one of us may experience one and not the other, or both and more. Some of us never seem to have this direct knowledge while others recall a sense of the Holy among their earliest memories.

If the words we use to describe the Creator can vary, an important test of whether or not we refer to the same Truth as early Friends knew is in how we describe its effect on the human soul. One of

A CONCISE SERMON ON THE MOUNT

The down will be up
You are supposed to be effective
You are supposed to be noticed
Don't do it to be noticed
Perfection=inside and out the same
Make peace
Get rid of whatever traps you
Give without limits
Tell the truth – all the time
Love without limits
Pray – simply and often
Forgive
Trust – it is the anxiety killer
Don't judge–
It makes you look stupid and
hypocritical
Ask persistently
Treat people right
This is simple but not easy
You may have to do it alone
Don't be fooled by imposters
Act on what you know
It is a foundation that will not fail

Peggy Senger Parsons
Pendle Hill March 2009

the basic lists of human attributes which point to the divine Seed is in Galatians 5:22: "The fruit of the Spirit is love, joy, peace, patience, kindness, generosity, faithfulness, gentleness and self-control." Friends have long used these fruits as evidence of flowering of the divine Seed, and still do, even if individuals don't attribute them to the Bible. Other gifts of the Spirit – the charismatic aspects of faith — are described In I Corinthians 12: prophecy, speaking wisdom and knowledge, healing, working miracles, speaking in tongues and the ability to interpret such speaking. This second list, while part of first-generation Quakerism, has been modulated since the late 17th century by the tensions between respectability and radical reliance on the Spirit, between rationalism and mysticism, between fundamentalism and revivalism, but has never completely disappeared.[26]

In the Sermon on the Mount, Jesus encourages us to meekness, raising up the downtrodden, making our lives visible (while avoiding glory-seeking), living with integrity, building peace, asking God for help and offering thanks, creating communities of trust, speaking honestly, and showing love to our enemies. This is not a bad recipe for recognizing God or for recognizing that of God in another.

Jesus Christ that died for them, and had enlightened them, that with his light they might see their evil deeds and their sins and with the same light they might see their saviour. —George Fox, 1658[27]

The children of God and the children of the devil are revealed in this way: all who do not do what is right are not from God, nor are those who do not love their brothers and sisters. – I John 3:9, 10

THE LIGHT OF CHRIST

The first Epistle of John describes some people as "children of the devil" – a concept offensive to many Friends and directly counter to belief in the Seed of God in all people. So how do I come to terms with this kind of Bible verse? This verse recalls Puritanical preaching, which makes certain we know that Satan is active in the world and that if we do not cling to Christ Jesus we will end up in hell. Fox answers this by separating the "flesh" and the spirit and urging all to move away from the external pressures to conform, the habits that ill-serve them, and other similar influences of the "flesh." Fox believed our "creaturely" natures would change as Christ formed within each of our hearts, making us more and more like Jesus. His faith contradicted the dominant Puritan view: he knew that the ocean of Light always flows over the ocean of darkness and is not consumed by it and that human beings could live free of sin.

George Fox spoke of Christ and the Light in many ways (I often use the list on page 44 as a reminder) and linked the Light unequivocally with Christ Jesus and the action of Christ in the human conscience.[28] This does not fit easily into my liberal cosmology and is easy to dismiss as irrelevant today. Speaking of "the Pure Principle" rather than Christ appeals to my rational side, but I am no longer so certain that the old words are irrelevant. Fox's words about the Light of Christ, which offers renewal in the image of God and shows us our wrongdoing, help me wrestle with the harshness of the verses from I John and see how I John relates to my faith. But first, I'll share my own experience of Jesus.

My Perceptions of Jesus

When my family moved from Baltimore to Philadelphia the children in the neighborhood wanted to learn about the new kid on the block and asked about my church. Apparently they knew nothing about Quakers and persisted, asking if we were Christians. My six-year-old answer was "No, we are not Christians."

In the 1990s when my mother faced a crisis in her health, I spent much time in prayer for her as she lived three thousand miles away. At that time I was reading *The Tibetan Book of Living and Dying*, which encouraged visualizing your loved one surrounded by light and love. As I did so I found I could see my mother in her bed. The love in that room was palpable and, as I looked to the foot of the bed, I saw Jesus standing over her with great compassion.

Today, Jesus embodies Light and Love for me even at the times when I attempt a Buddhist practice. I have come to understand how fully I am Christian even as I am affirmed again and again in my belief that God works in many ways — more than we can comprehend — to heal us and fill us with love.[29]

Reading the Bible tells me that we, as Friends, are Christian in the broad sense, no matter what our individual beliefs. All our practices, all our testimonies flow from the teachings and example of Jesus. Yet they are not simple repetitions of the words and teachings of Jesus, nor is our faith today a replication of a 17th- century faith. For instance, Jesus did not condemn slavery. George Fox urged slave owners to educate their slaves so they might read the Bible, not to free them. Nonetheless Friends, after decades of struggle, came to know the evils of slavery and could not accept slavery as consistent with God's way. Our faith and practice is leavened by the work of the Spirit.

One Seed or Two?

The question of what constitutes a Christian in the face of the assertions of the Book of John still remains before me. I am not an orthodox Christian and am not sure how first-generation Friends would respond to my theology. Yet, at times I feel a real affinity with them. They did not speculate much on the accuracy of the facts of Jesus' life even though many of them knew the Gospels by heart. They seemed to experience the inward Christ more as a principle than a distinct personality.[30] However, they did not deny most standard church teachings. Instead of focusing on such things as the virginity of Mary, their concern was about the risen Christ whom they knew inwardly, trusted and followed.

As I spent time with the works of Isaac Penington, I came across his description of "True Christianity,"[31] and was caught up by his use of criteria which have little to do with right belief. All his descriptors had to do with the inward state of the person and the resultant outward actions. After starting off by saying, "It is easy to pretend to CHRIST; but to be a true Christian is very precious," Penington listed some of the qualities of those who know Christ inwardly: a new creature; in the *new* covenant; inwardly circumcised with the circumcision made without hands; inwardly washed with clean water. Such a person feeds on the bread of life within, and drinks the water of life out of his own well or cistern; lives the Christian life; walks not after the flesh, but after the Spirit. And finally, this person who knows the Life, "doth not fulfill the lusts of the flesh, but hath the law of God written in his heart" and lives by faith.

Penington affirmed a faith strongly inward yet immediately evident in behavior and words. I hear in him the reality of a living and lively spirituality which nourishes the soul and guides our actions. He drew on the strongest thread running through the Christian Testament: our faith and salvation are weighed in regard to love. Just as Jesus said he would divide the "sheep from the goats" based on how they treated prisoners and orphans, a theme of Faith revealed in action is repeated and expanded on in the Epistle of James. Even I John 3 tells us at length that the children of God will be revealed by how they love one another before it adds a comment about believing in the name of Jesus Christ.

Timothy Peat Ashworth, who teaches the Bible at Woodbrooke, the Quaker study center in England, tells us that the Greek phrase usually translated as "belief in Jesus" could just as legitimately be translated "belief of Jesus." The latter I can unite with. Independent of the endless arguments about whether Jesus is the only way, a Quaker reading of the Christian testament tells us that if we cannot treat one another well, if our lives do not evince the fruits of the Spirit, we have not yet known the spiritual rebirth which makes us fully visible as God's children. The parable of prodigal son, however, makes clear that even those who walk away from this inheritance are God's children and the divine heart always welcomes anyone who turns towards love, no matter what kind of mess they've made of their lives.

What I know of our spiritual ancestors tells me that they affirmed God's love in all peoples they encountered when that love was evident in how they lived. Mary Fisher engaged with the sultan in Constantinople acknowledging the rightness in how he spoke of Allah and other Friends wrote letters calling on Muslims to live up to the teachings of the Koran and to treat well people they had captured. Fox notes in his *Journal* how he argued with a local official that the Great Spirit known by the native peoples they encountered in North America was the same God they knew. That much is easy for me to accept.

The language of the seed is helpful, in particular the references to the two seeds in each human heart: the Seed that is the Light of Christ and generates the fruit of the Spirit and the seed whose fruits are discord, hatred, and avarice. We each can turn to one or the other seed within

THE LIGHT
as described by George Fox

* Christ is the Light of the world.
* The Light is spiritual and universal. The Light is unchangeable Truth.
* This Light is within you. This Light enlightens every one.
* This Light will open Scripture to you.
* This Light will show you righteousness and unrighteousness.
* Wait in the Light that discovers sin and evil in you and reveals the secrets of everyone's hearts.
* This Light renews the minds of all people and teaches while we walk, lie down or work.
* Dwell in the Light, feel the Light, walk in the Light.
* The Light leads to the kingdom of God and gives entrance.
* All you who love the Light, love God and Christ. If you love and obey it, it will lead you into the way of peace.

[compiled by T. Canby Jones from Henry J. Cadbury, Annual Catalogue of George Fox's Papers, Cambridge University Press, 1940, #23, 51A, p. 47.]

ourselves, a process which requires self-knowledge and honesty. No one can make this choice for another, nor do the "weeding" for another, although we accompany others as they work and share techniques of gardening. I suspect we all nurture both seeds to some degree, but most of us come to a point in our lives where we want to weed out that which is not of Holy Love. The Inward Light shows us clearly the source of each interior plant and teaches us to be master gardeners. Plucking out my own weeds can be hard, painful work, leaving me sore and shattered for a time. At times the task seems too overwhelming even to start. Jesus also counsels us that it may be appropriate to leave the weeds rather than destroy fruitful plants in the process (Matthew 13:29).

An evangelical f/Friend once said that one of the most important characteristics of Quakers is our ability to hold, and even enjoy, paradox. I agree with her. We do not have to have everything tied up in neat simple answers. There is space for mystery in our relationship with God, with Christ and with each other for that matter. So one paradox I hold within is that Jesus Christ is the Way, the Truth and the Light, yet that same Way, Truth and Light is before the world was and is available to all people whether or not they know anything of Jesus or become Christian.

Friends,

And this is the word of the Lord God to you all, and a charge to you all in the presence of the living God, be patterns, be examples in all countries, places, islands, nations, wherever you come; that your carriage and life may preach among all sorts of people, and to them. Then you will come to walk cheerfully over the world, answering that of God in every one; whereby in them ye may be a blessing, and make the witness of God in them to bless you. Then to the Lord God you will be a sweet savour and a blessing.

Spare no deceit. Lay the sword upon it; go over it; keep yourselves clear of the blood of all men, either by word, or writing, or speaking. And keep yourselves clean,… that nothing may rule nor reign but power and life itself, and that in the wisdom of God ye may be preserved in it.
– George Fox, 1656[32]

And who is my neighbor? – Luke 10:29

THAT OF GOD IN EVERYONE

The response to the question, "What do Friends believe?" often seems to be, "There is that of God in everyone." When I ask the question "What is at the core of our testimonies?" people often give the same answer. By itself, this phrase irritates me and is not satisfying: without context, it tells me very little. As used today, it seems like all we only need to be good, smile, and think everyone else is nice – a tendency not confined to Quakers by any means.

I also find within this phrase the potential for burnout and frustration. Much of my struggle with "that of God in everyone" lies in the intensity of its optimism about humanity and temptation to over-expectation. It seems to encourage us to look only to the good in the other person even though I know within myself a push to do harm. I know how hard it can be not to give in to those negative feelings. And, when I look around me and see the condition of the world, I wonder how we can be so blindly and naively optimistic.

Yet again and again passages in the Bible admonish us to love our neighbors as ourselves. When asked "who is my neighbor?" Jesus responds with the story of the good Samaritan, a story where all the pious and proper folk ignore the beaten man lying by the side of the road and the despised Samaritan shows mercy. This parable, like so many other stories around Jesus, breaks apart people's assumptions based on nationality, religion and other such boundaries. Just as Jesus reached out to the tax collectors and prostitutes, we are to engage even the most unlikely folk with hope.

These words, and my heart, push me to break free of cynicism and prejudice. I am pushed to treat each individual with respect even when I do not understand his culture, or when my culture warns me of danger or says he is unworthy. I am pushed to change institutions and laws which treat any human being as less than another. There is no room for doing otherwise. Affirming that of God in all people is a powerful force.

Fox on That of God in Everyone

In 1656, George Fox wrote a letter to Friends using the phrase "that of God in everyone."[33] Fox expected us to nurture the Seed in the heart especially when the "other" seems ignorant, lies, or has done some evil. Our ability to "answer" others expands the more we have done our own inner work so that our "carriage" – our very way of being – becomes an example to others. As we act, we are not to draw blood with the sword but find creative nonviolent means to overcome evil. Fox stated in his letter, following the words at the start of this chapter:

> In the power of life and wisdom, and dread of the Lord God of life, and heaven, and earth, dwell, that in the wisdom of God over all ye may be preserved, and be a terror to all the adversaries of God, and a dread, answering that of God in them all, spreading the Truth abroad, awakening the witness, confounding deceit, gathering up out of transgression into the life, the covenant of light and peace with God. Let all nations hear the word by sound or writing. Spare no place, spare not tongue nor pen; but be obedient to the Lord God and go through the work and be valiant for the Truth upon earth; tread and trample all that is contrary under....

How easily I forget that in his call to answer that of God in the other, Fox expected us to evangelize and to bring all people into the presence of Christ Jesus. Yet even as I question the "bring to Jesus" aspect, I like the idea of the Quaker evangelist as "a terror" and "a dread" to their enemies by recognizing the movement of the Spirit in their hearts. Thus, all who wish to trample dishonesty and injustice have to simultaneously call forth love. They cannot intimidate others by fear, but instead demonstrate Truth. In this way, perhaps, they might throw those who live by violence into confusion and doubt.

Fox continued by articulating an important role for Friends: to support others who are trapped by their own wrongdoing, and to help them find the freedom of the Spirit:

> Bring all into the worship of God. Plough up the fallow ground …
> and none are ploughed up but he who comes to the principle of
> God in him which he hath transgressed. Then he doth service to
> God; then the planting and watering and the increase from God
> cometh. So the ministers of the Spirit must minister to the spirit
> that is transgressed and in prison, which hath been in captivity in
> every one; whereby with the same spirit people must be led out of
> captivity up to God, the Father of spirits, and do service to him and
> have unity with him, with the Scriptures and with one another.

For Fox, our personal struggle with the darkness in our own souls opened opportunities for each of us to "speak to all conditions" without condescension or condemnation. Having experienced transformation, Friends wanted others to know the Light. The use of pressure to convert others is totally at odds with all I know and I have had several lively conversations with modern evangelicals about how to share what we've learned about the Eternal without using fear or condemnation. Early Friends set a helpful example when asserting that the most they could do was to share what they knew inwardly: any more was between the individual and God. Sometimes someone will ask me to meet them for coffee and want to talk, asking me about my experience or telling me their story. My task seems to be to affirm in them all I hear which echoes what I know of God's way.

Fox's message to Quaker ministers, dense as it is and full of admonitions, is also a message of hope that we will come to answer that of God in all people. I constantly need to hear his encouragement to stay close to that which is holy and to live in it. He envisioned a joy which fills each soul but is not limited to human time and the human condition. He also warned us not to abuse our knowledge and strength.

Keep in the wisdom of God that spreads over all the earth, the wisdom of the creation, that is pure. Live in it; that is the word of the Lord God to you all, do not abuse it; and keep down and low; and take heed of false joys that will change.[34]

Fox did more than appeal to the good within. By "answering that of God" in others he was challenging the arrogance, greed and dishonesty he saw within each person alongside the Seed of mercy. Fox called attention to the "evils within" only that people might know and respond to the Light, as when he wrote in another letter in 1659:

[When Friends were brought before judges,] "If they give them the hat, it is a civil thing; it pacifies the rage of the transgressor … but break down his Idol, and bring him … to seek the honour which comes from God … and not give him this the hat honor … and he will rage."[35]

Here Fox was responding to the 17th-century convention whereby men doffed their hats to their social superiors as acknowledgment of social position. Quakers' refusal to show special respect in this way, even to the king, threatened egos — as well as the whole social hierarchy — often generating an enraged response. Refusal of hat honor was at its core a challenge to the "idols" of arrogance and false superiority, not a political act. Fox believed that doing this would make the "transgressor" – the person who depended on this social acknowledgment of his status – aware that all true honor comes from God.

Thus, the often unspoken dimension of "answering that of God" in others is to bring them to see how they are nurturing the wrong seed in their own hearts — an action which might well make them rage. A question I often ask is, "What is the hat honor of today?" – what simple, everyday action can prick the conscience of people caught up in the materialism and militarism which are so prevalent among us?

In the beginning was the Word, and the Word was with God, and the Word was God…. What has come into being in him was life, and the life was the light of all people. – John 1: 1-5

The Lord created me [wisdom/Sophia] at the beginning of his work, the first of his acts long ago…. and I was daily his delight, rejoicing before him always, rejoicing in his inhabited world and delighting in the human race. – Proverbs 8:22, 30, 31

… The spirit of God, which was given to every one to profit withal, … and which … teacheth them that obey it … to live soberly, righteously, and godly in the present world. – George Fox, 1674[36]

THE LIGHT THAT IS IN US ALL

In silent worship, I have heard words drawing on insights of psychology, the practices of Asian meditation, the rituals associated with the rhythm of the seasons and affinity with the natural world, as well as the traditions and faith of various Christian churches. In the expectant quiet of worship these multiple influences blend in complex ways that offer great potential and openness to the possibilities of life in tune with Eternity.

For many years in prayer and even occasionally now, I've asked what name I should use for "God." Although I don't phrase it this way, the underlying question is about naming Jesus Christ. Spending as much time as I have with evangelical Friends as well as living in a culture with strong Christian influences, a part of me worried that this was somehow necessary. My prayers have always left me with the option of naming the Eternal as I wished. The search for compassion, mercy and truth is not confined to profession of belief in Christ Jesus, or for that matter in the Five Pillars of Islam, daily yoga practice or Catholic Mass. The mystical meeting with the Divine Lover is beyond all words and creeds.

One evening, when I was leading the Multwood group of evangelical and liberal Quaker women, I raised the question of whether the experience of relationship with Jesus and mystical experiences which are described in non-Christian ways are, at the heart, the same experience. About half the women from each yearly meeting said yes, the other half, no. There is no way yet available to prove this in any scientific way, but I am one of those who says yes, there is an encounter with the love at the heart of the universe which can be described in many ways. How we speak of mystical experience, which is inherently beyond words, seems to be a result of our particular culture and context. Thus even when the effect — the emotional impact – is quite similar and perhaps even the same parts of our brain can be shown to be activated, the words and stories we use to communicate are particular to our community.

In my encounters with other faiths, I find it easy to spot commonalities and places where their tradition enhances my own response to God and opens up new perspectives. Both the phrase, "answering that of God in everyone" and use of "The Light" as perhaps the most common names for all that is eternal, compassionate and true, make it easy for Friends to reject a mandatory link between any particular creed or language and living in right relationship with all that is holy. Trained as a scientist, I find that laboratory methods and the desire for proof inform my relationships with the people and the world around me. This, too, is essential to my relationship with the Holy One. I am a person of my time, not a Jew or a Greek of two thousand years ago, or a Quaker of 17th-century England. Yet these all inform who I am. I cannot separate myself from them no matter how I might try.

Rufus Jones, more than any other Friend in the 20th century, constantly tried to articulate both the mystical and ethical dimensions of our faith. In his historical writings, he placed Quakers squarely in the mystical tradition, but always with the caveat of ethical action resulting from that holy encounter. He wrote of the vital connection which comes in the direct discovery of the will of God:

> ...The quiet spiritual communion, the sense of guiding Presence, the reality of Eternal Love, the consciousness that in my best moments of life I am the organ of a divine purpose – those aspects of life have been as much a part of my essential being as breathing and the beating of my heart have been.[37]

To be filled with this radiance, even once, penetrates all outward trappings of religion and custom. This Light carries in itself the desire to care for the world around us and to engage with others equitably and with tenderness.

The Mystical Connection

I still find it odd to call myself a mystic, probably because my hard-core rationalist self is still part of me even after having my life turned on end in the inward awareness of divine love. But those times when I am open so that the Light breaks through my resistance, I am aware of a connection totally unrelated to culture or to any outward profession of belief.

The opening passages of the Gospel of John as well as passages in Proverbs say this unequivocally: the Word, the Light, and Wisdom are present in the beginning with God, before the earth was (Proverbs 8:22); the Light "shines in the darkness and the darkness did not overcome it" (John 1:5). It is this Light of which I speak. It is this Light which Friends have always known at an unshakable level is available to all people of all faiths. Paradoxically, it is this Light, this Word of God, which the Gospel and most Friends identify with Jesus.

The Ethical Path

Much of my life the path I searched for was the ethical path. George Fox describes this way in terms of denying "ungodliness and worldly lusts" and living "soberly, righteously, and godly in the present world." Rufus Jones wrote of an "ethical mysticism" grounded in the Gospel. Modern liberal Friends speak of equality, peace, integrity, simplicity and community. I speak of compassion, integrity, justice, mercy and humility as universal values. This is an ethic described in a way drawn originally from the New Testament, just as the Light is, but with counterparts in many traditions. Knowing this path with the mind, the heart and the feet is part of living into the City of God, the Covenant of Love.

I am learning to explain the ethical dimension in terms of the first of the eight limbs of *Ashtanga Yoga*, the *Yama*, or ethical practices. The *Yama* teaches non-violence, truthfulness, non-stealing, continence and non-greediness. *Niyana*, the second limb, calls people to personal observances of cleanliness, contentment, self-discipline, self-examination and reverence. These sound quite familiar to my ear after nearly twenty years of practice, which paradoxically stills my mind while giving new range of motion to my body.

The eight limbs of Yoga also affirm the interrelation of meditation and awareness of the spiritual dimension of life with the ethical. Practice of the first two limbs lays the foundation for *Samadhi*, or complete integration – which I think of as similar to Buddhist enlightenment. In recent decades, I have found that the ethical and mystical paths illuminate one another. Each adds dimension and complexity to the other. As long as I am part of this world, I cannot separate the practicalities of life from my sense of the Eternal.

Universal Truths

Recognition of universal truths common to the varied writings and myths which are central to each culture is part of my learning. This is an area explored and articulated by many others. Tom Harpur, a former Anglican priest and professor of Greek and New Testament at the University of Toronto, has said words which feel right to me:

> "The *Christos*, though known by many names, is present within all humanity; it is common spiritual property, but not all Christians and non-Christians recognize it in their lives." He set the story of Jesus into a much broader context when he wrote that "The Gospels are really dramas about the *Christos*, with Jesus in the starring role as a dramatic personality. Jesus is the symbolic personification of the *Christos*."[38]

Both the mystical and the ethical dimensions of universalism are essential to understanding my faith. Some individuals emphasize one or the other, a few reject one or the other, but both streams flow strongly through Friends. What Harpur calls "the *Christos*" I see as the force of life, hope and love which is in Jesus, but is spoken of in virtually every culture.

The story of Jesus, his life and death, touch into something more than can be explained by calling him a prophet or teacher, although he was both and still is for many people. The statement that Jesus is born of God and the Virgin Mary is something I neither believe nor disbelieve. The power of Jesus's life is in his dependence on God throughout his ministry and his choice to accept the crucifixion. His death and rebirth speak to a profound experience which fortunately few of us will have to face literally, but which many of us experience inwardly and spiritually. The story of Jesus, I believe, speaks of something essential, that which is greatest in the human soul and humanity's relationship with all that is holy. Thus, someone like Tom Harpur gives words to the concept that Jesus is one expression of a human-divine relationship known to all cultures and in all times.

Finding Unity Amid the Many Voices

In 2008-09, I was part of the Way of Ministry (TWM), a year-long Quaker program which focused on the prophetic ministry, that is, a call that makes visible the City of God by holy faithfulness. We used the Bible for our common language and concepts, but our individual expressions of faith differed and we brought with us a blend of mystical encounter and ethical understanding. TWM was built on a presumption of the power of lives turned topsy-turvy. Be it in small increments or a sudden opening, the Light acting in the human soul shifts priorities and the call to faithfulness leads people into internal death of the self and rebirth. TWM asserts that each of us can literally live "in the virtue of that life and power that took away the occasion of all wars."[39] A constant thread throughout the program was that inward spiritual renewal is tied irrevocably to the way of justice and harmony.

I attended TWM at a time I felt the need for renewal. It was a time of testing and accountability — difficult processes personally as well as more broadly in this age which highly values individualism. Facing the Inward Monitor in such a public format revealed, and broke through, some of the traps set by my ego. Others pointed out when I was distracted by an inner voice that prevents me from seeing how my words can benefit others who are troubled by the same problem but think they are alone. In such struggles I grow. I can claim tiny bits of spiritual maturity each time I hang in there and follow through with what the Light has shown me.

In this community we were constantly pushed to dig deeper beyond words. We sought to feel the Power which guided each individual and know that same Mother teaching us to accompany one another in our unique ministries. If, as we say we believe, the Holy One can lead the group as well as individuals, then trust by the individual of the Spirit working in the gathered community is part of who we are, just as much as the willingness of the community to be prodded and challenged by one person's sense of leading. This is a challenge I feel especially in those rare moments when it seems my heart, mind and soul love God so fully that the divine way becomes my way. Reliance on the Source and testing in community are necessary grounds for a prophetic voice and authority in the world.

When I was a child, I spoke like a child, I thought like a child, I reasoned like a child; when I became an adult, I put an end to childish ways…. And now faith, hope, and love abide, these three; and the greatest of these is love.
– I Corinthians 13:8-13

And how do we grow up in Christ, but by the growing up in this seed and feeling this seed grow up in us? … Now we cannot receive this seed, but as we part with and deny our own wisdom and fleshly confidence;
- Isaac Penington, (n.d.)[40]

SPIRITUAL 10 MATURITY

Paying attention to others' journeys of faith, I become more aware of impulses which push me towards perfectionism one day and discouragement the next. The discouragement which comes from reaching for an ideal growing out of our own heads is visible in many old Quaker journals. In 1749, for instance, Elizabeth Hudson wrote in her journal while traveling in the ministry:

> After I sat down my spirit was covered with distress even to anguish, however [I] was favoured to prostrate myself at the feet of my master who knew if I erred it was not owing to the wickedness of my heart, but too great readiness to grasp at vision, which is no qualification to preach …[41]

Using a lens which senses the movement of the Spirit, not an abstract, intellectual one, both perfectionism and discouragement become evidence of my own fears. Attempts to make every little detail right and worries that I have failed are linked when seen in this perspective. Both are part of my tendency to forget the Inward Guide. It can be so much easier to focus on my own feelings or my desire to please others. Whether described as self-centeredness and codependency, or in old words such as "creatureliness" and "worldliness," perfectionism separates me from God when it controls my behavior.

Perfection, Perfectionism and Freedom

The early Quaker doctrine of "perfection" grabs my attention. It promises healing of the wounds which left me so full of hidden fear. Often I use the term "spiritual maturity," a term which captures some of the meaning of the Greek word *teleios*,[42] when I try to understand Jesus' call in Matthew 5:48: "Be ye perfect, even as your Father in heaven is perfect" (KJV). Thus, my focus is different than George Fox's emphasis on achieving perfection – meaning sinlessness – in this lifetime. He was imprisoned for blasphemy as a result and many orthodox Christians still strongly disagree with him. Even Robert Barclay softened his claims. What speaks to me about perfection is the thought that the Greek term used in the Bible for "perfection" is more about coming to completion, or wholeness.

As a child, I so wanted to please others by being perfect – being the brightest, being on time, never being wrong. I was trapped by this as much as my friend was by the church teacher who encouraged her to be "perfect" in word and deed so that she would not be a "stumbling block" to the salvation of others (I Corinthians 8:9). For both of us the emphasis was on details of behavior without any link to the inner being. To become "perfect" as Jesus meant is a process of growing into a maturity of spirit visible in our actions. And perhaps even more, it is a state of being open to God's love flowing through us to others. Perfect love is an inward state of being. It is about becoming part of the wholeness of life and an attunement to all that is divine so complete that it frees the heart from fear.

Another way I think about perfection is to ask myself: Am I to become whatever I want to be? Am I to become more like Christ? Am I to become what the God at work inside me needs me to be? And then to ask: Are these the same question? Or not? I think not. I used to think they were. My mind changed as I looked back and realized I am not the person I wanted to be. In fact, I find myself now enjoying the writing and public speaking which I used to avoid at all costs. I never imagined my life could be the life it has become. This total about-face is not true for everyone. I know that. So for some, the questions I posed may seem to be, or are, one and the same. But I have come to see how limited my imagination was, and is. How restricting my ideas were, and sometimes still are – both as to my outward actions and my inward state.

57

Tuning the Inward Ear

Only recently has it occurred to me to consider feelings as part of a theological discussion. "Theology" always seemed an abstract discipline and irrelevant to daily life. Heavy tomes arguing over nitpicking points are irritating and arrogant. They make me laugh at the thought of spending one's life writing about such things, even as I am called to a ministry of writing. I am learning that there are ways to approach conversation about the Eternal which open up the heart. The Quaker tradition of transmitting theological reflections in personal journals falls under what is now a whole branch of study, that of narrative theology. In telling our stories of encounter with God, we help point others to that essential connection and help teach one another about discernment.

Learning to separate impulses and feelings from the guidance of the Inward Light is at the core of the discernment that comes with spiritual maturity. How do I recognize the voice of the Light? What sound does the Spirit make pushing on my heart? With attention, I can feel the difference between my own hesitations and the hand of the Light holding me back – most of the time. Great contemplatives tell us that at times discernment can only be confirmed in hindsight, when we see the results of our actions. But through prayerful attention, it is often possible to know which way to move.

The well-attuned inner ear is evident in the journals of early Friends as they record stories of coming to a crossroads, stopping, waiting to see which way to turn, then finding themselves in the home of someone who needed their presence. Some traveling ministers were adamant, upon arriving at a strange town and Meeting that they not be told any of the local news. They preferred to rely on the Spirit and to respond in the moment, rather than be influenced by what they had been told. I do not have that faith, or that well-developed an inner ear (although I suspect a connection there) and want to speak with people when I arrive at a community to give a talk or lead a retreat. I may then say things I had not planned to say or shift the focus of a weekend in ways which surprise me. Gradually I learn to trust. Less and less do I organize everything tightly in advance.

Listening to the Voice of the Light is the central piece in this puzzle. It is what distinguishes between doing what I think I want and what the universe has in store for me — what might be called "Christ forming in me," even though I rarely would phrase it that way. Faithfulness to the Guide does something to the heart that no amount of money or fame can do. When I am acting and speaking in accord with the Light, my voice is steady, my actions sure, my words correct. The uncertainties and doubts drop away.

Living Out of A Place of Love

I can feel the consequences in my life resulting from the intense encounter with Love. For many years, I focused on being an example by doing things normally assigned to men: math, chemistry, competitive sports. I was one of a very few women, either in my work as a research chemist or as a maritime facility planner. I was determined to prove that all women should have that opportunity. Nothing wrong with the goal, but along the way I got pulled into the trap of trying to be like the men around me and to win on their terms. Theirs became the defining voices.

Seeing myself, beloved, in the eyes of the Inward Monitor was a shock and a relief. Little I saw was new. Yet, as months and years of exploration followed, fresh patterns of shadow and highlight were everywhere. So many assumptions about actions and feelings were turned on their heads. A fascination with words and a sense that I might actually have something to say replaced my dislike of all writing. Most important, I saw how damaging my own self-hatred was. That damaging feeling shriveled and dried under the intensity of a love so personal, so complete, so uncompromising, that no room remained for hatred, even self-hatred. The Light, which I had heard about all my life, came as both a searing searchlight and a comforting beacon when I actually experienced it. This beacon

LOVE
(I Corinthians 13)

Love is patient
Love is kind
Love is not envious or boastful
Love is not rude or arrogant
Love does not insist on its own way
Love is not irritable or resentful
Love does not rejoice in wrong-
   doing
Love bears all things, believes all
   things, hopes all things, endures
   all things
Love never ends

is so sure I go towards it without question. The searching is so intense I can't avoid the answers it gives and so persistent that years later it still is working its way through more and more corners of my soul.

Isaac Penington wrote a friend that while he might sit all day watching the young green corn, he would not see it change. But over the course of time that seed would form into ripe ears which nourished him and his community. Thus, the friend was advised to patience in his spiritual life and to know that it would come to fruition in its proper time. Patience is time and again noted as a mark of spiritual maturity.

Spiritual Growth

The best known of Paul's statements about spiritual growth is in I Corinthians, chapter 13, a passage which I memorized as a child in First Day School. Here, Paul describes the love which never ends. This love is complete. It does not rejoice in wrong-doing. In love we are known fully and come to know fully. It is in talking about such things that I appreciate other languages such as Greek which has multiple words for the various concepts we evoke by the word "love" — *agape, philia,* and *eros.* In English, different flavors include compassionate love, affectionate love, and erotic love, but I soon start shifting to words such as selflessness, neighborliness, constancy. But central is loving God with all our hearts, minds and souls, and loving our neighbor as God has first loved us.

We each come to spiritual maturity by our own paths and in our own time. The blind alleys and potholes are different. The specific answers are different and each of us must find our own way. The Quaker understanding of the Christian path is the way I know best, yet I see similarities in other faith traditions. The *sutras* read at the start of my yoga classes echo what I know from Meeting. In the ancient words of Patanjali, I hear words similar to what I have found through the Christianity of my spiritual ancestors. The modern Buddhist meditations of Jack Kornfield or Pema Chödron seek to bring us to this same place of forgiveness, loving-kindness and peace. The variations are infinite. The mystic encounters the one Eternal Presence and is drawn into the same way of being by any of multiple paths. Each soul drawn into this encounter, by mystical connection or by faith without the knowing, is also drawn to stand with others.

I do see the secret work of God going on in people's minds; look not at the work, nor look not at briars, nor look not at all the thorns, ... for it well may be there hath been no vinedresser nor plough man there; ... therefore the Lord hath set you forth to do his work – Margaret Fell, 1653[43]

Other seeds fell on rocky ground, ... when the sun rose, they were scorched; ... Other seeds fell on good soil and brought forth grain, some a hundredfold.
– Matthew 13: 3-9

BEING PRESENT TO OTHERS

The images of plowing and sowing central to the agricultural foundations of life transfer readily to the spiritual realm. Without the farmer, corn will not grow so profusely, nor tomatoes, nor any of the life-sustaining produce of our fields and orchards. The plow breaks up the hardened soil and cuts the interlocking weeds so the seed might more confidently fall on fertile ground. Do Friends today still feel any responsibility to be the farmer or the plow in other people's lives?

Wild foods long gave sustenance to bands of people, and still do in small pockets. In the wilderness, the natural condition of the soil determines what chance the seed might have to germinate and grow. As with the sower in the parable of the seed, so it is with the birds and other animals who drop seeds without conscious intent: some seeds fall on rocky ground, some on fertile soil, some yield fruit, others not, an image which speaks to the spiritual life as well as our physical well-being.

Matthew's image draws me into my own heart, where God often has to break up the hard soil of my life to make room for the holy seed to grow. Margaret Fell's caution makes me ask what my role is in the inward plowing and sowing which others experience: is a human "vinedresser" needed for the work of God to come to fruition? The knowledge of the importance of others in my own journey makes me open to Fell's prodding. I find it so much easier to feel "spiritual" while I am alone. The testing and the plowing seem to come when I engage, or don't engage, with the people around me. While solitude is essential, it is in the time of rough elbows in the ribs of my heart and the concreteness of my own outward response, be it helpful or wrong, that the deep plowing occurs. Sometimes, part of my call is to stand with others as they are made sometimes painfully tender as they mature, as their lives unfold to potential they had not known.

Reaching Out

I recall one evening sitting in a small group talking about whether we needed a new Meetinghouse to accommodate our growing community. There was disagreement as to whether growth was a good thing – shouldn't we all know each other well and be comfortable with each other? Someone then raised the question of whether or not we should list our Meetinghouse phone number in the telephone book – wasn't that too much like proselytizing? That evening, we finally all agreed that listing our phone number was just fine. Eventually we put a large sign on our building saying who we were.

What is the line between teaching and indoctrinating, between prophetic witness and insisting only our way is right? When is it right to share what we know and when should we simply stand with others while they find their own way? In these and many similar questions, we in the unprogrammed Friends Meetings have tended to err on the side of silence rather than raise any intimation of arm-twisting. We have shied away from changing individual hearts, more comfortable with activism targeting institutions.

In the early years of the 21st century, liberal Friends are asking ourselves many questions. Shouldn't we be more visible in the world if we think that what we have to say about living simply on this earth is important? If we believe we have learned something about peace and justice, shouldn't we be making that known? Shouldn't we let others know that Quakers are alive and well and have both a way of living and a perspective on the world which counters materialism and violence? Shouldn't we share what we know of spiritual matters?

Back in the early 1980s when I was clerk of the Yearly Meeting Outreach Committee I spent long hours supporting many isolated Friends and tiny

Meetings and Worship Groups in the Pacific Northwest. Groups which might have more children than adults and individuals living a hundred miles from the nearest Meeting were eager to find other Friends, or would-be Friends. Visitors were cherished and suggestions on how to meet others who would sit in worship on a Sunday were eagerly sought.

This experience is in sharp contrast to the hesitation about publishing our Meeting phone number. In the larger, urban community in the 1980s and 90s, few of us told anyone in our workplace or neighborhood we were Quakers or described how that affected our lives. Protest marches seemed the only place we were willing to make public statements. In peace demonstrations, gay and lesbian parades, and rallies against malicious harassment we carried signs proclaiming ourselves as being from Multnomah Meeting. While some Friends travel the world as mediators, find homes for the homeless, or work in prisons, speaking one-on-one about our faith seems harder. Over the years I have become much clearer about letting others know that I am a Friend and sharing what that means, but I still rarely invite anyone to attend Meeting.

In spring 2004 I attended a retreat on "Prophetic Ministry." In the extended, three-hour long worship that weekend, several people rose to speak claiming our role as prophets and the critical importance of Friends bringing our witness into the wider world. Little was explicitly said about what that meant, although witness against war in Iraq, not paying taxes for war, and similar concerns about our nation's policies were implied. We agree on our message to the world in these areas, but too often can't work with our fellow Friends in constructive, respectful ways. I find this latter work essential if we want to point to ways in which people who are passionate about their faith – be it Islam, Judaism, Hinduism, Christianity, or another faith – can speak their beliefs clearly, practice their faith without hindrance, yet respect that other faiths are valid. This vision is a crucial part of our witness.

The shift in consciousness about religion in the early 21st century is slowly ending our reluctance to speak out. Many of us are getting angry about the presumption that knowing Christ means deeming homosexuality a sin or believing that war is right. We are becoming more willing to speak up about who we are and the importance of spirituality in human life. We are saying that nurturing the Seed within will lead one to nurture truly loving relationships among couples no matter what their gender. We are saying that a lively, growing Seed of Christ within brings individuals to an inner peace wherein they can no longer take a human life or participate in war. We are learning that God is calling us to help nurture that Seed in all people.

Community

When I was working on *The Historical Dictionary of The Friends (Quakers)*, about 100 people contributed essays on Quaker history and practice. No one we (the editors) asked was willing to write anything about "community" – even though it is in the list of testimonies as summarized by Howard Brinton, one of the best-known 20th-century Friends. For more evangelical Friends, the answer was simple – the entry should be about the nature of the "church" and how Quakers have always understood the church to be the people of God, not a building. For others of us, community is certainly something we long for. But what is it — an extended family, a social set, a group of neighbors, a collection of peace activists, or what?

To the mild dismay of my co-editors, I insisted we include the term "familied monasticism" in the *Dictionary*, largely because it gives me a framework for considering how I see community among Friends. This odd term is a modern one, used by one of the former teachers at the School of the Spirit, Kathryn Damiano, to express Quaker practice as a melding of spiritual discipline and engagement with the world. It holds up an ideal, mindful of monastic practice, of people supporting one another in turning to the Light – through prayer, meditation, or devotional reading.

Today, at least in North America, Friends live apart from one another, raise our families, hold regular jobs, and otherwise live as most Americans do in many ways. We are not isolated from cultural pressures by living in a cloistered environment, nor do we have a clear set of rules of attendance at prayer and other matters which are enforced by those around us. We somehow have to find the discipline.

The spiritual community I call home, Multnomah Monthly Meeting, is a relatively large, urban Meeting. It is not unusual to have ten or more people introduce themselves as newcomers on a given Sunday morning after worship. Some are Friends from other parts of the country, but some are stepping inside a Meetinghouse for the first time ever, regularly confronting us with the question of explaining ourselves and engaging the stranger. Sometimes I wish we presumed, as many evangelical Friends churches do, that anyone with any serious interest in Friends will take courses about Quakerism. Whoever teaches at Multnomah has to be prepared for two people to show up when they hope for 30. Even so, programs on the basics of Quaker history and practice only touch a portion of the need.

In Multnomah Meeting I found a community determined to use small groups to help build trust and spiritual connection. I was trained in leadership without realizing it by participating in "Gifts and Discoveries," a program designed so we each took turns being in charge. When hard issues arose in the Meeting requiring careful consideration, "Zip Code Groups" brought me in contact with people I didn't know and encouraged us to penetrate beyond our initial reactions to the problem. I also cherish the small, spontaneous groups which offer intimacy within a Meeting of several hundred members and attenders.

In some ways, these small groups seem to replace the old practice of visiting with Meeting families in their homes to worship together and reflect on the guidance of the Spirit. At their best, many interlocking circles bring a variety of people together in fluid interactions and develop strong connections across the entire community. In my shyness, I remain conscious of the people "lost" around the fringes with few of us even knowing who they are.

The rough elbows most often bump in our Business Meetings. In this place which some find alternately threatening and boring, I find a plough at work. This was most painfully obvious when a man, a member of another Meeting and a recently released sexual offender, came to worship with us. We did not meet this test well in the midst of conflicting desires to welcome everyone and to protect our children and those who had been abused in the past. This period demonstrated that we inevitably fail when we try only to protect ourselves, and that we needed skill, intent, strength, and attention to the Spirit to answer that of God in the former convict who was worshipping with us.

At the end of three years of conflict around our responses to this man, a few people voiced thankfulness that we had been able to make this a public discussion, and that in so doing, we had given them the impetus they needed to face and to heal from abuse in their own lives. Some left the Meeting altogether rather than face the pain. Some, including me, were left bewildered or distressed, but with a growing conviction that we needed to find ways to preserve this open engagement with the harsh brokenness of the world but at the same time find surer ways to engage and to witness to God's way. Surprisingly, I have come to find at least some of the answers I need in the cross.

Taking up the Cross

ℒ TAKING UP THE CROSS ℒ

Friends are called to *take up the Cross daily* — not as a static symbol of Jesus' death at the hands of the Romans, but as the living reality of Truth present in our lives and breaking the bonds of egotism. The cross, as I have come to know it, speaks to something deep in the human condition and says something profound about the nature of all that is holy.

For a long time I carried with me a negative response to even thinking about the *atonement* – it struck me as some of the most outrageous theology in Christendom. Comparing my own reactions and the way early Friends considered the Atonement made a space where I might drop old reflexes and hear more clearly the underlying message of evangelical Friends. Whether one sees the cross as horizontal and vertical lines marking the intersection of the sacred and the earthly creation or as a sign of God's reconciliation with humanity through Jesus Christ, the cross points to the tension of separation and unity between the visible and the unseen aspects of our lives: the separation of humanity from God. The cross overcomes our fear of death and suffering. It speaks to us as individuals, but also to our deep connections with all of humankind as well as all creation. It draws each of us into being part of a world-changing response which overcomes violence. And it points to the reality of divine guidance and calls us to faithful listening against all opposition.

I resist some of what Truth asks of me and at times want to *flee the Cross*. All too often my head doesn't want to do what I hear the still small voice pushing me to do. My fears overwhelm me and my imagination builds up stories in my head about what might go wrong. When I respond to the sense of divine love flowing into me and through me to the world, I find myself stepping into a place of certainty and clarity where I know I move with a tenderness that is more than human. I am sustained in my soul. The love flowing through me touches others around me. My work is rightly ordered. Taking up the cross can having surprising consequences including a quiet delight at the beauty and glory of God.

"Taking up the cross daily" was a common phrase among Friends for centuries. But the immediate image this phrase long drew up for me – that of someone seeking out *suffering* — is not what they meant. To take up the cross is to be obedient to God which to me means being attentive to the Eternal Principle in every moment (or at least as often as we can manage) and to know that the guidance of the Spirit is more important than being successful in business, popular, wealthy, or influential. To take up the cross is to shift one's entire frame of reference about what is crucial in this life and what is not. It allows us to hold on to the world lightly yet identify with the pain of others. It also allows us to face suffering knowing that we will be upheld, and to accept that sometimes suffering is necessary if we are to be faithful witnesses.

And he that would... hear the voice of God in his true ministry, must first take up the cross to that part of him which is not of God, and receive from God the eye which sees, and the ear which hears. – Isaac Penington, 1680[44]

The obedience of the light of Christ Jesus is the obedience to the cross of Christ ... The cross of Christ, which is the power of God, is to crucify the affections and the lusts thereof, the world the flesh, and the devil. – Margaret Fell, 1660[45]

... But [God] said to me, "My grace is sufficient for you, for power is made perfect in weakness." ... for whenever I am weak, then I am strong. – 2 Corinthians 12: 8, 10

TAKING UP THE CROSS DAILY

What is the cross to me that I should spend an entire section of this book on it when I once cringed at the sight of a crucifix? Ever since having a clear leading that this was important to my sense of being a Quaker, I've found myself asking "What does the cross tell me about how I live my life?" and "What does it have to do with the way the world works?" To answer these questions I have to return to my early fascination with the infinitude of space, which for so many years I pursued by delving into science books. I delighted as liquid changed color when I slowly added colorless drops, or suddenly was full of solid materials when none were there before — all the small wonders of chemistry labs. I wanted so to know what the world is about, what makes it all tick, why things happen, even as I delight in the mystery opening before me.

In more recent years, that drive to understand and to marvel at the unexpected has shifted its focus. The miracles I see are in the human capacity to face suffering and still find purpose or even happiness in life. I am in awe of Dawn, the mother of a ten year old when she was diagnosed with an aggressive cancer. She was told she had perhaps six months with no treatment, maybe a few years with extensive chemotherapy and surgery. She wanted ten years (at least) and internally knew she would not have those years to enjoy with her family. My image of her is full of laughter, laughter grounded on a rock and full of knowing even when it was clear the pain was strong. She sought to break the secrecy which often accompanies the process of dying and asked others of us to accompany her in this time of approaching the shift to another form of existence. A small group formed to work with the book *One Year to Live*, knowing that for Dawn it was probably literally true. Even knowing she did not have those ten years to accompany her daughter, Dawn projected a certainty that she and those around her would be all right, a certainty which echoed words of early Friends as they faced what they believed was reunion with God.

Another friend, Peggy, is a Quaker pastor who a number of years ago took over a rural Oregon Friends' church with a congregation of 25 adults and children. The day after she started work there a young woman and her three small girls were murdered by their husband/father. All were members of the Meeting. The next hours, days and years tell us much about the resiliency of the human spirit as this small, tight-knit community upheld the extended family. Peggy was given a vision of God's community acting together and the clerk of the Meeting brought a commitment to reconciliation and non-violence. Much of the town gathered around the church and found a path of acceptance rather than turning to revenge and hatred. That year, the congregation grew to two or three times its previous size.

I have written these two stories in terms which speak of human capacities, but am certain that something more is involved. Dawn and Peggy are both Quakers, one who drew on pagan, Buddhist, and Celtic/Christian spirituality, the other a committed Christian evangelist with strong ties to the Holiness tradition. While their theologies couldn't be more different, I experience the same Spirit moving in both their lives. I know that both have regular, intentional, and intensive spiritual practice. Both reach out. Both turn to the Infinite and respond to what they hear.

So perhaps my question here is, "What do they hear and follow?" Next I ask, "How did that change their lives?" I ask these questions in relation to the cross after reading so many Quaker journals and other materials which lay out the cross as obedience to God, an obedience which opens each individual to divine power, unexpected and beyond our imagining.

Attending and Following

"Taking up the cross daily" does not mean that our every action puts our lives or relationships or property at risk (although we may have to). Taking up the cross is a state of being which means we are attentive to something more than our own needs, our own desires, our own logic, the demands of those around us. This inner awareness, this search for cosmic signposts (mostly tiny arrows marked in the dirt on some inner path), which is so crucial to Friends' spirituality, is the first action in taking up the cross. The second action is to follow that small arrow in the dirt even when it seems to lead to the cliff edge or into the heart of the blackberry bush. This combination of attention and response, listening and obedience, is a central aspect of what Isaac Penington and William Penn meant when they called us to take up the cross daily – to follow the signposts which lead us closer to union with the Eternal Presence.

The willingness to be alert to invisible signposts grew out of my response to a strong inward push towards vocal ministry despite a lifelong habit of silence. The long work involved in change often dredged up old pain. The gap between my once scientific self and this calling still amazes me.

While I was participating in the Way of Ministry program at Pendle Hill, Laura, one of the teachers, several times looked at me and with her hands, sought to draw me into speaking. One of these times was when I was sitting to the side, with my foot elevated after twisting my ankle. The group exercise just finished had involved milling around the room, then stopping periodically and engaging another person. People had to be reminded to walk to the side and include me in the exercise. It was as the group reflected on this that Laura turned to me and almost willed me to finally speak about my visible sense of separateness from the group. I also spoke to how being apart physically let me see others in the room who were apart from the group emotionally and seeking to avoid engagement as they moved.

It took a lot for me to speak of my own feelings about this — just a small glimpse of what obedience to the Holy is about. If I had been seeking what was comfortable, I would have kept my mouth shut. Once I spoke, I realized I was also speaking for others – something which happened to me other times during the program, particularly when I spoke of complex emotions which some of the exercises triggered in me.

This is where the cross comes in, the cross that is not stuck in theology about salvation from our sins, but rather the living cross. To take up the living cross is to respond to the Divine Voice and set aside self-will. Standing in the cross, we recognize the agony so prevalent in the world yet are not mired down in it. These concepts spell out the paradox of the cross: it is at once about holy obedience and about divine power.

My call to a ministry of writing and speaking is a cross to my desire to remain in the background — to be quiet, get lots of things done, but not be visible. I had to give up many comfortable habits of being and interacting. It would have been much more pleasant to go on without change. I had also to give up a focus on accomplishing things, something I was very good at. The lesson is not that planning is wrong and that we should simply hang around and let happen what will; that smacks to me of laziness and avoidance. Can we plan, yet hold plans lightly? If so, we can work hard and accomplish tasks while being conscious of the path, accepting that the wisdom of Love might have different aims than the goals we can define, just as John Woolman was called to faithfully deliver his message about the evils of slavery while knowing that the end result was in God's hands.

The Cross is the Power of God

Not long after I became presiding clerk of Friends Committee on National Legislation, (FCNL), the Quaker lobby group in Washington D.C., I was nearly taken aback when I suggested something happen and suddenly staff started to act on my words.

Power is an uncomfortable topic to bring up in Quaker circles except in the context of "speaking truth to power." Power has connotations of control – controlling others, to be exact. All too aware of the human tendency to want to be in control, we shy away from any use of power. What happens if we speak out *and* can make things happen? As I found out in a tiny way in the FCNL offices, it can be disconcerting. Several strands of my life played into this discomfort with any forms of power: the deference I was taught as a young girl; rigid expectations of what women can and cannot do; an image I carried of Quakers as a small, inconsequential group; the admonition of the Sermon on the Mount that "blessed are the meek"; and awareness of the ugliness and addictions which make people want to control other people's lives. The concept that the "cross is the power of God" was key in untangling the complexities of my reaction to the concept that I might have the power to change the world.

In *True Testimony*, Margaret Fell wrote that, "The obedience of the light of Christ Jesus is the obedience to the cross of Christ, … which is the power of God."[46] Okay. This sounds straightforward and not particularly revealing. She is telling me to give into divine power and be obedient to God.

"[It] is a mystery to the wise rabbis [teachers] of the world and all the disobedient ones that will not stoop to the light of Christ," Fell goes on to say. Such folks "exercise their fleshly liberty, pride and ambition, superfluity of naughtiness, vain glory and arrogancy, voluptuousness, pomp and vanity of the world." I enjoy her play with words using "mystery" here in its common sense, in contrast to other places where she named God as "Mystery," and her use of "superfluity of naughtiness," which should be enough to make anyone rethink their actions!

Fell continued by saying that, "The cross of Christ, which is the power of God, is to crucify the affections and the lusts thereof." In other words: stop running after celebrity or accumulating possessions, they will only pull you further into selfishness and cause more harm. The end result of living in the cross is to "bring forth the fruits of the spirit, which are in all, goodness, righteousness, and truth: yes, love, joy, peace, long-suffering, gentleness, faith, meekness, and temperance. Against such there is no law."

Sitting with these passages and the rest of her writing in *True Testimony*, something more arises in me. Margaret Fell is not talking about submitting to God's power and becoming helpless, even though our actions will become gentler and more temperate. This spiritual ancestor is really talking about the cross as entering into the power of God. Those who take up the cross are thus visible in their actions, and able to act in the power of God, a power which enriches and enlarges the well-being of all, in contrast to the powers of the world, which engorge a few.

Holy Power

What is it like then to accept that we might be powerful? Starhawk, the feminist activist and Wiccan, writes about power in groups, in leadership, in patriarchy, in ritual, in daily life and more. She names three primary forms of power: power-over, power-from-within, and power-with. She defines these as follows: "Power-over is linked to domination and control; power-from-within is linked to the mysteries that awaken our deepest abilities and potential. Power-with is social power, the influence we wield among equals."[47] She ties power-over with the estrangement that is prevalent in our culture, noting that witches have a saying, "Where there's fear, there's power." Power-from-within she associates with the unfolding creativity of small children and our deep connection with each other and the environment. Power-with occurs when someone speaks so that others listen willingly and act. It is filled with respect. She sets her awareness of each of these kinds of power in the context of being one of 600 women confined in the gym at Camp Parks after being arrested for participating in a nonviolent blockade of the nuclear weapons lab at Livermore.

Margaret Fell seems in agreement with Starhawk about the nature of power: we are not to have "power-over" others; "power-from-within" is that which rises from the Light within us; and "power-with" is to know that all people are equally loved by God. In addition, Margaret Fell would probably have insisted that the cross and risen Christ are central, not our human self, and perhaps be quite pointed in her remarks about witches. What might have happened if they had met? My mind likes to play with the possibility. I am certain, however, that they both know power in its various manifestations and are clear about which ones they chose.

So, how do I experience this holy power? The most obvious way is simply that I am sitting here and writing about it. Mind-boggling! Especially when I look back and feel the old fear generated when teachers called on me, or recall how few words I had for faith or for emotion. Words form a link, they affirm, they cut through bad assumptions, or they can do the opposite. The Gospel of John begins by saying, "In the beginning was the Word." In a reference work, *New Testament Words*,[48] I find a list of actions of *logos* – which means "word" in Greek and also refers to all of Jesus' message as well as being a name for Jesus. As used in the Christian Testament, words judge, purify and lead to belief. Logos is an agent of rebirth which must be heard and received, held on to and abided in. Logos must be kept and witnessed to as well as served, spoken with boldness and acted upon. I missed so much in my silence, yet just speaking is not in itself enough, for words may also be hollow, disbelieved, or used to manipulate. My gift of words is dependent on standing in that paradoxical place where holy boldness and humility intersect. This is one of many paradoxes which become evident when taking up the cross and learning of the power it carries.

The knowledge that I truly am loved, unconditionally, is one aspect of this power. Another is to recognize that my words have merit and that what I know from a deep source is worth saying. I can take my place as one among equals. A third aspect is the reality that, at least upon occasion, others find what I have to say worth hearing and ask me to take leadership. Thus, being empowered (power-from-within) and being given respect (power-with) are both part of my experience.

Fear, power, and love are all interconnected. Whether the first or the last of these is dominant determines the nature of the power. Fear gave too many people too much power over my life for many years. Sometimes fear still slips in, but I recognize its shadow more easily and am less apt to be swallowed up by it as the moon was last night by its total eclipse. There have been times and places when an eclipse elicited fear in humanity, fear of the unknown. Elaborate rituals were developed to reassure, and often to control, the people who were so afraid. So knowledge is also central to power – knowledge of the world, knowledge of others, knowledge of the self, knowledge of divinity.

Power Over Death

Yet another aspect of power is only on the edge of my experience: the power over death. I cannot deny the reality of this power, even as the reality seems complex, only to be seen out of the corner of the eye. If I try and look at it directly, I cannot see it.

A few years ago, a woman my age from Meeting learned she had cancer. She explored many possible treatments and made her decisions. Within months, it was apparent she would not live much longer, and she entered a residential hospice. A few days before her death, I joined in a small Meeting for Worship at her bedside. She was not visibly conscious, yet as we sat in worship I was filled with the knowledge that she was ministering to us, not us to her. She was at peace and largely in that space, whatever it might be, beyond the grave. I cannot explain it otherwise.

I do not have in me yet that freedom from fear of death. I am slowly more able to be around people who are close to death. I believe that somehow our spirits, our souls go on after the body dies. Bodily resurrection is outside my conceptual framework. My strongest experiences of God have been soon after death – the death of my mother as well as my father. So I know God in grief, and that in this absolute brokenness the Holy One molds the soul. More than that I do not know.

Standing Still in the Power of God

Turning to the Tao Te Ching, I find a wisdom which seems closer to early Quaker experience and understanding of the Gospel message than the theology which asserts that God sent his only son to die on the cross in order to save us from our sins. Stephen Mitchell's translation of Chapter 16 seems to convey the underlying orientation to the Pure Principle which is at the heart of the Quaker practice of taking up the cross.

Tao Te Ching (16)[49]

Empty your mind of all thoughts.
Let your heart be at peace.
Watch the turmoil of beings,
but contemplate their return.
Each separate being in the universe
returns to the common source.
Returning to the source is serenity.
If you don't realize the source,
you stumble in confusion and sorrow.
When you realize where you come from,
you naturally become tolerant,
disinterested, amused,
kindhearted as a grandmother,
dignified as a king.
Immersed in the wonder of the Tao,
you can deal with what life brings you,
and when death comes, you are ready.

I love the idea of being both grandmother and king. The humor of this translation tells me much about the state of being it seeks to describe.

It speaks of an integration of self, inward wholeness, and completion. I have felt this most strongly in Meeting for Worship when the hour is but an instant and the instant extends beyond. On the more everyday level, I am increasingly aware that my ability to make choices and see options increases when I stop trying to force things to happen and let the anxiety drop away. In this state I am conscious of more of the universe and am less apt to stumble. There is more space for caring. I am better able to deal with what life brings my way.

Taking up the cross is an inward state of being immersed in the Spirit. To hear the Inward, we must first learn to recognize it and know it as the Source of all being. Then we must still our mental gyrations. Mine are particularly strong, so I rarely get beyond the point of wanting to do this. My yoga practice helps. It is a time of intense concentration on kinesthesia, balance, breathing, and awareness of different kinds of pain. "When am I going to hurt myself?" is a very real question as I enter my sixties and attempt to do a variety of stretches and upside-down poses I could never do as a child. Recognizing and finding ways to counter fear is also an important part of my yoga practice. I've always been afraid of any kind of turning on my head, so headstands and handstands are a significant accomplishment. To learn to kick my feet up onto the wall in a supported handstand took years – my body was convinced I would fall over backwards despite my rational awareness of the wall. Sometimes responding to the beckoning of the Spirit is like that: fear and rationality, patience and persistence all get involved before I can move.

At times I hold up the words of William Penn as a reminder of how I am called to be:

> The cross of Christ is a figure of speech borrowed from the wooden cross on which Christ submitted to the will of God. The cross mystical is that divine grace which crosses the carnal wills of men. It may justly be termed the instrument of man's wholly dying to the world and being made conformable to the will of God. Nothing else can mortify sin or make it easy for us always to submit to the divine will.... Where does this cross appear and where is it to be taken up? Within. For, where the sin is, the cross must be.[50]

Penn drew upon a framework for viewing the world — a faith based in awareness of sin and salvation, hell and heaven — that is not always easy to comprehend, yet his words return me to awareness of standing still in the Light. To stand in the Light is to sink into submission to the mystery which is divine grace. This grace "crosses the carnal wills of men." It is about letting go of our desire to control and make the world conform to what we want. Knowing "divine grace" is returning to the source where we encounter serenity. Grace, I have learned, makes us "kindhearted" and "dignified", and is full of wonder. Given space, it allows us to deal with what life brings, and prepares us to face death — without fear.

And it was called the light … which let them see all their evil words and deeds and their sins, and the same light would let them see Christ to save them from their sin and to blot it out. – George Fox, 1657[51]

Have mercy on me, O God,
according to your steadfast love;
according to your abundant mercy
blot out my transgressions. — Psalm 51:1, 2

And you, that were sometime alienated and enemies in your mind by wicked works, yet now hath he reconciled … to present you holy and unblameable and unreprovable in his sight… — Colossians 1:21, 22 (KJV)

ATONEMENT 13

O ne of the lessons of these past dozen years is that when something seriously irritates me, or if I have a really strong response on the order of "I'll never do that!" this is a sign for me to stop and pay attention. Whatever it is that caused me to react negatively may be just the thing which unblocks another room in my soul. My irritation at the concepts of "The Cross" and "Atonement" is one of those places where shuffling as best I can through the dank pages of academic theology despite my initial distaste has well repaid the effort. I make no claims of expertise, only a desire to share what has broken down my resistance and made me more tender towards what was once alien. Others may well find that these are not stumbling blocks for them, but perhaps my process of allowing my intellect to grapple with concepts in ways which free my heart could be helpful.

The phrase "Jesus died for your sins" long made my skin crawl. A bit of this is in the head knowledge: I often find the Atonement a messy theology, complex and full of theories which make little sense. But the teeth-clenching response comes from somewhere else. A God who sacrificed his only son is an appalling concept that makes me run from

Christianity. Almost as bad is the idea that Jesus' death somehow bought my soul. But the crazy idea that there is a power which comes from accepting the cross, from being more like Jesus, from a God who suffers with us, lures me further in so that I am willing to sift through the dust of theory looking for the pearl.

Atonement

The word "atonement" speaks to reconciliation, and in Christianity "Atonement" refers to reconciliation between humanity and God through Jesus Christ according to various theological dictionaries I consulted. Apparently there is no official church dogma about the Atonement as there is about the Incarnation and Resurrection.[52] For a long time I associated the Atonement with sacrifice and thought it meant that Jesus was a substitute for the traditional lamb or other animal killed to appease a vengeful God. This idea is not far from the "satisfaction" theory described below. More appealing is the belief that atonement is about self-identification with the life and death of Jesus. Sitting with the academic, intellectual issues as well as the emotional and spiritual nature of the various questions raised lets me see which ideas upset me and where there is room for something which might touch my soul and clear the blocks.

My reading of these dictionaries[53] tells me that the three most widely believed Christian theories of the Atonement are as follows:

Ransom Theory: In this theory, identified as the "classical view" of Paul, the early Greek church fathers and the German reformer, Martin Luther, humanity is portrayed as enslaved by "sin, death, and the devil" — the powers of evil. God then defeats these powers through the crucifixion of Jesus and redeems humankind from these powers. Humanity has no active part in this reconciliation. All the initiative is on God's side: God changes "His" mind about His relation with humanity.

Sacrificial or "Satisfaction" Theory: In this view, connected with St. Anselm, and adopted by Roman Catholic and Protestant orthodoxy, humanity's disobedience is considered an affront to God's honor and thus God requires satisfaction (which sounds to me like an old-fashioned duel). Because it is impossible for God's creation to offer sufficient satisfaction, God must act. Therefore, "God becomes man in order to satisfy his own offended honor." In another variation on this (known as the Penal or Substitutionary Theory), mankind deserves to be punished, but Christ takes the punishment instead. This can also be seen as Christ sacrificing himself and taking the brunt of God's wrath which humanity really deserves. Thus, the practice of individuals taking on any kind of suffering is considered by some to be appropriate acceptance of punishment and part of "being saved."

Forgiving Love or Moral Influence Theory: This theory, identified with the 12th-century French philosopher Abelard, has Jesus as the embodiment of God's sacrificial love. By Jesus' death on the cross, humanity is freed from the fear of God and thus each individual is able to respond fully to that divine love. In accepting the cross, therefore, the individual is changed within as well as in their words and actions by divine love.

My explorations also led me to the Hebrew Testament where sacrifice was the outward form of atonement – reconciliation with God — restoring the relationship damaged by human sin.[54] But sacrifice of an animal was not effective without the cleansing or spiritual purification of the persons making the sacrifice. "After the destruction of the Temple [in Jerusalem] in 70 CE the only means of atonement were prayer, repentance, fasting, charity, and full restitution."[55]

Forgiveness and Divine Mercy: The Early Quaker View

Where did early Friends fit in all this? They believed Jesus' death on the cross was necessary for reconciliation between humanity and God, according to the late Quaker theologian, Wilmer Cooper.[56] However, unlike other Christians of their time, Friends also insisted that being sanctified, that is, coming to live more like Jesus in response to the Inward Light of Christ, is at the heart of salvation and increasing wholeness. The work of the cross — which they knew as the power of God in the human soul to act against all that is evil – occurs inwardly. They found that the cross transforms hatred and arrogance, opening space for tenderness to all people. The cross also gives the power to speak truthfully and calmly to Pontius Pilate as the crowd clamors for your crucifixion, or to meet for worship in front of a locked Meetinghouse knowing the king's soldiers are coming to beat you and imprison you. They named this God's power, not an act of human will.

Isaac Penington invited us, "So, come into this covenant, …there is no more remembering of sin there, but perfect forgiveness through this one offering, and so no more need of any more sacrificing"[57] Here, Penington described the Atonement as an act of forgiveness of sin and an end to the need to make sacrifice to appease an angry God. The death of Jesus on the cross is the sign of a new covenant with God, just as the rainbow was a symbol of Yahweh's covenant with Noah after the flood. In this new covenant we are to know and live out the law which is written in the heart rather than focus on conformity to the written law.[58] The written law is not in error, but it is not the total story. This knowledge of the inward source of divine guidance is that which fulfills or completes the written law and allows us to live out Way of Love in Spirit and in Truth.

George Fox spoke about mercy as much as forgiveness. He was also clear that God would blot out the sins of those who sincerely change. Blotting out implies that as far as God is concerned, the things we did wrong in the past never happened and the Eternal will never recall them or taunt us with them.

Fox knew how easy it is to be troubled by the multitude of impulses which pull us into seemingly easy but negative actions and how powerful the urge to backslide can be: "Friends: Whatever you are addicted to, the Tempter will come in that thing. When he can trouble you, then he gets advantage over you, and then you are gone." Knowing this, Fox gave simple, lovely advice to "stand still in that which is pure, after you see yourselves, and then Mercy comes in. After you see your thoughts and the temptations, do not think but submit." What then might be the result? "Then the Power comes."

Fox repeated and summarized his advice thus: "Stand still in the Light and submit to it, and the other will be hushed and gone. Then contentment comes. When temptations and troubles appear, sink down in that which is pure, and all will be hushed and fly away. Your strength is to stand still…"[59]

Here I hear how strong the pull of rationalization can be – how easy it is to talk ourselves into going along. "Just doing this little thing won't hurt" or "I'm much too busy to . . ." I know I have honed the skill of finding reasons to not call people, even when I know someone is lonely. Fox yet again said not to rationalize, but to stand still and take up the cross.

"And then Mercy comes in." This is what makes Fox's words resonate. Elsewhere he wrote, "The mercies of God are known when we are under judgment and hungering for the right way of life."[60] This evokes in me a gentle rain of love washing over me when I yearn for doing what the Inward Teacher has encouraged, but at the same time know I have not done it. When I turn away from whatever I have been doing and move in the direction of that Teacher, I know a support and rightness which well might be called mercy. Refuse to change and guilt gets pretty heavy in me. So Fox's language describes my experience better than language of sin and forgiveness.

William Penn's book, *No Cross, No Crown*, has a message particularly apt for today's middle-class Americans. Penn wrote about pride and its excessive desire for knowledge, its longing for power and personal honor: concerns not surprising for a man brought up to wealth and power. Covetousness and the desire for luxury — luxury in "diversions" (entertainment and recreation), as well as material goods and adherence to fashion are the other major concerns he addresses. I sometimes think of pride as a bulldozer in my life: it keeps me going when everything seems to have disintegrated into rubble, but the crudeness of it means I miss many precious details and can crush the pain and hopes of others in its passage.

Penn was absolute in his assessment that "none must do evil that good should follow" and in linking the excesses of the wealthy to the agony of those left to toil.[61] Penn did not mince words: "O you pretended followers of the crucified Jesus! Examine yourselves. Don't you know that if he dwell not, if he rule not in you, that you are reprobates?"[62] But Penn does not end with condemnation, rather with the assurance that all who do take up the cross will know God's kingdom.

My Response

All these theories give me much to chew on. What gets in the way of my relationship with God? What drives my prejudices against Christianity? The last question is important to me, for I don't believe I can be truly loving without facing the way I slip into defensiveness upon hearing only a few words about someone's relationship with Jesus. And I want to find more ways to sort out my own prejudices from honest disagreements. Coming to more clarity in my heart about the Atonement involves reconciliation with my past, but this is only a part.

If I cannot see reconciliation of God and humanity as defined by some cosmic sacrifice, or penalty, or purchase by death on the cross, what approach might speak to my condition? While I know that faith does not depend on intellectual consistency and rationality, my gut cannot accept that *only* the act of Jesus dying (out of all such self-sacrifice in the face of unjust punishment) is sufficient to bring God and humanity together.

Yet the yearning in my soul says that the death of Jesus on the cross is the Way bringing the holy to fruition in humanity. This particular death lives before us as the alternative to self-serving actions, to vengeance, to hatred, to greed. It replaces the ongoing punishments of "an eye for an eye and a tooth for a tooth." It supplants the conviction that *only* my family or my nation are what matter. If Jesus is truly God, then the Eternal is an extraordinary kind of Love, a Truth that is hard for me to comprehend. This Rock, as made visible in the person of Jesus, is not afraid in the face of the most appalling threats. The Defender speaks truth with gentle conviction no matter what the consequences. This Power will not impose itself, or even defend itself, by force of arms or coercion.

I am so easily separated from God – at least it feels that way to me. I so easily imagine the worst in any situation and look for things to go wrong rather than trusting. If sin is about missing the mark, about separation from God, then sin is a regular part of my condition. Ways to restore the sense of the Holy in my life are essential. Is that why some people love altar calls and go forward again and again, seeking reassurance that the Comforter loves them? My life feels full of back and forth motion between bleak awareness of my limits followed by rest and reassurance that all is well. Yet even in the bleakness I can often tell that I am upheld. I can feel the breath of the Spirit on my neck even as I am tempted to indulge the arrogance which says I don't need to do the preparation needed to be faithful to what I am called to do – an indulgence early Friends would name as fleeing the cross. This urge to flee comes in infinite forms. My reason can dig incredible ditches for me to fall into. Being too busy can stretch a tarp across the void, but nothing strong enough to walk upon for long. Only tender Mercy can support me, and sometimes I need other people – or even jarring concepts – to point this out.

Consider whether ye did not flee from the cross, in your transplanting into New England, ... and gave advantage to that spirit to get ground in you, which you outwardly fled from. –Isaac Penington, 1660[63]

And going a little further, he threw himself on the ground and prayed, "My Father, if it is possible, let this cup pass from me; yet not what I want but what you want." Then he came to the disciples and found them sleeping... –Matthew 26:38-40

FLEEING THE CROSS

Just a few minutes ago, after I opened this file, I "minimized" the word processing program and played a game of solitaire rather than starting to write. Most of my resistance is on this level – putting off for a few minutes, or a few days, my writing, phone calls I know I should make ... the list goes on. What is it in me, in all of us, which can make it so hard to do the apparently simple tasks that I know are mine to do?

I wish sometimes I were part of the Jewish tradition where people are encouraged to argue and even bargain with God. This seems to make God more alive and at the same time makes me more of an agent in my own fate. Slowly I am learning to do that sometimes, but this is a fairly recent thing. For much of my life, I simply ran and hid.

"My Spirit Revolts"

I love the stories of early Friends in part because they offer many examples of strong resistance which arises even when knowing an action is right. Rachel Hicks, a 19th-century New York Friend, reported, "... the language was sounded intelligibly to my mental ear, 'If faithful to My requirings, thou wilt have to speak in My name to the assemblies of the people and travel extensively in the ministry.'" She went on to say how "This was an unexpected and unwelcome message. My nature revolted, and I said in my heart, 'This is a service I cannot perform.'"

She then noted that when, about a year later, she felt an intimation that she was to stand and speak she responded by silently asking God to let this pass. She felt God grant this request and "a sensible feeling of His presence was withdrawn, and long was I left, as a dove without its mate, moaning my condition, and longing for the return of the Beloved of my soul."[64] It was more than twenty years before she gave into the original requiring, and stood to speak in worship. Since I was in my forties before I first spoke in worship, I most definitely identify with such stories of resistance.

What is this resistance about? When I've been aware of it, I know it makes me miserable. I want to respond, but often can't make myself. At times I work hard to comply with the strong inward sense that this is what I am to do or say, then fail and am remorseful for long periods after. Other times I simply cannot face the whole thing and duck into the oblivion of mindless, distracting tasks. It is amazing how many things need doing when this inner resistance raises up. I can get lots of yard work done! Fleeing the cross has its benefits.

It can seem that fleeing the cross is much easier than taking it up. But on a deeper level it is much more painful to turn and run. This is not a rational thing. Actually, I think neither response has much to do with rationality or even with immediate happiness. I can know fully that I will be at ease in my soul if I take a certain step and still not be able to act. Thus to flee the cross is to flee happiness. I can also know at other times that the action God asks of me is incredibly difficult and I might face immediate discomfort and the displeasure of others. So taking up the cross can be to turn away from happiness as well. It all sounds like a no-win situation when I start thinking this way.

One of the things I am called to do these days is to speak positively of evangelicals to liberal Quakers. Some of my friends dismiss the Bible as nonsense and irrelevant, a thing of the past that no rational person would pay attention to. Others lump together all Christians into a highly fundamentalist camp while others struggle with (or condemn) my lack of Christian orthodoxy. Some patronize me for my quaint, misguided efforts. Some are thankful to have me speak up. I rarely know what reaction I'll trigger. It has taken a lot of time and practice for me to find some ease at taking this position, one that used to totally embarrass me. This is a small thing but it speaks directly to the divine call to love one another and a willingness to take up the cross for one another. When I do so, my heart knows it.

What Are We Fleeing?

In the words at the start of this chapter, Penington asked the Friends who had fled their homes to settle in New England if they did this for the right reasons. He asserted that if their purpose was wrong, they did not stand in the true cross – in the power of God "by which ye may witness all that to be crucified which is contrary to the will of God"[65] — no matter how much they might be persecuted or suffer. Personal problems and focus on the self were not what is most important. Penington goes on to say,

> Consider, when ye came to New England, whether tenderness grew up in you, and was abundantly exercised towards such as might differ from you: or whether ye were as eager for the way that ye thought to be right, as the conformists ye fled from were for the way they thought to be right.[66]

Penington wanted these Friends to be clear if they simply fled persecution, or if they fled the "persecuting spirit" in themselves. Here he was referring to other British settlers in New England who fled to the American colonies to avoid persecution, only to treat other newcomers as harshly as they had been treated in England once they were safe and in charge. He was aware that if we simply replicate the behavior we flee from, and if our hearts are hardened towards others, we are not taking up the true cross. This is a pattern we see again and again, when oppressed people overthrow a tyrant and then allow a new one to arise from among their ranks.

Taking up the cross is to break patterns. These patterns may be those which affect nations, and raise up successive autocratic governments. These patterns may be cycles of revenge for harm done. Or the patterns may involve the inertia of laziness when we are aware that the homeless shelter needs help, or self-indulgence when we buy a fancy dinner, bypassing the call to give to the food bank. These small acts of resistance may not have any broader implications, or they may signify our participation in a greater evil. Yet, I suspect even the saints spent time resisting the call to take up the cross and live in the way of peace and generosity.

When Is It Right To Flee?

As in so many other aspects of Quaker practice, there are not simple boxes to check and know I've done this right. Discernment of motives and awareness of a calling are inward processes. While the inner ear increasingly becomes attuned to the voice of the Light, sorting is often needed, sometimes with the help of others.

In trying to sort out what it is to take up the cross, I'm particularly conscious of the push to fit the roles defined by others. While the message is somewhat changed now, those of us growing up in the 1950s and 60s *knew* we were supposed to become wives and mothers. For women in particular, it is hard to sort out when taking care of others is right and when it is simply allowing someone else to take advantage of our good impulses. There is the long-held stereotype of the dedicated woman being praised for saying "this is my cross to bear." In my world, at least, only recently have women been encouraged to weigh carefully when it is right to stay and when to leave in difficult family situations. Similarly, when people are dealing with painful issues which generate strong feelings, when is it right to leave and protect oneself and when does staying present with the pain allow old wounds to be healed or respect to develop and new actions to come to the fore? These and many other situations point to the confusion which can surround the concept of "taking up the cross."

Thus, it helps to have Isaac Penington (at the start of this chapter) mention that not all "crosses" are the right ones. He was not addressing the situations I mention above, although I think his comment is pertinent to them.

Distinguishing the "right cross" asks us to be aware of what is driving us and to be conscious of the consequences of the actions. There are times when it is absolutely right to flee painful situations such as abuse, rather than "bearing it" for the sake of some preconceived notion or an imposed sense of guilt. Escaping danger is rarely fleeing the cross.

Yet there are times when it is right to bear painful witness perhaps to protect children or to stand for an unpopular but just solution or in response to a clear leading. The early Friends did the latter when they continued to meet for worship at the appointed time and place even knowing that soldiers would come and beat them or haul them off to jail. When we find ourselves totally unwilling to take action, even knowing it is right and it is ours to do, then we flee the cross.

Whether living in 17th-century New England, where Quakers were banished on pain of death, or in 21st-century suburbia, where the accepted lifestyle has significant consequences for the planet, the cross calls us to act "for the love of the souls of all people," in the words of Margaret Fell. Even if the outward actions are similar, the difference between giving freely of oneself and being *trapped* into "giving up · the self" and serving others is huge, particularly when surrounded by individuals who thrive on other's selflessness. The cross is not about resentment. Nor retribution. Grudging or forced self-sacrifice only engenders more bitterness and self-seeking, except among the most loving people. Freely giving to others is a gift to the world. True justice restores the dignity of the soul. Taking up the *true* cross is an act of choice, motivated by compassion, and an action coming out of inner strength, not weakness.

Choice

Freedom of choice is essential to "taking up the cross." The cross is something we can accept or not. At times the direction is absolutely clear, especially for those used to listening for the movement of the Still, Small Voice. Coercion is a clear marker of unholy forces at work. Other times confusion rules or, despite knowing what the leading asks, fear steps into the equation and the impulse to flee is strong. I have come to believe that practice in the small, everyday moments helps build the spiritual muscles, the habit of obedience if you will, which makes it more possible to step forth into more demanding situations. Thus, I close this chapter with a brief meditation on the everyday.

When I sit to write it is a choice. Even though something deep inside me will not rest until I write this manuscript, I struggle still with the old voices: my mom saying, "Dear, don't work so hard," or classmates mocking my opinions. In the writing I encounter the paradox that God gives us free will, yet knowing divine love makes the answer so obvious that there is no real choice.

I am thankful for the flock of sparrows darting around the camellia outside my window as I write. I note the chickadees in their midst and search for the finches which I hope are nearby. They settle and focus me on expressing what I know. I don't always do it well. Many of the words floating in my head are transplants from outside, just as the sparrows are invaders from Europe. So I come back again and again to awareness of my native habit of the heart and the beauty which belongs there.

Choosing where to spend my energy or which words to write is a matter of discernment. Listening to the sound of the Seed growing within mirrors watching for the chickadee outside my window. First I had to learn which was the chickadee, which the finch, which a common house sparrow. Similarly, the voice of the Spirit has its own color and texture. The slight breath of its wings against my heart, the flutter in my inner ear, and the smoothness of its touch all help me know which way to move my fingers. These delicate, firm indicators help shape the outline of each book and tell me what to do next. I choose to follow. I have no choice.

Then they put me in Prison, where I lay upon Straw, on the Ground and when it Rained, the Water and Filth of the House-of-Office ran in under my back: And they Arraigned me at the Bar, and bid me plead Guilty, or Not Guilty: And I answered, that there was no guilt upon any ones Conscience for what they did in Obedience unto the Lord God. –Barbara Blaugdone, 1691[67]

Here is my servant, whom I uphold,
my chosen, in whom my soul delights;
I have put my spirit upon him;
he will bring forth justice to the nations.
He will not cry or lift up his voice,
or make it heard in the street;
a bruised reed he will not break,
and a dimly burning wick he will not quench;
he will faithfully bring forth justice.
He will not grow faint or be crushed
until he has established justice in the earth;
and the coastlands wait for his teaching.

Isaiah 42: 1-4

SUFFERING

In 2007, I had the privilege of spending a few days with a well-to-do extended family. They owned an apartment building where the family members lived side by side, each with their own apartment yet with the doors open all the time, meals shared, and kids running in and out with great freedom. They lavished me with good food, showed me their city with pride, and I joined them in the Easter week celebration at their church, where one of the families accompanied the priest through the stations of the cross, carrying the symbol of Christ's crucifixion.

The last night I was there, they sat me down in the living room and started to speak of their lives. They told of soldiers occupying the building where I was now staying, and in their occupation destroying the plumbing and ruining much of what was there. They told of a neighbor, a young mother, stepping onto her own balcony for a moment and being shot and killed for stepping outside during curfew. The father showed me his damaged hands, which meant he could no longer create the jewelry which had been his main livelihood. Their story was long and immediate. A condition of living in Ramallah. They were able to put the pieces of their lives back together, although one daughter was still visibly suffering from the trauma. They had rejected revenge and sent their children to the Friends School where they were taught about peace.

Once one has experienced such suffering how is it possible to go forward, balanced between the pulls of despair and revenge without succumbing to either?

I inhabit a place in this world and a time in history when physical suffering is alien to daily life for most of us. It is a tragedy– an accident or illness or criminal act– and I am among those who have rarely been directly touched by these. War fills the news, but it is continents away, as is mass starvation and other happenings which tear apart whole societies. As a person of privilege, how am I to stand with the people who hosted me in Palestine? If – when – my circumstances change, how will I respond to pain and anguish in my own self? And on top of this, my spiritual ancestors tell me I am to take up the cross, an action which can cause me to voluntarily enter into a dangerous or painful circumstance.

The cross is a messy theology, full of contradictions and used to justify everything from self-flagellation to crusades. But one thing I get from sitting with my spiritual ancestors, is that the cross is not to be used as an excuse to harm anyone else, nor is to be used to seek out suffering. However, suffering may come as a result of taking up the cross, as Barbara Blaugdone found out centuries ago. The inward sense of rightness which comes with taking up the cross is distinct from our modern efforts to seek external comfort, as when we ask in Meeting for Business if "Friends are comfortable with..." whatever is the decision of the day, rather than explicitly considering whether this is what we are being asked to do.

"Knowing All Conditions"

18th Century Friend and abolitionist John Woolman approached worship, at least in part, in ways I rarely think about. In particular,

Woolman saw the intense silence of worship as a time when our defenses might be broken down and we might participate in the suffering of Christ and of humanity.[68] Woolman was never a slave, yet somehow he entered into their suffering in a way sufficient to change his life. Am I to do this? Are we all to do this? Is entering into the suffering of others inherent in worship?

George Fox expressed something similar when he declared that he was drawn into knowledge of all kinds of horrors so that he "might speak to all conditions." By his example, to live in the cross is to live with awareness so that other people, all creation, and faithfulness become central, rather than our own desires.

There are moments when what Woolman called a "feeling sense of the condition of others" arises during Meeting for Worship."[69] On Sunday mornings I have sat in worship and had the strong experience of the need for a certain kind of prayer, then felt the reality when either the need was expressed directly, or that prayer was offered by someone else. Numerous times I've sensed a message needing to be given and then heard it either from one person or bits of it from several people expressed during the time of worship. So I know that sensing the condition of others is possible, and that I don't have to focus on helping someone by promoting what *I* want to happen.

Standing in the cross thus is to share in a divine perspective, rather than clinging to our own limited view.

Woolman included the slaveholders as well as the slaves among those who were suffering. Woolman did not rant against slave owners as evil. He met with them in their homes to appeal directly to their consciences. Then, before he left, he paid them for the services he had received from their slaves. This direct, simple action was meant to make clear to the host both Woolman's unwillingness to benefit from slave labor and his concern for the soul of the host whose ownership of another human being had put him at odds with Truth.

Woolman wrote of entering into the sufferings of the oppressed as "Christ's peaceable government." Redemption, at least in significant measure, was to be found in the transformation of the world to relieve that suffering. It was not enough to simply feel, one must act for change as well.

Living in the City of God begins with entering into the sufferings of others. Michael Birkel, a Quaker who teaches at Earlham College, yanks away the illusion that we are in control, saying, "We are not the initiators because the process is already under way; we are asked to join into a sacred unfolding." Birkel goes on to tell anyone who feels a call to stand against wrong-doing that, "to participate in the ongoing redemption of the world takes us to the edge of our selfhood as individual persons. The very boundaries of the self become very permeable, as they can become when we have the privilege of being with someone at birth or at death." He concludes by saying: "To bear the cross in this way is at once painful and joyful. The suffering is intense, but we do not bear it alone. We are suffered through. The power of Christ bears us up."[70]

Strength

George Fox reassured us that there is an infinite ocean of Light which flows over the ocean of darkness.[71] When I am discouraged, it seems that I can only stick a toe in this ocean of light and maybe splash around a tiny bit. But no jumping off the safety of the boat or even wading into the waves. No immersion. No real, full commitment. Fear is still there. I won't leave the security of the beach I stand on and I won't let free, won't ride the waves, won't dive through the waves as they roll in. I start to go in and get part way, then jump out again and watch.

This power of the cross is not just the power to listen to others from time to time and speak to their condition at a particular moment. It changes lives and overcomes death – death in all its aspects, from the death of the ego to the death of the body. How might I write about the resurrection? I know it is true in some way shape or form, and I have experienced it in small ways. But it is more than I fully comprehend. This is the power which frees from horror and fear, the power which breaks the bonds, and releases the traps. Somehow I have to step into it. I know I do better jumping into the water than gradually easing myself in. But where do I jump?

Here is where the strength lies. In the trust that the Eternal Presence will catch us when we jump. When I am empty of the need to be self-protective, I can sit as I did in Ramallah and listen to the way soldiers, funded — at least indirectly — by my country have caused deep suffering. In that moment I held them in prayer. In the longer term I spoke about the damage done by the Israelis as well as the Palestinians.

The risk to myself is not great in this pattern of prayer and speaking, although the actual doing can be quite difficult and at times I encounter angry response to my words. My role is to adhere to the truth as best I know it, while reaching to the kernel of truth which underlies the anger. Developing inner strength seems not unlike my youthful experiences learning tennis or swimming: muscles need to be used to build up power and practice is needed for gaining specific skills. Slowly, I build the spiritual muscle to hold steady in the midst of emotional upheaval.

Risking All

This is where I have no experience of my own to draw on. Risking my home, or even precious belongings, such as the Navajo rugs which link me to the desert Southwest, is something which thankfully has not been in front of me. I don't know if I have the strength to take that risk, much less risk my life. I can only name what I know from my spiritual ancestors and hope they might guide me if I ever am in that position.

The 17th-century Quaker theologian Robert Barclay wrote about the "Purpose of Christ's Earthly Appearance," speaking words from 2 Corinthians 4:10-11 and Philemon 3:10:[72]

> Our ancestors drank from the spiritual rock that followed them, and the rock was Christ. Christ also suffered for us, leaving us an example, so that we should follow in his steps. For we are to carry in our bodies the death of Jesus, so that the life of Jesus may also be made visible in our bodies. For while we live, we are always being given up to death for Jesus' sake, so that the life of Jesus may be made visible in our mortal flesh. And so we know Christ and the power of his resurrection and the sharing of his sufferings by becoming like him in his death.[73]

The Quaker sense of Christ as both come and coming is a radical statement which impels us to create a better world, not to wait for the destruction of this one. Barclay described an inward reality that is more than imitating the written stories about Jesus. It is about Christ alive in us and guiding each one of us now. It is definitely not about waiting for some specific "return of Christ Jesus" in the millennium. *And*, most importantly, this Inward Guide is available to all people in all times and places. To know at the center of one's being that there is a Way which knits together death and life is something early Friends declared. We only need take the plunge. If we give up all our expectations of what this might be, our hopes for our human lives, our desires to control the world around us, then we might know something of this death which is at the core of life.

Visualizing the Freedom of the Cross

The closest thing I have to an image for the cross is something I expressed in the oddest vocal ministry I've offered so far in worship. It was at the Way of Ministry program. As we gathered, we had a non-verbal check-in where each person indicated their emotional/spiritual condition by some physical movement. Then we settled into worship. A strong, but lightly articulated message about the cross was present and in fact one woman came to the center of the circle and knelt with her arms spread wide. Near the end of the worship time, I felt something rising in me, but set it aside. However, just about then, a woman across from me caught my eye and motioned for me to stand. I shook her off, but she repeated the motion. So I stood. Then I asked two others to stand with me as "spotters" – people to help me see the center and keep my balance. I then moved into a basic yoga pose – standing with my arms outstretched. I stepped out to one side, rotated onto one foot and placed my body parallel to the ground with my arms spread wide – the image of a bird in flight.

I found this odd ministry to carry two central messages. First was the transformation of the cross into freedom and power. The moment of standing in the cross as preparation, was followed by the pose which spoke of a bird in flight, and also is known in the yoga tradition as "Warrior III." Thus in the cross, we begin to be freed from suffering and hopelessness. The movement to accept the cross is a decision that can, like Jesus' refusal to give into the power of Satan or to use violence even to save his life, ultimately opens into the strength which transcends death.

A second message was surprising to me. As I was shifting into this delicate balance position, I wobbled and one of the spotters reached to brace me, but I noticed I needed to ask her to step back. Her attempt to steady me was only making me more unstable. This seemed to me a reminder that while it is essential that we stand with one another as reminders of where to find the center, if we intervene too soon when someone seems to stumble, we can interfere with the release of new life and capacity. Part of this freedom is the letting go of that which traps us and blocks us from full movement.

The New Creation

❦ THE NEW CREATION ❧

We are called to live in the New Creation, a life lived in accord with the Beatitudes and other teachings of Jesus. A life of simplicity and integrity evidences a life transformed so thoroughly that neither greed, nor fear, nor the opinions of popular culture remain central. In such lives, in such communities, the Light shines so clearly that the *City of God* becomes visible.

The City of God is visible in everyone who lives Truth in all things. The blessing of the City is visible in the tree whose leaves are for the healing of the nations. The City is a place for *justice*, where all people know respect. Here we also come to know our rightful place in the dynamic system that is the earth and all its creatures. And the existence of the City can only come about through the "Lamb's War," which rejects all violence and knows only the weapons of kindness, gentleness, truth, peace, joy and compassion. Above all, it is the way of humility and faithfulness to divine leading: a willingness to do that which is ours to do no matter how strong the pull to take on all the ills of the world.

Raising up the New Creation and seeking to live it out on earth puts us at odds with popular culture and much that is happening around us. Yet this vision is not unique to Friends: it is the way a significant number of people read the Gospel message and is consistent with what I know of Buddhism as well as the teachings of the Yoga sutras. It is a way of being that many people have reached through many faith traditions. The particular take any group has on this vision is its own, but we share much in common. It is a path at once very lonely and full of fellow travelers.

Justice and peace are intertwined in any concept of the New Creation. If the least of us is not cared for, harmony is superficial and temporary. Friends' testimony to the wonder of the City of God and its manifestation on earth means nothing if we are not alive to justice. In my life this feels more like a tale of failure than a true witness, yet without just acts, all my words mean nothing. Similarly, we are all called to commit to living as peacemakers. *responding to violence* without being lured by the temptation to do violence is our most distinctive calling as Friends.

At this particular juncture of history, in this country, such a path rarely forces us to choose between honoring God's law and human law in a way that puts us at significant risk of injury, loss or death. That may be a sign of the tolerance around us or a sign that we are not fully alert to the leadings of Light and Truth. We live amidst temptations of wealth and ease which draw us away from Jesus' words. We each have to find our way in conversation with the Inward Guide and Monitor.

In the immediate future, the rapid onset of global climate change and the swiftly evolving technology around genetics both have unforeseeable and potentially massive consequences. While I speak to where I am now on this inward conversation about these issues, I am also clear about the inadequacy I feel in the face of the changes scientists are predicting. I ask questions about the ways our faith might shape our response to the threats to the *wholeness of the Earth* as we know it. Many of us need to ask these questions again and again in the coming years. Similarly, I touch on the practical realities of answering that of God in everyone in a world where humans are literally (re)shaping life.

[The angel] showed me the holy city Jerusalem coming down out of heaven from God. It has the glory of God and a radiance like a very rare jewel, like jasper, clear as crystal ... I saw no temple in the city, for its temple is the Lord God the Almighty and the Lamb. And the city has no need of sun or moon to shine on it, for the glory of God is its light, and its lamp is the Lamb. The nations will walk by its light, and the kings of earth will bring their glory into it. Its gates will never be shut by day – and there will be no night there. People will bring into it the glory and the honor of the nations. But nothing unclean will enter it, nor anyone who practices abomination or falsehood, but only those who are written in the Lamb's book of life.

Then the angel showed me the river of the water of life, bright as crystal, flowing from the throne of God and of the Lamb through the middle of the street of the city. On either side of the river is the tree of life with its twelve kinds of fruit, producing its fruit each month; and the leaves of the tree are for the healing of the nations. Nothing accursed will be found there any more. — Revelation 21: 10, 11, 22-27, 22:1-3

We lay these things upon you ... you who are in the place to do Justice, and to take off oppression which you may do while you have time, if you live in the power of God. – 7000 Handmaidens of the Lord, 1659.[74]

... And this must convince the World that we are of God, because we love the Brethren. – Dorothy White, 1662[75]

THE CITY OF GOD

Realizing the City of God on earth[76] is to me the end point of Quaker mysticism: a union with God which is engaged in the world. At times Quakers speak of "practical mysticism" or "ethical mysticism" or even "familied monasticism" to describe an approach to life that is grounded in spiritual practice as disciplined as that of monks, but lived out in ordinary homes among the pressures of the everyday world. Similarly, the Buddhist pacifist, Thich Nhat Hanh has spoken of "engaged Buddhism" to convey the need for contemplatives to respond to the world around them.

The 46th Psalm has been central to my vocal ministry at times. It provides me with a glimpse of the City of God in a way which reaches beyond words. Verses four and five proclaim:

> *There is a river whose streams make glad the City of God,*
> *the holy habitation of the Most High.*
> *God is in the midst of the city; it shall not be moved...*

The Psalm goes on to point out that while nations may be in an uproar and kingdoms tottering, the City of God is safe from such things. The power of God is more than any human or natural force. God devastates human plans by destroying weapons and making wars to cease! The Psalm goes on to tell us, "be still and know that I am God."

That complex, disturbing book, Revelation — the last book of the Bible — has the fullest vision of the City of God. It is most definitely a holy place, filled with the divine spirit, "coming down out of heaven," to be squarely part of this earth. (Revelation 21:2) This City is clear and transparent. No hidden places exist there: no secret deals in back corners, no lies, no covert control by malicious (or even benign) forces.

The New Jerusalem has twelve gates, which seems restrictive to us today. But two thousand years ago this was an image of an open city where all may come and go freely. Most cities then were walled, heavily guarded, and had one, or perhaps as many as four, gates depending on their size.

There are no temples in the city. This recalls John 4:24, where Jesus tells the woman at the well that a day will come when people will no longer worship on the mountain, as her people did, or in the temple, as the Hebrew people did, but all would worship in Spirit and in Truth. Passages from the gospel of John and Revelation underpin the Quaker refusal to consecrate churches or otherwise assert that one could only worship in certain places: the important thing is how we worship and our awareness of the Spirit present among us, not the place.

The Blessings of the City

The New Jerusalem of Revelation has a stream flowing through its streets, as does the city of the 46th Psalm. This stream is the water of life.

This is the spiritual water that refreshes the soul. It quenches our thirst to know eternity. When we drink of it, every cell of our body absorbs truth and compassion.

On the banks of the stream grows the tree of life, "and the leaves of the tree are for the healing of the nations." This is one of the most compelling images of the Bible. At the heart of the City of God grows a tree whose purpose is to produce a balm for the animosity and violence which separates nation from nation. In just the last decade of the 20th century and the first one of the twenty-first, the killing, rape and torture which have grown out of hatred between peoples divided politically, ethnically or by religion is appalling. We – however you define "we" – have done a lousy job of reconciling peoples. Too few people have taken the risk to step forward and say "this has to stop" at crucial times. In the New Jerusalem, violence is not answered with more violence. This is what we are to live for. To be part of a city, a city which encompasses all creation and sets a tree of healing at its center.

A Place of Justice

Revelation, despite its images of violence, is full of the call to love, to endure patiently, to live righteously, and when you have done wrong, to recognize this and change your ways. The well-known center of this book is a vivid portrayal of the destruction of evil– personified as Babylon, the "great mother of whores"— and many avenging angels, beasts and woes. Yet those who are obedient to God's voice are protected.[77] Early Friends saw corrupt institutional churches or governments as Babylon destined for destruction if they did not change, but they were clear as well that while evil would be defeated, destruction and vengeance were not outward, human actions. They refused to cooperate with evil and sought to live out the Kingdom now, calling others to join them.

Justice is at the heart of the biblical message, both in the fairness of the justice system to individuals and in a vision of equity: a balanced society where all might be at home. Above all, we are to remember that we (again, whoever "we" are) have been and may be again among the dispossessed. This is said in many ways: in Exodus 22:21, "you shall not wrong or oppress a resident alien, for you were aliens in the land of Egypt". In Leviticus 19, "You shall not steal; you shall not deal falsely;

and you shall not lie to one another," In Deuteronomy 27:19, "'Cursed be anyone who deprives the alien, the orphan, and the widow of justice.' All the people shall say, 'Amen!'" This message is in the prophets, the Psalms and Job. And in Jesus.

Limits of Human Efforts

The tension between reason and feeling for much of my life has not been an even battle – for years I turned to reason, a reasoning tied to conformity to worldly aims and which ignored feelings. So perhaps when I ask, "When does action in the political arena become an act of faith?" the first response lies in self-knowledge (or the lack thereof) and an articulate awareness of the moral grounds which sustain me.

At Swarthmore College during the 1960s, S.D.S. (Students for a Democratic Society) was a big thing. They spoke out against the Vietnam War, for civil rights, for justice and an equitable world. Their aims were appealing, but while I marched and tutored children from nearby slums, I hung back on the edges despite my own deep caring and the passion I saw around me. The unease I felt was borne out in later years as several campus anti-war leaders became involved in violence. And as the sexism among radicals became evident, this fueled my growing passion for women's rights.

After graduating, I married and Carl and I moved to Chicago, then southern Virginia. I helped elect women to office, then became a legislative aide for the first woman elected from Norfolk. I was convinced of William Penn's admonition that our faith should be visible in the world, seeing this as a call to action. However, my model for establishing the "kingdom of God" here on earth was the colony of Pennsylvania mixed with a goodly dose of modern politics. I was not conscious of my spiritual state. The absence of a line between Sunday morning and the rest of the week was illustrated in the old Quaker joke about making *New York Times* headlines a focus of Meeting for Worship – a sharp contrast to knowing prayer as the underpinning of action.

Later, reflecting on this time, the words of Isaac Penington seem apt:

> The Lord hath been kind to me in breaking of me in my religion, and in visiting me with sweet and precious light from his own spirit; but I knew it not. I felt, and could not but acknowledge, a

power upon me, and might have known what it was by its purifying of my heart, and begetting me into the image of God; but I confined it to appear in a way of demonstration to my reason and earthly wisdom.[78]

Looking back I can see that my impulses were right, but I was missing both a sense of God within and any way to sort out which actions grew out of faith and which were simply following a fallible human agenda.

The Lamb's War

The City of God does not appear suddenly in a blaze of destruction and glory as Revelation seems to promise. That realization became clear to early Friends by the 1660s. Instead, they came to anticipate a time of inward struggle for each human heart. They used the language of warfare from Revelation, but did not interpret this language literally. They believed that the victory of the Lamb could only be won using the "weapons" of Christ: humility, the power of mercy and justice, and the force of compassion.

What a direct challenge – to see the coming of the eternal City as an active process, not a passive waiting. It requires our energy. It is a position of engagement and relationship, but one that turns conventional expectation on its ear. Above all it is a creative process.

Jesus once told us that when someone strikes us we are not to strike back. Rather we are to turn the other cheek. This is the kind of instruction which at first glance makes the concept of non-violence seem passive and simply a matter of not resisting aggression or other evils. Biblical scholars tell us otherwise. In first-century Jewish culture, clear rules existed about how one person strikes another. A person of high status strikes someone below them only with the back of the hand. Thus, to turn the other cheek actually creates a dilemma for the aggressor. If he is to strike again, he must either hit the person with a fist, as an equal, or with the back of the other hand. This latter action serves to make the striker "unclean" and requires that he undergo ritual cleansing. To turn the other cheek, then, is to change the rules of the interaction and challenge the grounds of the aggression. It is not about meekly submitting. We know that their words and actions earned Quakers much wrath, disownment by their families, imprisonment and loss of friends.

Neither the Lamb's War nor Friends' testimonies are about naming people as victims. Rather they are about opening way for all to live in the power of the Spirit. This is a radical call to live out the same ethic. No matter whether we are impoverished or are among those who hold outward power, we are to do unto others as we would have them do unto us. The Lamb's War is drastically different from the too-often-seen pattern of upheaval where people have identified injustice and acted, but get caught in the trap of using violence to generate change, then only have the tools of violence and the old patterns of tyranny to guide them once they gain power. Breaking totally from the past and living into a generous peace is a hope not often realized.

Being in right relationship with God often turns upside-down the conventions of the world. Listening to the word of God in one's inward ear can result in surprisingly creative responses whether to the tensions of daily life or the prospect of weapons in space. No aspect of life is too great or too small for the power of God to leaven. Our relationships and the words of our mouths witness to the attention we give to that still small voice. In these ways we build the City of God.

A Recipe for City Living

In the city – be it a place where millions live or only a few dozen — we bump elbows. My particular "community" has taken multiple shapes, ranging from neighbors on the block, to the city of Portland. It extends to the whole world. Each community makes different demands. I can pack up and leave the neighborhood if things get rough. Other communities, like Multnomah Meeting and my adopted hometown of Portland, I know I don't want to exit no matter how rough it gets. Spiritual community offers connections with the power to shape me and show dimensions of the New Creation, but also it requires work to be sustained.

In his famous statement of the Peace Testimony, Fox referred to the lusts which, according to James, are at the root of all war. When I eventually read the Epistle of James, I found he has other useful advice about human relationships – what I've called "A Recipe for Life in the City," always remembering that recipes are guidelines which need adjustment based on local conditions or available ingredients.

A Recipe for Life in the City of God

✳ Give to all, generously and ungrudgingly. See to the physical needs of those who have nothing.

✳ Endure temptation. Don't be lured by your own desires or be fooled into thinking that personal wants are the same as holy direction.

✳ Be quick to listen, slow to speak and slow to anger.

✳ Match your words and your actions. Just as the body without the spirit is dead, so faith without works is also dead.

✳ Don't show favoritism. The richest person in your gathering is no better than the beggar at the door. Both should have a seat among you. In fact the poor are richer in faith and heirs to the kingdom of God whereas the rich too often oppress others and drag them into court.

✳ Love your neighbor as yourself. Mercy triumphs over judgment.

✳ Watch your tongue! It can get you into no end of trouble.

✳ Do not let bitter envy and selfish ambition take over your heart as these lead to disorder and destruction. Live and act with the gentleness born of wisdom.

✳ Be humble before the Spirit and recognize destructive impulses within your own heart. Disputes and conflicts arise from inward cravings: desire for what others own, lust for pleasures of the flesh, jealousy, and double-mindedness.

✳ Don't speak evil against one another. Do not judge one another.

✳ Do not boast. Do not hold false confidence that tomorrow will be better, living in a delusional mist.

✳ Be patient. Strengthen your hearts. Do not grumble at hardships and suffering.

✳ Let your "yes" be yes and your "no" be no. Do not swear.

(continued)

⁂ Pray for one another. Let your heart sing out with praise. Be humble and do not hesitate to admit when you have done wrong.

⁂ If someone wanders from this, God's way, and does harm, reach out to them and draw them back onto the path.

Summary of James by Marge Abbott

I've not experienced what James asserts: that there is a God who sits in judgment over humanity. But the all-too-human tendency to judge everyone around us – to separate people into "us" and "them" by some criterion which makes sense in our heads – is one of the most damaging traits we all share. Surprisingly, I find comfort in the concept that there is some kind of eternal judgment grounded in compassion. Giving judgment over to God helps avoid being thrown about by my emotions or generating false judgments about other people, the world or myself.

To be empty of the desire for revenge and for control over the behavior of others is a lesson taught in many faiths, Friends and Buddhists being only two examples. This attitude of trust in God's way is one response to the voice of the Light. Similarly, the "recipe" for living gives many ingredients to leaven human interactions.

If these are the ingredients, Meeting for Worship for Business is the cooking school. The standard practices of campaigning and voting, or using Roberts Rules of Order, too often form the way we expect decisions to be made, although more and more people have had some experience of consensus. Friends' manner of doing business together involves (or at least invites) the entire community to participate and assumes that each person is able to sense where the Spirit leads us. To work at its best, I find this process asks us to be faithful in small things: being fully present, knowing the facts, being clear about what is being asked of the group, a willingness to help others, taking a deep breath rather than reacting to something which makes us angry, and being centered.

My Meeting has been heavily involved in actions to stop wars and twice rebuilt and expanded our space using the Quaker process of seeking the Way of Love for making corporate decisions. We offered sanctuary to a family fleeing persecution in their own land. And we regularly deal with ordinary business such as budget and membership. We took perhaps a decade to agree to marry same-sex couples. We wrestled with mixed results for three years over how to be welcoming to a man convicted of child sexual abuse while changing our own practices to better protect our children and gaining wide awareness of the numbers of adults among us who were similarly abused. Such issues are not solved easily or without facing our own anger and hurt. We still have much to learn about forgiveness.

Making decisions about the present and future of a community tests each of us in many ways. Are we polite – for real or with an edge? Do we talk over others and ignore them? Do we want decisions made quickly by someone else (who we can blame if we don't like the results)? Or do we fight or manipulate to control the action ourselves? Do we listen to others and focus on what is right for the whole group? Do we have the courage to bring complex and difficult questions into the open and take the risks which come from seeking truth? For most of us, realizing the City of God arises out of a shift in the inward stance of the heart which opens in us a tenderness to all potential citizens of that land.

*When I had staid the firstday's Meeting there, which was very large and precious,
there being a ship ready, and the wind serving, we took our leave of Friends;
parting in much tenderness and brokenness, in the sense of the heavenly life and
power, that was manifested amongst us... .*

*A good, weighty, and true people there is in that nation, sensible of the power of
the Lord God, and tender of his truth, and very good order they have in their
Meetings; for they stand up for righteousness and holiness, which dams up the
way of wickedness. –* George Fox, 1669[79]

*When the ear heard, it commended me, and when the eye saw, it approved;
because I delivered the poor who cried, and the orphan who had no helper. The
blessing of the wretched came upon me, and I caused the widow's heart to sing
for joy. I put on righteousness, and it clothed me; my justice was like a robe and
a turban. I was eyes to the blind, and feet to the lame. I was a father to the needy,
and I championed the cause of the stranger. I broke the fangs of the unrighteous,
and made them drop their prey from their teeth. –* Job 29:11-17

JUSTICE

George Fox set a high standard for justice, but even he did not always
find it easy. In his *Journal,* he reports how he felt he was supposed
to go and speak with some justices and tell them to give servants decent
wages, but put off confronting them. When he came back to speak with
them, they had gone and Fox was struck blind. Only after he persisted to
find the justices and go after them did his sight return, "and I went and
ran thitherward as fast as I could."[80]

I long tended to dramatize acts of justice –seeing in terms of Fox's
actions or Martin Luther King Jr. In the words of an old hymn, justice
seemed to me "like mountains high soaring above."[81] When I had my first
opportunity to speak up for women's rights on the radio, I found myself
tongue-tied. I was in the odd position of being in a leadership role, but
possessed neither the skills nor personality for being a spokesperson.

Looking back, I can see that what I had to offer was organizational skills and a willingness to stand with others. Engaging with Job's encounter with the mystery of God's justice has deepened my understanding of this complex concept.

Cosmic Justice

The book of Job, one of the classic stories about cosmic justice, tells of injustice: God and Satan work out a deal whereby Yahweh wreaks havoc on the life of a good man. This man, who is honest, just, merciful, faithful and humble, loses in quick succession all his children, his servants and his wealth. In his mourning, friends come to comfort him and do so by sitting in silence with him. After several days they speak words that anger Job rather than comfort him. The friends insist that Job must have done some great wrong to bring God's wrath down upon him and his family. Job rejects this view of the Creator and insists he has done no wrong.

The story of Job brings into tension two major ways the Bible speaks of God: the God of judgment and the God of compassionate mercy.[82] Deuteronomy 11:26-28 tells us that if we obey Jehovah we will be blessed, and if we do not obey His commandments we will be cursed. In contrast, in Isaiah 49:15, God says:

Can a woman forget her nursing child,
or show no compassion for the child of her womb?
Even these may forget,
yet I will not forget you.

Job's story fits my belief that every natural disaster shows us that good people suffer illness and loss just as disreputable people do. Obeying the Ten Commandments increases our chances of living a sound, secure life, but the natural world is governed by its own laws: an earthquake shakes the house of the just as well as that of the unjust. In the end Job confronts Yahweh, secure in the knowledge that he is a just man, demanding an answer. Job is answered by the awesome, unknowable majesty of God, and – almost as a footnote — God restores his life.

If I had to believe in a Creator who sends blessings only on the just and curses only on the corrupt in order to find value in the Bible, I would reject it. The Infinite Giver of Life and Breath that I know is both the God known by Isaiah, one who loves each of us more than a mother can love a child, and that which is unexplained Mystery.

Both Job and Isaiah affirm my own sense of the world that cosmic justice is not about reward and punishment through wealth and misery. The more I apply my scientific bent of mind to the world, the more conscious I am of mystery. Job was answered with power, a God who answers out of the whirlwind saying, "Who is this that darkens counsel by words without knowledge?" (Job 38:2). God rebukes the friends of Job who gave false counsel—the friends who said that God lives by certain rules—and upholds Job's righteousness and integrity through all adversity. Job's response is one of contrition and humility.

Justice is central to formation of the City of God. While the Bible offers the mystery of Job and the straightforward injunctions to feed the widow and the orphan, humanity has developed alternative views of what "justice" involves. While I am not trained in humanity's myriad interpretations of justice, I know that if my first priority is to attempt to practice God's righteousness, then it behooves me to know that the rain falls on the evil as well as the good. I also know that it is wrong to deny aid to the helpless just because they are outside my community or don't fit my definition of merit. What I know of divine justice has little to do with justice as a free-market exchange, something my spiritual ancestors confirm.

Openness, Integrity and Respect

This sense of bringing respect and integrity into dealings can affect every aspect of our lives. In 1661, George Fox wrote an Epistle to "all Friends everywhere," about living righteously and acting justly towards all people.[83] He asks Friends if they speak truly to all people and treat all people equally. Fox does not mince words. Deceit, hardheartedness, guile, and fraudulent dealings are all strongly condemned. Writing to merchants, dealers and husbandmen, he admonished them not to cheat or covet what is not theirs – actions which so permeate American society today that in 2008 and 2009 this form of injustice destroyed many lives and almost the entire economy.

Fox's boldness presents a lesson for us today. More and more I've come to realize how essential it is to have space to openly address questions of injustice rather than making excuses or simply avoiding them. It is my way to emphasize commonalities rather than differences. Over the years

I have had to learn the value of not being pulled into a bland "niceness" that covers up real differences and is ultimately destructive.

In the 1980s, when pressure grew in my Meeting to recognize same-sex marriage, my initial reflex was to avoid the question and all the strong emotions which surrounded it. Once again, I found myself in a position of leadership, this time because I happened to be absent during some major confrontations. Marriage was the main topic of business for the two years when I was clerk of the Meeting. I had to let go of my own notions of what should happen and trust God, at least a little. In so doing, I found help as others in the Meeting stepped forward. Many were able to hear hard things being said. More than any dramatic action, time was needed for people to change internally, along with the deep listening which allowed reconciliation, at least for those willing to remain present. The decision to accept all loving, reciprocal relationships needed open conversation as well as space to grow. It could not be forced if it was to hold meaning.

Integrity is also critical at the personal level. When a man who had been in and out of mental hospitals for years began to regularly attend functions at my Meeting, those of us running the religious education program were torn between his obvious need for companionship and the discomfort of most of those present in the face of this man's tattered clothes and odd manner. We learned quickly, however, that he appreciated clear guidelines for behavior and was normally quite good about respecting them and everyone relaxed more. But at times, he would be so agitated that all we could do was to find someone with the confidence and understanding to accompany him to another room where he could tell his story. Usually, it was about the maltreatment he had received – being kicked out of public buildings because people objected to his appearance or otherwise being denied the normal access to services that most of us expect.

Over the years many of us from the Meeting have taken action on his behalf. For example, various of us accompanied him to his storage locker when the management found him too discomfiting, even though he had done little wrong, and wanted to evict him. We argued to allow him to keep his storage unit. Too often his uniqueness trumped justice and too often he had violated some minor rule which gave them the power to prohibit his use of the facility.

Responding with respect rather than dismissal applies on the world stage as well as in our local communities. In 2007, President Ahmadinejad of Iran stood ten feet from me and bowed politely, despite our very different concepts of how women should behave. He was in New York for a meeting at the United Nations and a group headed by the Mennonite Central Committee, the American Friends Service Committee and Friends Committee on National Legislation had contacted him as part of a follow-up to previous meetings in Iran and New York. I had the opportunity to be among the 100 or more people who gathered at a chapel across from the U.N. to converse with this extremely controversial man who at the time was treated with sharp hostility by the U.S. government and by many Americans. Those behind this gathering were convinced that we must be able to dispel myths and to converse with others labeled as our enemies and find ways to treat them justly even as we voiced our grounds for severe disagreement. Our encounter with him stood in stark contrast to Columbia University, which had invited him to speak, then the university president proceeded to condemn the man and his country under the pretext of introducing him. In our encounter with President Ahmadinejad, we hoped to offer a precedent for respectful official actions, something which did not happen until the U.S. administration changed.

If part of acting justly is to honor trust, then there is also the need to make amends when trust is inevitably broken. Without being aware of, and responsive to, the need for humility and making amends, communal and global relationships will not be mended. A question we regularly need to ask ourselves individually and as a society is: When have I made a mistake and what steps did I take to make things right? I cannot claim always to make amends or even to see when amends need to be made, but I value those who make apologies, and replace what is damaged. On a larger scale, Americans of European descent have still not come to terms with the damage done to the people already present on this continent when it was "discovered" or to the people enslaved to pick cotton and sugar cane.

Finding Simplicity in Our Actions

Questions of justice are rarely easy to answer. Simply by living an American middle class life I am destroying forests, and using disproportionate amounts of energy and water. What I do has ripple effects around the world. Responsibility to correct the injustice so broadly obvious in this nation and the world weighs heavy. Infinite ways to act exist: Friends in Burundi offer trauma counseling and work for reconciliation. Other Friends buy cows for widows in Kenya, seek to stop the destruction of Palestinian homes or visit prisons. In this country, Friends work to rectify the mismanagement of the Native American Trust Fund, and build low-income housing. Any of us only need to look around us with eyes and ears attuned to the Spirit to find openings, yet at the same time not all concerns are ours to carry. Without a sense of leading, action can easily be brittle or patronizing.

None of us has more than a glimpse of divine purpose and totality. But it is all too easy to take a drink or pop a pill in the face of hurt and loss rather than sink into the reality of divine compassion – often my "drug" of choice is excessive work combined with overeating. Even taking one step with integrity, as simple as saying "I'm angry," strengthens the holy spark within me. Such steps break apart the fear which wells up and seeks to crush us with its force.

The New Creation, the Kingdom of God, the Holy City, or however we name the condition where we see the Spirit active in the world, is a complex state I enter into at moments when I am expecting something else. It is a point of utter simplicity and clarity. It is a glimmer. It grows in us. In some it can hardly be imagined or even seems to be denied. In some it feels full grown. We are each invited to know it fully.

So when they came to anchor, they went to trim and dress themselves as usual; this took up some time. I was under a weight of trouble; and when they were ready to go on shore, a marshal came aboard, with orders from the governor, that none should come ashore, ... The governor sent for the master of the vessel, who was no Friend, and bound him in a bond of one thousand pounds sterling, to carry us back to Antigua. But there came on board us one Col. Stapleton, who was governor of Montserrat, and several men of account with him.

I told them, it was very hard usage, that we being Englishmen, and coming so far as we had done to visit our countrymen, could not be admitted to come on shore, to refresh ourselves, within King Charles' dominions after such a long voyage: Colonel Stapleton said, it was true, but, said he, we hear that since your coming to the Caribbean islands, there are seven hundred of our militia turned Quakers; and the Quakers will not fight, and we have need of men to fight, being surrounded with enemies, and that is the very reason, why Governor Wheeler will not suffer you to come ashore. – **William Edmondson, 1672**[84]

Blessed are those who hunger and thirst for righteousness, for they will be filled. Blessed are the merciful, for they will receive mercy. Blessed are the pure in heart, for they will see God. Blessed are the peacemakers, for they will be called children of God. – **Matthew 5: 6-9**

When they had brought them, they had them stand before the council. The high priest questioned them, saying, "We gave you strict orders not to teach in this name, yet here you have filled Jerusalem with your teaching and you are determining to bring this man's blood on us." But Peter and the apostles answered, "We must obey God rather than any human authority."—**Acts 5: 27-29**

RESPONDING TO VIOLENCE

My father, a lifelong Quaker, spent World War II in Baltimore working for Bethlehem Steel Co. He was an engineer with skills useful to the construction of ships and other military necessities, so he did not have to decide about whether or not to fight. His brother and his three Quaker first cousins were military officers during that war and among the many military-age Quaker men who enlisted.

Today, Friends often name with pride men, like the late Steve Cary, who were conscientious objectors during World War II and were instrumental in running Civilian Public Service (CPS) camps or doing relief work with the American Friends Service Committee. Men such as Cary made a strong witness for Friends' advocacy of nonviolence. In contrast, we have heard little about those men who felt that their faith called them to stop the evil actions of Hitler by actively taking up arms.

My father never spoke about why he chose to work in the shipyards rather than refuse to engage in the war effort at all, an action some men felt was their responsibility as Christians (as most Quakers of that time would have described themselves.) A few of those men spent the war in prison, and even those in the CPS camps were despised by many Americans. Their treatment echoes what William Edmondson experienced centuries before while traveling in the ministry to the American colonies. Much of my father's generation is dead, so it is unlikely I will ever learn much more. But Quaker response to World War II raises the same question facing us now when explosions wrack cities far removed from any war zone: how should a group of people who believe that violence is wrong respond to people or nations who act violently?

I find myself committed to nonviolence. It is a practical consideration – it is rare that violence does not sow the seeds of continuing evil. And it is a matter of religious conviction – the Holy One at work in the heart allows no room for violence. Even as I say this, I know I have not been tested in this faith. Will I live up to that measure of Light I've been given? My practical head often argues with my heart, and at times I do not know if nonviolence is the right response, particularly when it comes to the protection of others.

Taking up Arms

In 2004 and 2005 a discussion developed in *Friends Journal* about the use of police power. One Friend, John Spears, argued that George Fox would be supportive of the use of "police power" to respond to civilian bombings. Another Friend, the historian, Larry Ingle, explained

Fox's position by noting that while Fox was "personally opposed to participation in war, he recognized and accepted the authority of the state to use the sword." Fox described the power of the state as, "a terror to the evil doers who act contrary to the light of Lord Jesus Christ." "The magistrate," Fox said bluntly, "bears not the sword in vain." Hence Fox was not a pacifist in the modern sense that he utterly rejected participating in all violent conflicts. He could not imagine himself bearing the sword, at least under present circumstances – he spurned a 'mortal crown' like the one some wanted Cromwell to wear – but he also believed that someone must wield the sword against evil doers.[85]

Thus, Quaker history provides a complex understanding of the pacifist position. Fox saw a governmental duty to restrain violent and abusive actions. He also was totally committed to government tolerance of the freedom to live in obedience to God's will – which included the call not to take up the sword. That tension still confronts us; even as we seek to prevent evil, we are confronted with evil-doing. Which must we do: stop the killing even if violence is required, or refuse to use violence even though children will die when no other obvious option is open? Do any of us truly know what our actions will be in the face of violence? We hold no official endorsement of a "just war:" the goal is to realize the City of God on earth where neither evil nor violence will have a place.

In some Meetings there is great pressure to take an absolutist pacifist position, whereas elsewhere the pressure may be the opposite — where Friends say yes, pacifism is the ideal, but it is totally impractical. While we leave the decision about personal actions in situations of violence up to the individual as long as the centrality of the peace testimony is not denied, we would all gain by asking ourselves about our personal commitment to acting without doing violence and seeking to imagine what that would look like in practice.

My Monthly Meeting in Portland held a special Meeting for Worship immediately following the attacks of September 11, 2001. Approximately 60 people attended on a few hours notice. Next, we engaged in public dialogue about how to respond nonviolently. We wrote letters, met with our Congressional delegation, and organized public demonstrations. We looked for ways to address prejudice against Muslims, asked our government to address the causes of such violence, and expressed concern about erosion of civil liberties. By the start of the Iraq War in 2003, we were strongly committed to opposing a spectrum of U.S. government actions. In these responses, we sought to be as the yeast which Jesus likened to the kingdom of heaven (Matthew 13:33).

Structural Violence

John Woolman knew slavery could not be justified no matter how wealth it generated, an analysis which still stands us well today. Much of his ministry was actually among wealthy and powerful Friends: the slaveholders he visited over the years as he worked firmly yet gently to open their hearts to the evils of that institution. He saw how slavery damaged the souls of the powerful as well as the powerless as it corrupted all human relationships within its bounds. Stories tell of apparently kind individuals finding themselves destroying families as they sold individuals to pay bills. Whether by denying the right to learn to read or physically battering their workers, each slaveowner damaged another human being. For decades the economy of North America was heavily dependent on this institution.

John Woolman did not do an economic analysis of slavery.[86] His tenderness to the plight of the slave led him to see it could not be justified. His approach began by examining each individual's condition in order to see how every one of us contributes to the system. None of us is free from participation in the institutions around us. Most pay taxes which go towards building up the military. John Woolman recognized many ordinary goods were made with slave labor, so he gave up use of

---

**WOOLMAN'S APPROACH
TO ADDRESSING STRUCTURAL VIOLENCE** ══════

※ Self-examination of the roots of injustice in our own lives

※ Knowledge that war has its roots in greed for wealth and power

※ Setting aside personal desires in order to attend to justice for others

※ Acceptance that true harmony is grounded in universal love

※ A commitment to minister to the wealthy and the powerful

---

dyes for his clothing and sugar for his table. Today much of our concern is around excessive use of oil, but could legitimately extend to many other purchases we make daily. Thus, we have to ask ourselves about our own level of commitment to eliminate our contributions to the institutional injustice we wish to end.

Awareness that war has its roots in greed for wealth and power seems almost a cliche today. Even today's incidents of genocide and civil wars which seem based on religion, ethnicity or tribal loyalty are often rooted in a desire for owning a source of wealth (minerals or oil); the unjust distribution of food, water and land; and a process of dehumanizing of "the other," whoever that may be. All three can be linked to desire for control in some way and an unwillingness to give all people respect and freedom.

The third and fourth points which Woolman made, giving up of the self and moving forward grounded in unconditional love, are not easy or always straight-forward actions. Trust in divine love and the ability to be faithful to where that takes us grow out of grace, careful listening for traces showing the creative power of that love, and spiritual discipline.

Finally, Woolman's example pushes us to engage the powerful in the wrongness of their actions. Woolman met with slave-owning families in their own homes, labored with them, respected them, and without being confrontational, made visible the damage done to them by slave-owning. Before leaving, he paid them for the services of their slaves while he was among them. This is the same kind of engagement in wrong-doing that Jesus urged when he told people to "turn the other cheek" (make the other hit you as an equal) or carry a load a second mile (when it was illegal for Roman soldiers to make anyone carry goods more than a mile).

Taking Away the Occasion of All Wars

One of George Fox's most famous statements is, "I lived in the virtue of that life and power that took away the occasion of all wars." At the time he said this, he was being pushed by some soldiers to be their officer. A "yes" on Fox's part would have released him from prison, yet he chose to say "no." He was not willing to take up arms.

Friends are a peace church. Friends are mystics. Both qualities are part of living in the City of God and are so intertwined in our faith that attempts to focus purely on one inevitably fails. The late Adam Curle, a British Friend, Buddhist, and internationally respected peace activist, gave sound practical advice on being a peacemaker able to face difficult situations. He also told us much about the self-discipline inherent in radical peace-making. His principles of peace making are laid out in *True Justice*, whose title is taken from the Epistle of James 3:18, "True justice is the harvest reaped by peace makers from seeds sown in the spirit of peace."

Curle saw peace as impossible without justice: the true justice which blends temporal concerns of equity and integrity with the state of being just in the eyes of God. His principles were made visible in large and small ways when I spent time in Israel and Palestine in 2007.[87]

Among those we met were two men, each of whom had lost a child to the violence. One was Jewish, one Muslim, yet they traveled together with the common purpose of letting everyone possible know that the hatred must end. Their respect for one another was visible in their words and faces. Acknowledgment of that of God in everyone is an attitude which promotes the expression of the holy spark in other people. Acting out God's way does not include manipulating others, nor does it leave room for self-centered behavior. "[U]npeacefulness can only be healed through those involved in the situation acting in accordance with God's will, that is to say, manifesting the Christ within... if action is based on the illusion that the isolated, separate human being is the mover, only confusion will follow."[88]

During that time in Ramallah, Palestine, as my host showed how his hands were broken by Israeli soldiers when they occupied his home, I was so aware of my need for attention to God if I were to listen without being overwhelmed and running from the room or seeking to respond with trite words. Curle wrote that, "The most essential preliminary to peace making is prayer, or meditation, or whatever is the suitable term. I mean that purposeful stillness in which we sink through the turbulence and the scum of the surface–the anxieties, isms, and preoccupations–to the eternal, the Light of Christ within, through which we are joined to the eternal Christ."

My four days in this Greek Orthodox home made clear how much might change if Palestinians and Israelis were to listen to each other one-on-

one in this way. In this active listening, we can move away from fear and become grounded in love. Thus we may come to listen attentively, with the ears of the Eternal Witness, to those around us. Attentive listening means learning to keep our minds from wandering so we can hear what is spoken as well as receive non-verbal cues without filtering out words and impressions. Attentive listening involves an attitude of prayer. When we are in this attitude of prayer and listening, our words and speech may arise from this same holy center, rather than from political posturing, fear, a sense of superiority or other human needs.

Curle also identified integrity and the grounding of the individual as essential even though as Friends, we may have an entree because of our reputation. "Peace makers must earn acceptance by those among whom they would work." Walking the city of Hebron, even for a few hours, with a member of the Christian Peacemakers Team made clear how the only possible way to be a true peacemaker is to enter the situation in true humility. Without the ability to remain centered in a crisis, I do not see how these men and women could hold to their sense of humor and humility so that they might be trusted by both Israeli soldiers and Palestinian neighbors.

The day I spent with Bil'in villagers showed how necessary persistence is. Faithfulness and constancy are other words to describe their regular Friday vigils at the wall, guarded by Israeli soldiers, which separated their village from their olive trees. Each Friday, they have stood for years in non-violent witnesses to the injustice they face. Curle noted, "One may judge the authenticity of [people's] ideals by the strength of their refusal to give in to discouragement....We cannot resign from our involvement with the relief of suffering although circumstances such as age may lead to our manifesting it differently."

I do not envy the task of the teachers at the Friends' School in Ramallah who want their students to remember that all beings are one in God. These children have seen too much violence and injustice, and their lives are constantly on edge. How do we suggest that when they find themselves in disagreement with those around them, they must be willing to search their hearts in humility? Yet this is the way of peace: a truth that can be dangerous beyond our experience as well as counter to all popular opinion. To quote Curle again, "If, after the most careful consideration, we are convinced that we are doing right, we should continue, neither deflected by the disapproval of others, nor upset and antagonized by it. Instead, we should understand [our adversaries'] feelings and try to explain our actions – to tell the truth, in fact, not harshly but with loving concern for those who have good reasons for finding it hard to accept." This is something we cannot teach if we are not willing to live it ourselves.

Discipline, which Curle also named as essential to a true peacemaker, is something each of us might know. We might also describe this as a process of spiritual formation whereby we might become more like Christ in our lives. The process of formation is usually described by Christians in terms of undertaking the disciplines of regular prayer and Bible study, and surrender of the self in accepting Jesus as Lord and Savior. The discipline Curle described is similar in practice, even though his absolute rejection of anger in all circumstances may be closer to Buddhism. Christians have the example of Jesus overthrowing the tables of the moneychangers. But even that was a response to desecration of the temple, not the act of an individual lashing out of control.

The thread which runs through Christian spiritual formation and through Curle's Buddhist/Christian teaching is an increasing habit of dependence on God. Such faithfulness leads to growth, integrity, self-knowledge, and breaking down the ego- or world-driven way of living. With each step we take under divine guidance we become more tested and grounded in the Spirit and gain in spiritual maturity. As we mature, the Seed of Truth and Love grows within our hearts and shapes our behavior. The fruit that comes of the Seed is a life which reflects God's Way on earth.

God's Law and Human Law

I was excited a couple years ago when I heard Marcus Borg, the Episcopalian theologian, describe Jesus' entry into Jerusalem on Palm Sunday as a well-thought-out social and political witness. Jesus' entry into the east gate of the city mirrored the Roman governor's military procession into the west gate. The latter was with soldiers and banners and evidence of physical force. The former involved palm fronds, peasants and a statement of the power of holy love: the army of the

Lamb's War.[89] This resonates with how I understand the early Quaker witness: politically sophisticated, relevant, readily understood by the people around them, challenging directly but non-violently actions which are contrary to the ethic of the City of God.

Gil Skidmore, a British Friend who has done much historical study, lists several core aspects of early Friends' approach to living out the testimonies and making public witness to their faith.[90] This process is similar to the one used in the U.S. civil rights movement of the 20th century when Martin Luther King Jr. wrote of the basic steps—collection of facts, negotiation, and self-purification—which proceed any direct action.[91]

Even among early Friends, not all individuals followed every testimony to the letter, but all were part of this public witness in some way. Simply by

---

CIVIL DISOBEDIENCE: EARLY QUAKER WITNESS

❊ An understanding of the public nature of their stance and how they witnessed to the truth of the Inward Light.

❊ A willingness to hold to their testimonies and witness to justice and mercy despite severe repercussions. "They were so resolute and gloried in their constancy and suffering."[92]

❊ A willingness not to resist when beaten or dragged off to prison. They were, however, clear and articulate in their protest of miscarriage of justice.

❊ The compilation of evidence to back protests of injustice. Meeting for Sufferings documented the sufferings of Friends at the hands of the state and actively sought to obtain the release of Friends from prison as well as turn public opinion.

❊ A commitment to ground their actions by testing them with other Friends and by reference to biblical witness and the commands of Jesus.

❊ A willingness to "take up the cross" to assert their right to be faithful to God's will, by actions such as continuing to worship in public or in private homes at known times and places even when it was illegal.

Paraphrased from Gil Skidmore

---

their manner of speech, they were identified as Friends and thus subject to the same harassment and persecution. Individuals who acted contrary to Friends' testimonies were labored with by the group and publicly disowned if they continued to act and speak in ways damaging to the Meeting. This disownment was not a shunning – these individuals were still welcome to worship and socialize with Friends – but they could not speak for Friends nor could they participate in business decisions.

The boldness and openness of the early Quaker witness simultaneously brought both strong negative reactions and a respect which drew others to join them. They were beaten and imprisoned in large numbers. However, rather than hiding when their worship became illegal in 1661, they continued to meet at their appointed times and places. This often resulted in some or all of them being hauled off to jail – once, reportedly, all the adults were carried away but the children continued to meet for worship. Nonetheless, their numbers grew rapidly during the early years. Their courage amazes me. Their perseverance and steadiness point to something strong which sustained them – a certainty which could not be shaken.

A Modern Perspective on Civil Disobedience

Quaker public witness is an act of integrity and truthfulness taken in response to a leading of the Inward Guide. During the time of economic sanctions against Iraq, several of us in our Meeting individually undertook civil disobedience in response to an American Friends Service Committee initiative in protest against deterioration of the health of Iraqi children and adults. We spent our own money to provide water purification systems to Iraqis. This step echoed the time years earlier when our Meeting had previously decided to offer sanctuary to Central Americans fleeing persecution in their homelands. This very visible and illegal action relating to Iraq was taken knowing the potential consequences in terms of huge fines and jail sentences. Each one of us who contributed funds also signed our names to a public statement as part of our witness as the Meeting as a whole considered its action in the course of Business Meeting. In this case there was extended conversation throughout the community, although increasingly, individual unprogrammed Friends make use of queries or ask for clearness committee as they weigh their own sense of leading and consider undertaking actions.

Every impulse in me is to be law-abiding, but there are times the call to witness is stronger. Supporting the provision of water systems was done openly, in accord with the compassion at the heart of all great faith traditions. It was done with a willingness to accept the consequences, although in this case there turned out to be none. I also had to weigh my desire for "radical credentials" – many people I know and admire have spent time in jail for their beliefs and test how much that was motivating me. So once again, I found myself sorting true leadings both from external pressures and from internal fears and self-serving impulses in hope that my words and actions are as much as possible taken in the Light, with honesty, courage, and the inward calm of God.

God is in the life of every creature, though few there be that know it.
– James Nayler, 1656[93]

... And wait all in the light for the wisdom by which all things were made, and with it to use all the Lord's creatures to his glory. – George Fox, 1653[94]

God made the wild animals of the earth of every kind, and the cattle of every kind, and everything that creeps upon the ground of every kind. And God saw that it was good.... Then God said, "Let us make humankind in our image, according to our likeness; and let them have dominion over the fish of the sea, and over the birds of the air, and over the cattle, and over all the wild animals of the earth, and over every creeping thing that creeps upon the earth." – Genesis 1:24-27, 31

THE WHOLENESS OF THE EARTH

How might Friends today articulate a theology and accompanying ethic which can shift the focus from the latest in hybrid cars to more fundamental change? Where I live we can easily see the glaciers receding on Mt. Hood: summer skiing is no longer such a certainty and massive flooding has done huge damage in the Hood River Valley. The orchards are threatened by drought caused by changing snowmelt conditions. Frogs in the Cascades are disappearing. The environmental consequences of human activity are so varied and intermingled that sorting out the cause for massive swaths of dead trees is not always simple.

"God is in the life of every creature, though few there be that know it" were the words of James Nayler over three hundred years ago. John Woolman's decision to walk rather than ride in public coaches in the 18th century because of the poor way the horses were treated is only one example of the way Friends have been sensitive to the world around them. Today, among Friends I see a mix ranging from passionate caring and commitment to a general awareness of the need to protect the environment. In the wider world, hype around preventing climate change often feels like a fad blanketing the real efforts to remedy the damage humanity is inflicting on the natural world.

"Sustainability" has become a widely used phrase, but it is not always clear to me what it means as a principle for environmental activism. "Sustaining" (or "restoring") the earth, or even relatively small portions of it, so it will be exactly as it was — before the advent of humanity, or a thousand years ago, or even as it was when we were children, is not feasible. This globe we live on is constantly shifting. The climate does change (even without human help), new animals and plants appear, glaciers advance and retreat, mountains and islands form and erode into nothing. Environmentalists and creationists all get themselves into trouble when they view the world and the creatures on it as static. A literalist Christian perspective encourages us to perceive the natural world in this static way by asserting that creation happened in a finite period and was complete long ago. Environmentalists encourage this kind of thinking when they focus on protecting and preserving particular areas in the form they happened to be at a certain time. Neither stance is ultimately helpful in responding to the realities of a rapidly changing climate and the multitude of other factors disrupting lives and ecosystems around the globe.

It is easy to think of the human species as relatively immutable as well. We are what we are! But genetic science is on the verge of throwing our perceptions into chaos. The growing ability to manipulate genes and clone animals is challenging ethical and moral guidelines. The phrase "playing God" shows up regularly. Who does get to make decisions affecting human health? What constitutes a disability? When does the "soul" come into existence? (and what is the "soul" anyway?) Who gets to make decisions literally about life and death?

"To sustain," the dictionary tells me, can mean "to undergo, experience or suffer (injury, loss, etc.); endure without giving way or yielding." It can also mean "to supply with food, drink and other necessities of life" or "to uphold as valid."[95] All these definitions are helpful in thinking about what we might hope for. I approach this question remembering the City of God and its tree for the healing of the nations. The Holy One also invites us into a process of integration watered by a perfect love showered on good and evil alike. Healing, love and coming to wholeness are all dynamic concepts which can adapt to changing conditions and apply to relationships on many levels. They offer me a grounding principle for action. In this context I can ask how humans might be oriented so that this world can continue to support familiar kinds of life in a way which reinforces the natural resilience of the earth.

The Earth Around Us

"Do all creatures have souls?" This was a question asked me by a woman whose mother is Hindu, a faith that long has identified animals as sacred. I have no clear answer to that question. Animals all have a spark of life. Is that the soul? Does a soul require free will? Language? The ability to love? The ability to reason? The ability to sacrifice oneself for another? My only response is that we are to act with respect, care and concern for the long-term integrity of the earth — as if, as Nayler said, "God is in the life of every creature."

I find it easier to bring an attitude of respect, gratitude, obligation and reciprocity into personal behavior, and harder to expand this to community action and civil government. Yet all of this relates to theology – how we know God (or whatever we hold most holy) and what our relation with God says about our relation with creation. Even using the word "Creation" implies a holy action at the core of the universe. This may or may not mean a Creator exists, a God who made the world. For me, knowing God present in the world does not preclude evolution. Nor does our ability to cherish or destroy the earth much as we please mean that the world was meant to be dominated by humanity. And I am certain that the creation of the stars and of this globe and all that are on it involves something holy, filled with mystery. The more that gets explained by science, the more wondrous it all seems.

Respect implies a two-way relationship. When we take something from the world around me, can we find a way to compensate for what we have used so natural systems can continue to function? Most of the natural world exists in this reciprocal way, gaining nourishment and giving nourishment back into the overall system. How can we continually take without returning, without paying attention to natural forces, to the limits of the system? The consequences come: homes swept out to sea, lost species, contaminated waters. My concern is not so much that the world is changing, but the speed and direction of the change indicates that the globe is losing much of its natural resilience and ability to rebound from damage in a way which will continue to support humanity and other life we hold dear. From a biblical perspective, we were given stewardship over the earth and the things which inhabit it, and we are learning that our short-term focus and attitude of dominion and entitlement have harsh consequences.

We have many names for pending disaster – global warming, the energy crisis, species extinction, bird flu, genetic modification. Fear can overwhelm us, pushing us into defeatism or denial. Or, we can step forward aware that we are part of something sacred — part of creation — and that we have responsibility to do what we can to restore and sustain its resilience and wholeness.

Those of us who are privileged can consider how we use what we own. Clearing debris, picking up trash along the road, and hand-thinning over-crowded woods so native trees can grow more freely and trillium can prosper are among the things I regularly do. Sharing what we have with others is another dimension of making places where we live more hospitable for all creatures. All this does not change the fact that we as North Americans benefit from way more than our share of the world's resources, but offers one tiny way such benefits can be returned.

But these easy steps are not enough. Once in the midst of crisis, naming and acting on what is just is so much harder. Practice in taking up the cross and building spiritual muscles can help prepare individuals to take action. The prophetic role of witnessing to that which is in front of us, lamenting its coming and offering a vision of a more comprehensive way to respond, grounded in generosity rather than fear, will take testing and practice, as many of us are learning.

Orienting Myself to Respect Creation

How do I know if I am living as if God were present in all creation? "Simplicity" is one way Friends witness to this attitude: to live lightly on this earth; to know when is "enough;" to live with our children's children's children in mind; to know that all things are holy.

"Do we center our lives in the awareness of the presence of God so that all things take their rightful place?" This is the opening query in my

Yearly Meeting's *Faith and Practice* under "simplicity." "To live so that all things take their rightful place." Those words put the desire for that new car, or great new dress, in perspective. Often my answer is, "No, I don't really need or even want that." When I think about where my money is going, I am willing to pay the higher price for buying organically raised food and shade-grown coffee, knowing that these kinds of decisions have personal dimensions as well as political ramifications. I walk a lot, however, the "I'm too busy" excuse gets in the way of always taking the bus every time I can. I use my car knowing it pollutes the air and water around me, around the refinery, and near where the oil was drilled. My conscience is pricked by the presence of a woman in my Meeting who not only does not own a car but refuses to accept any rides. But not enough to join her yet.

It is tempting to equate "nature" with "good," as well as seeing God present in all creation. My faith somehow has to embrace the sense of humanity made in God's image, the reality of the way we can mess things up, and the fact that our very existence is interwoven with that of the earth and everything on it. A satisfying theology of the sacred has to account for the ruthlessness of nature as well as all the glory. Jesus states in Matthew 5:45 that God sends rain on the evil as well as the good, just before he admonishes us to love our enemies. How might we live into loving our enemies as water runs short, crops dry up, and tensions grow.

How Hard It Will Be!

The Oregon Ocean Policy Advisory Council (OPAC) was for a time a bright example of cooperative efforts to protect the coast. I was delighted to be part of it for a decade. The bureaucrats, fishermen, environmentalists, local government officials, and others concerned with the fate of the Oregon territorial sea made decisions by coming to agreement on actions, without taking a vote. We energized citizens to take responsibility for the spectacular coastline we are so proud of and educated people about the damage they were doing without realizing it.

It's funny how once I was caught up in something I passionately believed in, hours spent going over boring details of regulations were invigorating. The tedious becomes important when it connects with a visible hope, a potential concrete result. I felt good about working cooperatively with people who live on the coast to create protections that they believed in. They readily took over monitoring for disturbance of protected bird nesting areas and stepped forward to educate beach-goers about the ways their feet damage mussels and their desire for souvenirs leads to buckets of dead starfish.

OPAC gave me hope for civil government, but success quickly turned sour. Years of efforts to propose small protected areas – marine reserves – off shore were blocked by one OPAC member. The process broke down just as my two terms ended, right after federal fisheries management authorities mandated a series of short or closed fishing seasons. Anger and frustration over fishing issues spilled into OPAC work. As a result, efforts to create an experimental marine reserve came to a screeching halt as people perceived they might lose their livelihood, even in the face of evidence that marine reserves enhance fisheries in many areas. It is in such volatile situations that patience and commitment are tested. To stand both with those who fear losing their fishing boats and with the protection of sea creatures pushes the mind as well as the heart.

(Re)shaping of Life?

Humans have been changing animals and plants by deliberate breeding for thousands of years, creating or enhancing the meat and vegetables which grace our tables, and the animals which are companions or assist in our labors.

A new piece in the mix is the human capability to directly manipulate genes. Genetic modification is in itself neither good nor evil. It is a tool. But it is a powerful one whose implications for the human species and the whole ecosystem we little understand. Theologically, it is all tangled in whatever reactions we might have to the story of the creation in Genesis: is humanity made in the image of God (and thus somehow perfect and whole?); and what does it mean to eat of the tree of knowledge?

As someone trained in chemistry and as half of a couple who chose not to have children, I am particularly struck by the myriad choices now possible for us as human beings. The choice of how many children to have has global implications. The choice of whether or not to carry a particular fetus to term has personal emotional, spiritual and moral dimensions. Even the language I use – "fetus" or "baby" – increasingly is entering the legal as well as ethical realm. The knowledge of our genetic code and the uses of that information have ramifications we have not yet imagined. All of these questions can and do trigger strong emotional responses in many people, including me.

Human Wholeness

At college I had a friend who lost her sight soon after birth. In her first days on campus, I took her around the myriad paths she would need to traverse as she memorized each one with the help of her cane. She got her braille typewriter set up and arranged for people to read her textbooks aloud. She brooked neither sympathy nor concessions to her "handicap." Today she has a PhD and is an ethicist, teaching in a large city whereas in many times and cultures she would have at best led a severely confined life. Humanity's sense of disability and ability changes over time along with definitions of who has full rights in society.

In the 17th century, Friends challenged the notion that women had "no more soul than a goose." Yet it was almost a century later before large numbers of Friends actively opposed enslavement of other human beings. Looking back, it seems amazing that some people thought such things were normal. Not long ago people who were blind, deaf or using a wheelchair were tucked away in institutions and dark corners, considered unable to deal with life. Now the deaf are recognized as having their own language, it is national policy to provide access for wheelchairs, the blind have more and more resources for independent living and attitudes slowly shift about Down Syndrome children. Today we seek words other than "disabled" to refer to individuals who need extra tools to interact in the community at large. And some people see "ability" as a temporary condition because most of us will face significant loss of hearing, or mobility as we age or when we are ill or injured.

My central premise of the wholeness and sacredness of life leave me open to accepting genetic changes which will alleviate suffering, that is, find ways to neutralize the deadly effects of inherited conditions such as Huntington's disease or cystic fibrosis. At the same time, I find it difficult to justify the prospect of modifying the human genome to change eye color or enhance some other characteristics the parents desire. Recognizing that each of us is a complex whole – genes are not all of who we are by any stretch of the imagination – and that our scientific knowledge is far from complete, I remain cautious. We have the potential to create untold, unexpected side effects for us or for future generations. That which seems beneficent can generate damage or misery.

There are more questions than answers now. Above all, we need to be reflecting on these new tools of science in light of what our faith tells us – and here I note that there is no unified "Quaker" position on what the answers are. Seeking answers which not only are consistent with what we know of God, but also allow others freedom of conscience is not easy in a world where groups exist, such as the Raelians, who believe that their faith calls them to affirm cloning and genetic enhancement. We must continually ask, "When do our actions pull us away from relationship with Compassion and kinship with all humanity in favor of some culturally-determined external factor?

Who Thrives and Who Suffers

Humanity is rapidly gaining the power to change and respond to the world around us. We do amazing things to increase productivity of grains and other basic foods, but poor farmers cannot afford the enhanced seed. Possible consequences of some genetic changes raise fears, worsened by how little we know of the reality. Scientists have developed vaccinations to protect against most diseases, but we breathe in manmade, damaging chemicals. Life-saving machinery and entertaining toys surround us, and many of us seek huge homes and cars, often using vast quantities of energy or otherwise contributing to climate change. The list goes on and on. The American ethic is to do it because we can. My faith tells me that we must weigh the individual actions in the balance of the whole and make considered choices based on all we know about the City of God. My rational sense agrees with those who advocate the "precautionary principle" which argues that the proponent of a activity, especially one which might cause harm, bears the burden of proof before actions are taken.[96]

The decisions we make now about what human life is, where humanity fits into the natural creation, and whether we are willing to change, all have long-term ramifications. Will our children continue to see ourselves as separate – separate from people of other nations and faiths, separate from the environment we live in, immune from the shifts in a dynamic system? Can each human being instead see her or himself as one part of a dynamic whole, and thus responsible for how our ways of life affect that whole? Can we accept our responsibility to our children's children? Can our race accept our role in healing the damage we have caused to the earth and to humanity, and the need to be wiser, more principled and more caring in our future decisions?

Retirement

ℰ RETIREMENT ℰ

Friends are called to take times of retirement from the world and to respond to opportunities to worship amidst the bustle of daily life. Who among us does not feel the weight of "too much" when we are raw, tender and wearied of the world? Too much to do. Too little time. Little opportunity to prepare our battered souls to be tender to the Spirit. It is easy to claim this weight as an ill of the modern urban age, and to some degree it is, especially when compared to a farming life where individuals and families have fallow months when there is no work to be done in the fields. Often this fallow period is crucial for making repairs, mending or taking odd jobs to bring in cash in the cold times. It might be the only opportunity for education. For many people now, and over the centuries, days are filled with long hours of literal servitude and the eight hour workday is luxury beyond imagination. We who have this luxury often fill our hours tight, but much is optional. There is always more to be done than is possible to accomplish. That has always been true, especially for one who feels concerned to change the world. How much is truly ours to do?

William Penn articulated well an understanding of the need for times of *solitude* and retirement – whether one be an admiral's son or a housemaid – as part of a life of faith attuned to the Inward Guide. Retirement is a conscious stepping away from the pressures of all the relationships around us, good as well as bad, and away from the need to "do," to accomplish, in order to spend time in *communion* with God. Each of us can benefit from frequent times of retirement, times of solitude and prayer, when we might be renewed in the Spirit.

Retirement in this sense of renewal is something which might pepper our days when we follow Thomas Kelly's advice "to pray always." A simple turning of the mind to God, or even taking an extra breath, can reset the heart into a quieter beat. Similarly, two or more people conversing or working together might find or create "opportunities" by dropping into a brief time of worship in the midst of whatever else might be happening, or by visiting one another in our homes for such times of spontaneous worship.

Yet in the solitude much can arise that has been hidden. Old pain, fears, and desires dance in the symphony of silence and fill the space left when our chit-chat and activity stop. Here is where the *hard work of retirement* begins, when we can no longer hide from ourselves.

Inherent in the willingness to experience periodic times of retirement is a need to *be gentle with yourself.* Not to ignore wrongs or errors, but to lift both joys and failures up to the all-loving Eternal Presence, ask for guidance, and hold lightly to our human ability to control the outcome.

In the morning, while it was still very dark, [Jesus] got up and went out to a deserted place, and there he prayed. – Mark 1:35

Not that I would be thought to slight a true retirement, for I do not only acknowledge but admire solitude. Christ himself was an example of it; he loved and chose to frequent mountains, gardens, sea-sides… divine pleasures are found in free solitude. – William Penn, 1669[97]

SODE

Several of us in my Meeting look to Asia for techniques for stilling the mind. Buddhism and Hinduism have much to teach us along these lines. An integral part of my day is to spend time doing a variety of yoga poses, from downward dogs—which my golden retriever does better— to handstands, which I only learned to do in my fifties. This combination of the physical, mental, emotional and spiritual disciplines suits me well. Relearning this connection in times of retirement allows our strength to rebuild and hold when we most need it. Yoga helps me to center, but prayer and listening teach me of dimensions distinctive to Friends.

The most important lesson of my yoga practice is learning to breathe. I often forget about this, especially under tension, until my body forces me to let my breath out in a large gush. Our teacher keeps saying "breathe" while she pushes us to stretch further or hold a pose longer. This teacher also keeps reminding us to relax and stop attempting to hold the pose with our jaw muscles. Another wonderful spiritual discipline for me. I do tend to be grim!

Learning to breathe, even with Asian wisdom to guide me, has been difficult. When I first experienced Buddhist walking meditations, where the teacher would specify how to breathe, I found myself in a panic. I could not remember how to do it. This conscious attention to the breath was threatening. I am better at it now. But paying attention to my breathing can still set my breath off in funny directions and is not always soothing. It's often easier to listen for the blood pounding in my ear or feel the pulse as it moves through my body. Doing this, my breath remains steadier and I am drawn closer into that space of wordlessness and mental calm.

So entering into the silence is not necessarily an easy thing, even with external methods to help. Many traps await in the absence of the din of the world and the babble of our own thoughts. Terrors, inner contradictions, and hidden things of all sorts readily rise to the surface. The mind readily seeks ways to cover up emotions and memories which are threatening.

One aspect of silence, in fact, is its cleansing nature. If we have the courage to stay present to whatever arises within us and can hold these dark things in the Light of the Inward Teacher, these things lose their power over us. George Fox's contemporary, Margaret Fell, did not mince words when she told Friends:

> Now Friends, deal plainly with yourselves, and let the eternal light search you … for this will deal plainly with you; it will rip you up, and lay you open … naked and bare before the Lord God from whom you cannot hide yourselves…. Therefore give over the deceiving of your souls.[98]

Recognizing this process makes it much easier, although the process is never painless or simple. Even Jesus had to face temptations – and it is crucial here to remember that these temptations came to him as he was alone in the silence of the desert.

Yet, I don't find solitude to be a time of feeling deserted or isolated. Perhaps it is my introverted nature or a lifetime of worshiping in the silence. But solitude as Quakers understand it is a discipline meant for extroverts as well, as is the silence of worship. An empty time alone – isolation – is full of fears, as "oughts" and "shoulds" run riot. Imagination takes minor words or actions and erects billboards across my inner landscape touting my errors or the faults of others.

William Penn extolled times alone as a way of being strengthened so that we might be "with more power over [our] own spirits enter into the business of the world again."[99] Penn could easily have been trapped in myriad ugly feelings during the years he spent in prison. Instead, in this unpleasant enforced time alone he learned the *Fruits of Solitude* (as he titled one of his books).

Learning to be present in the silence is one path to self-knowledge and to bringing the soul into alignment with all that is holy. The more deeply this is experienced, be it through listening to others or in prayer, the more thorough the inward cleansing and the more solid our grounding in the Pure Principle.

Listening to Others

I once thought of being introverted as a fixed condition. Coming to learn otherwise is something of a miracle in itself. I had not realized that I could find energy in the company of others rather than always being drained. When I first took the Myers-Briggs test I was almost off the scale on the measure of introversion. When I took it a second time, 10 years later, I was approaching the center line dividing introversion and extroversion. I see this change as a gift of the Spirit.

The Meeting community years ago held a retreat where listening skills were taught, including lots of practical suggestions such as don't be preparing your own response before the other person has finished saying what is on his or her mind. This kind of advice, drawn from mediation training programs, is quite helpful and blends well with the passionate advice of 20th-century Friends such as Thomas Kelly and Douglas Steere about a deeper kind of listening with attentiveness to the divine presence.

What a gift it is when others are willing to listen even when it is uncomfortable. Over the years, one on one, in small groups, or in the various worshipful gatherings at Meeting, others' respect for my words gave me respect for them as well. Their enjoyment of me was echoed in new ways for me to view my self. In very tangible ways, their willingness to listen demonstrated the absolute care the Holy One gives each of us. Their willingness to affirm, point out another perspective, or note where I was wrong, showed their respect and integrity. It also conveyed the message that I deserved respect and valued my own integrity. Even as I grew from experiencing others listening me into fuller life, in listening to them I learned to be more open to the divine presence and be aware of the motions of the Spirit.

Prayer

Who among us hasn't lost attentiveness to the Inward Teacher in the pressures of work, errands and the multitude of things-to-be-done which fill our lives each day, no matter how strong our intent? Consciousness of prayer in its many dimensions helps nurture this awareness. One of the gifts of this time of intense focus on my inner being is learning that prayer is not formulaic, nor is it necessarily the kind of intercessory petition I associate with born-again Christianity. When asked to offer a favorite prayer by an interviewer for a documentary on mysticism, I had to say I had none to recite, that my prayers are most often without words. I pray at times in conversation with God. Sometimes my prayer is angry, or full of delight. My prayers may be as simple as groans of pain or smiles at the beauty of a bird in flight. Prayer is as basic as breathing. The habit of prayer is reinforced by a community which cherishes the Inward Teacher, and can remind me again and again to turn towards the Light. I need those willing to listen me into Life as I experience the ongoing cycle of dying to self and being renewed.

One morning in worship a woman spoke of being overwhelmed by fear and agony to the degree that death seemed the only answer. Somehow she had found the courage to simply sit in the intensity of the feelings through the night, giving in neither to the desire to end her own life

QUERIES ABOUT LISTENING

❋ *Am I preparing and rehearsing my response while my companion is still talking?*

❋ *Am I second-guessing what my friend will say?*

❋ *Am I comparing who is smarter, or more knowledgeable, or hipper?*

❋ *Am I filtering out the parts I don't want to hear?*

❋ *Am I making remarks to myself about how this statement was not worth hearing or that the speaker was unqualified?*

❋ *Am I determined to show I know the "right" answers?*

❋ *Am I shifting the conversation to avoid my own feelings of discomfort or to control the outcome?*

❋ *How have I labeled my companion – as an expert, as a housewife, a foreigner? How does that affect my reaction to their words?*

❋ *Am I aware of the Spirit present as a third party to the conversation?*

nor the impulse to hurt others, a matching impulse which seemed to promise relief. Neither the finality of the former nor the vengeance of the latter are the answer faith offers. So she lay, in faith, in the darkness, trying simply to be present to these pressures and to be tolerant of them. So she lay in the darkness seeking to feel the space between her muscles and her bones, inviting God into those spaces in her being. In the morning she slept. When she awoke, she knew she had learned much about tolerance and the painfulness of coming to be a person of peace. In her being, in faith, she knew something of what each person in Iraq, or Israel, or Palestine, or so many other places, must face in themselves to be a person of peace.

This woman understands what Penn asked of us. To sit alone – not savoring the agony, but accepting it and asking God to step in. Prayer can be a matter of pouring out our hearts as Mary Penington did as a young girl in 1637 when she reported, after hearing about two men who were facing an agonizing ordeal, "I was strongly unable to sit at my work, but was strongly inclined to go into a private room, which I did, and shutting the door, kneeled down and poured out my soul to the Lord in a very vehement manner." Here, as Penington found, the moaning of a broken spirit can bring one into solitude – a time directed towards the Spirit and not fed by desire for revenge or an urge to satisfy a craving. She went on to report, "I was wonderfully melted and eased, and felt peace and acceptance with the Lord; and that this was true prayer, which I had never before been acquainted with."[100]

Approaching Prayer

My approach to prayer is often quite simple. It may start in cries of frustration as I am doing ordinary chores around the property. It is there when my being calls out, "Hold the ladder, tight, when I'm this high," clambering over the roof and brushing down the chimney. Knocking off fir needles and branches. God seems quite close even as I am nailing siding. Hacking away the willows, dead and dying. Declaring that Scotch broom should be banished.

I find it hard to accept a version of prayer that aims at satisfaction of small favors. Chit-chatting at God, some man said, nothing is too small. Pray for the parking meter with a quarter still to go. That is not what

I believe will happen (although I may at times succumb to asking). Mostly my calls for help are simply letting the frustration and anger free, giving that burden up to the Spirit, a prayer for patience, or steadiness, or persistence, whatever is needed to keep me going rather than any expectation of specific results. And then come the wonderful times of sinking into thanks.

Action and accomplishment are so ingrained in me that I lean towards the thought that prayer ends in labor and labor ends in prayer. My rational self prefers to see effort at cooperation, where others might see a miracle. Stories of how Jesus turned stones into bread conflict with my impulse that there is no substitute for toil. Work gets done. We do it. Yet when faced by my friend risking losing her husband to cancer or even with my own inability to do what I intended, I find that prayer touches into something beyond my comprehension. Prayer exposes joy. Yearning. Soul to God, God to soul. I know it may be a groan, offering all. In prayer I seek stillness and come to know faith.

One of my semi-regular practices is to sit quietly, intuit which book to pick up, often a Bible, and then open it and see what the pages have to say to me. I may transcribe a short passage into my journal, then continue with my own reflections. Or I may simply sit with it a while and let it sink in. Sometimes these readings become a central part of my writing for the day or leaven other writing projects. I continue to be surprised how often such an exercise can free up a writing block or open a new topic. A significant early Quaker practice was a variation on this. Early Friends knew so much Scripture by heart that while they sat in worship or prayer, some passage would often rise up which spoke to their condition. They might hold this internally, or share it with the rest of the Meeting if it were given as part of a message for the community.

Prayer may be the discipline of emptying the head and stilling the mind so that the whole body might listen for the whispers of Creation in the inner ear. Such things are a long way from my old-time prejudice about prayer as "petition" — constantly asking God to solve all the problems of the world for us. That view of prayer, which still sometimes pops up fully formed in my head, conjures up images of passivity and self-righteousness: asserting "Well, I prayed for that!" but not doing anything about it myself. Yet petition to the Holy Spirit is sometimes the only response available to us, the only thing we can do. I pray I might recognize when that is true.

I actually find myself asking, petitioning God on a fairly regular basis. Sometimes I even slow down enough to notice a reply. The response often confounds me. I seek strength and find I am weak. I seek understanding and am confused. I seek to *do* God's will and can only listen. I seek power and find I am vulnerable. I seek understanding and am bewildered. I seek to act and learn to wait. I seek strength and find I am held. I seek understanding and glimpse dimensions beyond measure. I seek action and find salvation.

At times I know prayer as suspension — suspension of thought, anxiety, or control. A release of both hope and fear. A release granted. Begged for. Prayed for. Uncalled for. I love the affirmation in the 139th Psalm that we are totally known and completely loved. It speaks of the darkness which is as light to God. There is nowhere to flee from God. In darkness, in heaven or hell, at the end God is with me, unto the uttermost parts of the sea. The only possible response is praise and thanks, thanks for the assurance that we are, each of us, fearfully and wonderfully made.

Prayer forms readily as the words of Psalm 139 become my own: "I have taken the wings of morning, dwelt in the uttermost parts of the sea." Remote. Even surrounded, alone. Yet You are with me. I longed for your Spirit, saw your Presence in the stars. Now I know how I am known, that You have held me in your hand.

I have awakened to find You there, felt warm winds reach heart and soul. Night shines as day to You. My days written in your book, my form wonderfully made. Nowhere can I flee from You. As I stop my doing, You are there in my soul, more abundant than the grains of sand on the shore. Would that I would listen, hear your command.

In Solitude With Others

During the retreat prior to attending the 1991 World Conference of Friends, I began to be conscious that one of my own internal "markers" – warning signs that I should pay attention to – was an intense desire to get away from people. When I feel this desire, most often the best action for me is to visit a friend, or at least pick up the phone. Entirely counterintuitive, this marker has been quite trustworthy and done much to foster my own healing and growth. Too often, when the urge to run away arises, it means I am close to a point of change or want to hold on to an old way of being/doing that is damaging to myself or to others. If I reach out, that pattern breaks and possibilities open up.

I use the phrase "in solitude with others" because I have learned that neither the solitude nor the silence which constitutes worship are about being physically or spiritually alone. They are about a state of being where the awareness is wholly centered on our communion with Truth, whether through prayer or in the reality of that divine spark in every human being. It is a kind of solitude which can happen on a busy street or in a room full of people. In this solitude, all who participate are part of the unity of being.

Be still and cool in thy own mind and spirit from thy own thoughts, and then thou wilt feel the principle of God to turn thy mind to the Lord God, whereby thou wilt receive his strength and power from whence life comes, ... which moulds up into patience, into innocency, into soberness, into stillness, into stayedness, into quietness, up to God, with his power. – George Fox, 1658[101]

"Be still, and know that I am God! " – Psalm 46:10

COMMUNION

At times I lead conversations about silent worship. When participants are asked how they center into the silence, a delightful array of practices is revealed. Some use a mantra. Some practice breathing techniques. Some silently welcome each person who enters the room. Some use a song or a Bible verse or a poem. Some visualize a beautiful object. Some offer thanks. Some use the silence as a time for quiet review of the week or thinking through a problem. Everyone at times gets frustrated and makes a "to-do" list or plans their week. When I am too restless and cannot focus on any but the most superficial things, the quality of the silence is affected for me. I can't sense the Spirit's presence or truly worship.

To explain the process of discerning when to speak during worship is to describe how we sense the movement of the Spirit. I most often find words arising, words which evolve in the silence. Thus, I find myself sorting through the words inside me. What have I picked up from the radio or the pressures of daily life and what comes from the Spirit? Are words given by the Spirit for me, personally, or for the gathered group? The trembling I feel always used to be nerves, but now more often seems a response to a divine motion – something I may feel when I have a message or as I listen to someone else's words. Fear is most obvious in my upper chest and I find myself either breathing quickly or not at all. The movement of the Spirit starts with a sensation moving up through my legs and into the rest of my being, a tremor which links me with the speaker and beyond.

A Shared Experience

Encounter with the Seed is multidimensional and full of paradox. Humility and awareness of my own failings are accompanied by surprising power to act and speak. Joy mixes with grief. In a state of mystical awareness, beauty is made more intense by my bare feet making their way on the broken glass of the world. Holding fast to Truth is somehow central to this process. This bare, raw honesty at times fills with me despair. Worship and its companion, prayer, turn despair into hope.

It helps to know that I am not alone in this. Steve Smith, a lifelong Quaker, found his life in shambles, reached a crisis, and was able to straighten his life out in part.[102] But it was only in entering into Zen meditation, and Quaker worship, that Smith found the discipline of stillness – stillness of body as well as mind which opens the being to the fullness of the Light.

Steve learned that the Light, while full of love, was also harsh. It revealed, "the barrenness of my former life [which] arose from my concerted efforts to be 'more than God hath made,' from refusing to bear the reality of my life." Similarly he found that, "Arrogance is just this: pretending to be more than one is. Straining to be elsewhere, running from the truth."[103]

Steve and I share an appreciation of Douglas Gwyn, the Quaker scholar, who wrote of the "harrowing, annihilating path," and early Friends' "spirituality of desolation." In Gwyn's words, "Quaker preachers offered not sublime mystical transport but a traumatic passage through death to a realm where God's will is known first-hand and the power to obey is received." The desolation Gwyn describes is that of the self. It "must take place on the inner landscape before one comes to know the Christ returned."[104]

Smith experienced this inward annihilation when he started the practice of Zen meditation at a local zendo when on sabbatical in Hawaii. In the silence of that discipline he had to face the worst within himself before space could open within him for love. "It returns me to myself, and to the unspeakable beauty at the heart of all things," he wrote in his journal in 1986. Facing that which holds the most pain and fear — the desolation— followed by increasing awareness of the Infinite were lessons of Buddhist practice, yet in this practice he recognized a way inherent in his own

Quaker faith. He had simply never seen it. Returning to Friends, he found that Quaker silence was not what he had once thought. It had depths and power beyond imagination when approached in its wholeness. Doug Gwyn's study of early Quakers was one beacon tracing the way.

So I remain open to finding something other than I look for when I settle into worship. The time alone and the time with others seeking the Eternal Presence inform each other, strengthen each other and complement each other.

Worship Standing Still in the Light

Stand still in that which is pure, after you see yourselves, and then mercy comes in. After you see your thoughts and the temptations, do not think but submit. Then the Power comes. Stand still in the Light and submit to it, and the other will be hushed and gone. Then contentment comes. When temptations and troubles appear, sink down in that which is pure, and all will be hushed and fly away. Your strength is to stand still... George Fox (1652)[105]

Some Sunday mornings when I get up, my dogs are full of energy and bouncing around. On those same mornings it seems that the noise from the nursery on the ground floor of the Meetinghouse reverberates unusually loudly in the room upstairs where we worship. Even the adults have a hard time settling into the silence. My physical body responds to the energies in the atmosphere more than I ever want to admit, but that is only one of many factors which affect the quality of the stillness.

The more I study yoga, the more I think that our spiritual ancestors knew (consciously or unconsciously) what they were doing when they put those hard, straight-backed benches in the old Meeting rooms. Most every old painting and picture I've seen shows Quakers sitting upright, exuding a sense of still energy and contemplation. The yogi masters believe that the upright posture allows spiritual and emotional energy to flow more freely through the body. Physical discipline is part and parcel of spiritual discipline. This is part of why yoga appeals to me – I'm a lifelong sports enthusiast. Yoga is explicit in linking the inner and outer states of our beings. And it makes me even more conscious that the disciplines I learned in sports are helpful reminders for the discipline of the spiritual life, including the memory of how sore muscles can get as I'm training and how long it can take to build up strength and endurance.

The relationship of physical and spiritual is visible in the words "stand still in the light." Stilling the body is part of learning to still the mind. Are you aware of the itch on your nose? The breath as it rises and falls within you? Are you unable to get your legs comfortable? Do you hear the rhythm of blood pulsing in your veins? Are you focused on the coughing and shuffling noises around you? Can you hear the hymn rising up in your soul? The discipline to focus more and more inwardly is one that is learned. Attuning the inner ear and focusing the inner eye has never been automatic for me, as much as I might wish it were, although there are days when it seems like it happens with no effort at all on my part. Then I complain to myself on days when the traffic is too loud, or the baby makes too much noise, or, or, or – I have to make myself remember that I *can* center in the midst of shuffling, snuffling, and annoying words.

When the mind's focus is on the surface, each noise, each muscle twitch becomes central. Often then the mind is racing, either in tasks, cataloguing things to do, or in a cover-up job – keeping busy with words and images which hide a deeper emotional or spiritual reality the mind doesn't want to deal with. The Buddhists speak of the "monkey mind." Douglas Steere talks of a "hummingbird on holiday." It is a universal condition of humankind, this tendency of the mind to fill up all the space available.

The discipline of the Spirit includes the practice of bringing that hummingbird to a steady perch where it can rest its wings and stop beating the air. When that happens the empty space can be beautiful. It may also be strange, or frightening. In the void, when the familiar inner chatter stops, dark thoughts or emotions can rise up. I have come to learn that when they rise up and I allow them to swamp me, I know why the mind tried to keep them at bay. If they rise up in worship or prayer, then I am able to face the truth they hold: it is time to let go anger over old hurts or the need to make amends for my loose tongue. The Light reveals us in blunt honesty — both how we have been and how the Eternal Presence promises we might be. Here is a portion of true worship and prayer: bringing all we are before God and asking to live in faithfulness to the divine Way.

Knowing Our Own Weaknesses

Confession is considered essential in many churches, but rarely mentioned in Friends Meeting. Confession deservedly gets a bad name from the horror stories of medieval confessionals and from the twisted way Maoists used the public practice of confession in the mid-twentieth century. The confession I speak of is a state of standing naked in the Light which loves every pore of our being. None of us is free from words and actions which call for forgiveness by those we have harmed—no matter how inadvertently—by the Eternal Presence, by our neighbors, and by ourselves. This forgiveness asks that we make a true inner turn away from damaging behaviors. Offering praise and thanks to the universe is a practice which can shift the stubborn will. Here is the peace within where we also find delight and thanks for all that is. The fancy names we place on such processes are not relevant, but the underlying truth is.

To stand still in the Light is to be humble and vulnerable. It is to know that true strength is not our own. It is to be turned from our own purposes, saying instead, "Your way, not mine." In this place of stillness, we are gathered together in the presence of Infinity. We are covered by the Spirit. We experience communion and share in the body and blood of Christ Jesus. We are truly empty of everything except being. The essence of all life flows through us and nourishes us.

The enemy kindles a great distress in the mind, by stirring up an earnest desire, and a sense of a seeming necessity, to know…. Therefore, retire out of all necessities, … and as thou abidest here, thou wilt abide in thy soul's true rest.
– Isaac Penington (n.d.)[106]

Then Jesus was led up by the Spirit into the wilderness to be tempted by the devil… "If you are the Son of God, command these stones to become loaves of bread." But he answered, "It is written, 'One does not live by bread alone, but by every word that comes from the mouth of God." – Matthew 4.1-11

THE HARD WORK OF RETIREMENT

It doesn't take much experience leading retreats to learn how varied people's responses are. I have been with people who get extremely upset at the use of the word "Jesus" and others who, like me, find the Buddhist instruction to pay attention to your breath disturbing. One time I led a retreat where ten of us spent a weekend at a mountain cabin following the rule of silence. Our only words were a simple recitation of the Lord's Prayer in various translations from the Aramaic before meals, then a time of reflection before we headed home on Sunday afternoon. For a few people, this time of silence among friends was a time when they could face the most wrenching, destructive moments in their lives and find grace. Others were at ease and rested in the lack of distractions and freedom from the press of ordinary business. In contrast, one person was distressed by the silence, but could not find solace. In this one weekend I gained much respect for the complexity of the inner life.

Jesus may have been beset by temptation in the desert, but it is in groups, especially groups of dear friends and supportive people, that I run headlong into unexpected corners of my life. The theological conferences of evangelical and liberal Quaker women somehow cut through my defenses. Rather than the temptation to be great and exercise total power which Jesus faced, I have struggled with the apparent comfort of seeing myself as powerless. This applies to how

I deal with the world and also how I respond to dark thoughts or old memories as they arise within. This latter choice can be terrifying in the moment and I have learned that I can face the fear and temptation openly when I am surrounded by people who I trust and who I know have the strength and skills to support me if need be.

Space for Light to Break In

I cannot pretend to predict what might trigger inner work for myself much less anyone else since for one it will be crowds, for the next, solitude. Times of retreat may be a place for rest, filled with rich visions and inspiration, or the space may allow harsh memories or troubling desires to rise to consciousness. Sometimes I find myself thinking in terms of "demons," not literal creatures, but shorthand for the past events and strong emotions which set our lives askew. Most of us are conscious of some of our demons. Most of us have some lurking outside our field of vision. One function of times of retirement is to allow space for these hidden demons to show themselves in a context where they can be seen for what they are and their power dispersed and broken.

The danger of being alone comes when we have few resources, our inward strength flags, or our faith feels far away in the face of emotional turmoil. Unending loops of fear or imagination can lay traps that are hard to break. Many of us have been with people who are frightened by someone else's revelation of pain or emotional turmoil and then lash out or change the topic quickly. These people may be lured by the same temptations which haunt us and tell us to ignore healthy advice. Such problems can occur at many levels: active dismissal of a reality you know is damaging and mocking laughter at the idea of spiritual guidance are only two examples. A community leavened by individuals with sensitivity and good sense is a treasure.

I am buoyed by people who have the strength to live into the New Creation in the face of indifference or hostility. I have heard people tell of occasions when their discernment felt entirely right and they had the resilience to act without help from others. While leading a workshop, a man told me how in his teenage years it became totally clear to him that to kill another person was contrary to his faith. His pastor and everyone else he knew told him it was right to enlist in the army and fight to protect his nation. Despite this, he knew he could not. He was able to hear their arguments while remaining true to the Guide, holding fast despite disapproval, taunting and worse. More frequent are the tales of individuals who found encouragement when their courage failed or had someone who asked a crucial question that made evident convoluted thinking or the lure of an easy out.

Unknowing

To stand still in the Light. To rest in a place of unknowing. Such advice from the mystics can be difficult even when it is right. The dimension of retirement which opens up the space to face what Penington called "the enemy" can build endurance and courage to take up the cross and find the freedom this offers. Or it can crush those who stand still but make no space for the Light to work.

At one talk I gave, 1,500 miles from home, a man who was present would break into my words with comments which appeared off base, and I quickly felt others present getting nervous. Somehow, drawing from the time of prayer I took before speaking, I felt empathy rather than annoyance. It must have been evident to him as his comments shifted. He spoke of visions he had and the story of his time in mental hospitals came out, but without the anger, intensity and duration I could tell others feared. Later someone told me that he had come to other events and totally disrupted those discussions, and she was so thankful he had not dominated this evening.

The line between mysticism and mental illness is not sharp. The visions which may arise during times of retirement can be foundational or can detach a person from reality. Attention to the inner life can be illuminating or become an obsession. Friends have long been sensitive to the needs of the mentally ill and Friends were among the first to treat such people with respect and care. In 1796, the Quaker-founded The Retreat in York, England, established an entirely new and humane method for the care of the mentally ill. Today, pharmaceuticals – illegal as well as legal – add their own complications. Knowing rightly what is holy and being able to taste reality when it includes the unseen world is a balance I can't yet describe well. And I know that in many times and many places even mentioning such things as visions generates laughter, hostility or a message that one is delusional. There is reason to resist standing still in the Light. At the same time, having visions is not central to being a Friend. However, there is much to be gained when our Meetings become places where matters of the soul are honored.

To give up the self asks that we have a strong sense of ourselves to begin with. Jennifer Elam, in her study of Quaker mysticism and mental illness, notes that "the language around obedience, giving up ego, being selfless is very confusing and has caused harm to many people." She goes on to say that:

> Ego strength gives one a sense of who to talk to about what and when. It gives one a sense of caring for that self and body that God made, the temple of God's spirit. There is a built-in meter that guides behavior away from those things that might be destructive to that temple. At that fork in the road, the input of others can make a difference.[107]

Penington described unknowing as a protective state. He wrote of times when the Spirit leaves us blind so that we will not let loose the part of our mind which excels in rationalizing, and that Satan strengthens that tendency in us. His solution was to rest trustingly in that place of unknowing. I find this to be one of the hardest of spiritual disciplines. Whether it be waiting for a doctor to give a diagnosis or for grades to be distributed at school, I have never liked being in suspension. I want an answer and will work hard to find one. My mind, when set loose, tends towards envisioning tragedy and sets me off in a cycle of fretting and defensiveness.

What a relief, or even joy, to sit with my eyes closed in the place of unknowing, watching the play of colors on the back of my eyelids or attempting to hear my heart beating and feel the blood moving in my veins. Somehow in doing this I find trust and security. It is a form of prayer and a way of placing myself in God's care.

Look not out but within; let not another's liberty be your snare; neither act by imitation, but sense and feeling of God's power in yourselves: crush not the tender buddings of it in your souls, ... Remember it is a still voice that speaks to us in this day, and that it is not to be heard in the noises and hurries of the mind; ... Two enemies lie near your state, Imagination and Liberty; but the plain, practical, living, holy truth, that has convinced you, will preserve you, if you mind it in yourselves. – William Penn, 1691[108]

*... Their soul fainted within them
then they cried to the Lord in their trouble,
and he delivered them from their distress;
he led them by a straight way.*
– Psalm 107:4-9

BE GENTLE WITH YOURSELF

William Penn, in his somewhat dense 17th-century language, offered advice to young Friends, encouraging them to actively wait upon God in a focused way, not distracted by flirtations and foolishness. Penn told them to look within, for that is where God's blessings will be visible. Don't imitate the people around you, he said, but sense God's power within yourself. Don't crush the tender, initial intimations of divine love or overwhelm them by your desires for loud music, hot cars, cool clothes, or even academic achievement. "Remember it is a still small voice that speaks to us in this day, and that it is not to be heard in the noises and hurries of the mind."

I don't think it is ever too late to pay attention to Penn's advice. After Dad died, it was only after I decided to attend worship alone rather than sit and talk with family that there was space for the tender Witness to break through my reserve. In the following months, I found I was pulled in two directions. As Penn noted, I had to sit with the experience and simply be alone listening for the motions of love, just as Jesus did from time to time. Jesus set an example of going out into quiet spots in nature, avoiding "hurries and crowds" and sitting "loose to the world." Yet I also needed people who could stand with me out of care for my well-being even if they did not comprehend what I had experienced. For years I rarely turned on the television — it was too overwhelming and harsh to my ears – and rarely even turned on the radio, my head was so full of music without it.

Forces That Pull at Us

Penn asserted that two forces pull us away from nurturing the Divine Spark: imagination and liberty. I take these to mean the influence of the wandering mind which is full of false desires, doubts, and imagined troubles, as well as lack of self-discipline. Penn advised plain, practical living and holy truth as the way to go forward. He advocated the discipline of bringing our various thoughts and inclinations into the Light, to see if they come from God or if they grow out of arrogance, codependency, self-centeredness, bitterness or other human failing.

In practicing self-discipline, we may develop a way of tapping into another dimension of sensory perception. This inner awareness becomes another sense, like taste: to sense peer pressure, pride, or any of so many other impulses which lead us away from God. Here lies the foundation. This treasure offers a holy fellowship with all who have gone before us. This practice teaches us what to do and what to leave undone.

"Two enemies lie near your state, imagination and liberty." That's what Penn wrote. I think I understand his caution about liberty better than imagination at the moment. Too many options are the bane of our modern American lives. Paralysis can come from being pulled in too many directions. This may not be at all what Penn was thinking about, but it is certainly true. How many hours have you spent at the mall or even the grocery store trying to choose, not to mention buying all kinds of things you never intended to get?

The freedom of our lives fills us with a mega-mall kind of disorientation. There may be too many things "to do," but few ways to sort. What takes precedence? Large parts of our inner grocery lists may be valuable, important, fun to do, or rewarding in some way. But the effort of figuring out "what next" can consume huge energies. It is so much easier to simply to garden, do other useful but small things, or simply sink into the distractions of solitaire. Guilt thrives in the awareness of all the things we "should" be doing and aren't. We rarely have time to consider another way to live.

Perhaps this is another place where "imagination" comes in, in the negative way Penn used the word. We imagine that someone else has found a way to save the world by doing incredible amounts of invaluable work and we should be doing the same. Anything less seems not worth doing. Or we imagine we can hold a job, raise children, volunteer at school, volunteer at in our faith community, spend time with friends, and do social justice work simultaneously, then collapse with exhaustion and frustration at the very thought. Or, perhaps more often, we imagine we are not worthy, not able, not lovable, and certainly cannot do anything worthy of being called a "leading" or…, or…, the imagination goes on and on.

So what now? How do we begin? Few of us walk the desert as Jesus did, even when we love the desert landscape. Even as we spend time in the mountains or along the sea, how many of us can go on retreat for forty days? Grand spiritual practices and experiences aren't for everyone. They are certainly a mixed bag if you do happen to be the one who experiences them – they can lead one into all kinds of difficult and painful situations, as well as "glory," whatever that may mean. Fortunately, for most of us the call to action is gentle and leads us to undertake small, humanly possible tasks.

So often an inner conviction that this is the action I must take is a push is to take a single step. A larger calling might be visible only in retrospect.

The first brush of a holy wing across the ear, which pushes us in an unexpected direction or which eventually grows into a calling, may be visible in the everyday, if we only pay attention. Reassurance can come at a depth beyond sense by the words of a rock song on a car radio. Picking up the phone and making a call in response to an unexplained inner urging, and finding a friend in pain. The urging of Spirit can be so simple we overlook it. I remember one woman who insisted she never experienced any mystical openings or felt divine nudges. Yet when she started talking about her life, it turned out she had a sense of an angel on her shoulder periodically, helping her forward.

Penn also stated that faithfulness to Christ is counter to the freedom of the world. And that in this obedience we will find true freedom. We can turn, even for a moment in the midst of a busy day, maybe asking a "please help me get through this day" prayer. In that moment we may turn and simply ask "what now?" or give thanks for what is. This turning is a true gentleness to the self. It reminds us that we are not alone, no matter how lonely we may feel. It reminds us that we don't have to work miracles on our own: we only have to do our part and miracles will occur as is right.

Temptation

How much easier to go with the flow – to ignore the homeless woman at the library entrance, to kick aside the empty bottle on the sidewalk, to presume we have no power to change our government. Whether it is in ads for designer jeans or opportunities for an instant of fame on reality TV, the pressures against simplicity and integrity surround us. However, I don't often hear the folks I know talking about "temptation," particularly not in the spiritual sense. That word implies a passé belief in the devil, or some such thing. No man in red with a pointed tail exists in my neighborhood except on Halloween. Yet the pressure to tell small lies to salvage our pride, to make friends, or to outsmart co-workers is constantly among us. To step outside of the expectations of the world around us invites scorn, displeasure, or scoffing – the modern forms of persecution, now that lions are out of favor.

Hannah Whitall Smith, a 19th-century Philadelphia Quaker and best-selling author whose books are still in print today, wrote that we often mistake the way temptation works. "First of all, people seem to expect that, after the soul has entered into its rest in God, temptations will cease;" she said. But "when they find the Canaanite [enemy] still in the land, they are utterly discouraged, and think they must have gone wrong in some way." Then people tend to make things worse as "next they make the mistake of looking upon temptation as sin, and blaming themselves for what in reality is the fault of the enemy only. This brings them into condemnation and discouragement;"[109]

Smith's language is mindful of the old Quaker language of the Lamb's War, a "war" which asks us to side with Christ to fight the enemy

– whether internal or external – that is Satan. The Lamb's War uses
only the weapons of the cross: love, forgiveness, honesty, gentleness,
mercy and justice. For most of us today, it is more natural to use either
psychological concepts here or else the Buddhist approach of self-
emptying. But I will stick with traditional language for the moment,
speaking of Christ perhaps as the great Sufi poet, Rumi, did when he
said, "Christ is the population of the world, and every object as well.
There is no room for hypocrisy."[110] Christ and self-knowledge are aids in
resisting evil.

The shorthand of referring to "inner demons," or "fighting temptations"
helps when other words or concepts escape me. Other times I slide into
talking of "temptation" and the "enemy." I so easily blame myself for not
living up to my own expectations, or some image of what I "should" do,
that I know well the despair which Smith talks about. It is a relief to read
her words and say to myself, "Hey! Maybe I'm not so unusual. Maybe
it is not my fault that I am like this. I can do something about this." Her
words give me perspective.

That perspective helps me accept the times of inner struggle, which
perhaps become more intense the closer I follow the Voice of the
Light. That often is my experience. When I do not give in, when I take
one step forward, I have a palpable sense of the Spirit enfolding me
and carrying me. Why can't I remember this sense each time I feel
the discouragement, the self-doubt, and the pressure to give up? One
friend's response to my description of this internal thrashing around was
a hearty laugh and delight that so much resistance is there. He found
the resistance to be a sure sign that my work is holy work. He believes
in Satan as an active force of evil in the world, a force which fights hard
against any act centered in divine energy. His laugh was a clear marker
for me as I pulled my leg out of the swamp of self-recrimination and
sought solid footing to move forward.

Hannah Whitall Smith concurred with my friend's reaction when she
said:

> As a fact, temptations generally increase in strength tenfold after
> we have entered into the interior life, rather than decrease; and no
> amount or sort of them must ever for a moment lead us to suppose
> we have not really found the true abiding place… We also make

another great mistake about temptations in thinking that all time spent in combating them is lost. Hours pass, and we seem to have made no progress, because we have been beset with temptations. But it often happens that we have been serving God far more truly during these hours, then in our times of comparative freedom from temptation.[111]

Each of us, in our own fashion, faces the task of fighting the "devils" which beset us and it can seem endless. I do welcome the assurance that these times of struggle with temptation have positive benefits, a lesson those in twelve-step programs know well. And I am certain we are to resist the testing of nuclear weapons and differential tax-cuts for the wealthy. Perhaps times of temptation are times of strengthening internal "muscles" which don't get used enough. In fact, in Christian literature there is a concept of "spiritual exercise." I am probably not using it in the technical sense, but it is a lovely concept that I must practice in order to gain strength and stamina— a kind of practice which is essential whether one is training to be an artist, or seeking to nurture God-given gifts. Spiritual strength does not simply fall out of the sky full-blown any more than does mature artistic expression. So, patience is essential.

Being willing to sit with the doubts and the pressures and let them wear themselves out may be integral to growth. Can I invite them into my inner space when they knock on the door of my mind and accept them as part of life? Sometimes this seems impossible, foolish. Since they return and return, no matter how much I think I have banished them, I cannot move forward free of doubt simply by kicking them out. Trying to ignore them seems ineffective.

There is an ancient story of a hermit besieged by demons as he sat in his cave meditating. Eventually he found he had to invite them into the cave before all the clamoring could stop. Inviting them in does not mean giving them control! It places them in perspective so that they are recognized as part of being, but not part of what determines words and actions and certainly not something which can hide the reality of faith for more than brief moments.

Is this not what spiritual "warfare" ultimately is about – loving one's enemies and doing good to those who would harm you? So dealing with demons makes sense in a way that defies conventional logic: the practice of setting a table in the presence of one's enemies (Psalm 23) is a long way from advocating violence as a legitimate means for opposing the evils of the world. This inward and outward testimony to peace is central to the radical nature of the way Quakers have always understood Christianity: the root of faith is Christ — the Lamb, the Way, the Truth — which is counter to violence, dispels fear, and grows us in love.

To Be **Broken** and **Tender**

✒ TO BE BROKEN AND TENDER ✑

The words *broken and tender* speak to my spiritual condition. They describe much of what I've been through in the past dozen and more years. They tie me to my spiritual ancestors as well as to other Friends today. In these words I also learn of changes needed in myself and in my spiritual community: the brokenness which needs to be fixed, as well as the brokenness which is the precursor to wholeness. They tell me that I may feel raw and tender as my heart expands and learns to be tender to the movement of the Spirit in other souls.

Fear is alive and well in the world. I have no doubt of that. Many people are willing to play on that fear and use it to their advantage. In the heart of faith is the knowledge that *something broken got fixed*. One mark of Truth is that while it may point out fear and make it visible, it is not based in fear. It destroys the power of fear. We hide behind barriers in false hope of protection. The breaking down of these barriers is a sign of God at work in the soul.

Fear often feels raw as it rubs off the hard edges of the heart. To be tender is not always pleasant. Nor is being broken. I often back away from both as fast and hard as I can. But desire draws me back, offering a promise of *breaking the fear of death*. Desire for being held in the circle of Mercy. Longing for the water of Life. A wish to move out of the muck and step onto solid ground.

Ultimately, each of us is part of a community and in each community as well as each individual there is *that which must be broken before finding peace* with one another. The practices we have for engaging with one another have in them the aim of fostering tenderness in our actions and words and breaking the worldly habits of aggression and self-interest. We stand in the odd intersection where *God's way and human will* clash and sometimes merge. My hope is in the integration of our way with the way of Truth and Love.

Here had never been a Meeting before, nor any within a great way; but this was a very precious one, many were tender, and confessed to the truth, and some received it. – George Fox, 1672[112]

If any want to become my followers, let them deny themselves and take up their cross and follow me. For those who want to save their life will lose it, and those who lose their life for my sake, and for the sake of the gospel, will save it. – Mark 8:34, 35

BROKENNESS AND TENDERNESS

The word "broken" has negative connotations today, as it probably had three or four hundred years ago. I can break a watch, or a glass – one can be repaired, the other gets swept in the trash bin. For much of human history anything which could possibly be saved was either repaired or transformed into some other use. Today, it costs too much to fix things. I have to be persistent, and willing to pay a fair amount, to find someone to repair a broken toaster, much less a toy. So aside from antiques and handcrafts, only large, expensive things like refrigerators and cars tend to be fixed.

What does this tell a child about being broken? To be broken is to be worthless. If I tear my dress, it gets tossed, not mended. I don't save good material from an old skirt to make into a quilt. Move on, get something new! That's the media message. Being broken and then being made whole again is not a regular part of daily existence. I'm reminded daily of the way we can remake fragments into a new whole by the beautiful quilts on our beds, which come from one and two generations before my time. When do today's children see broken objects being made into something new, beautiful and useful? Who has time!

In 1956 my family visited a farm in the Midwest, where I saw a chicken running around with its head cut off. It didn't make any sense to me – it was supposed to be dead! In 1991, in the Kenyan countryside, I sat in a car with too many people, a paper bag of fresh eggs and a chicken squawking on the floor as we drove to where we were to have dinner. These glimpses of dinner ingredients are rare enough in my life to remain extremely vivid after years and decades. I am a city person and urban life doesn't leave much room for experiencing the cycles of life. A broken egg is either a mess (on the floor), or breakfast (in a fry pan). I don't know when I last saw an egg become a chick. Even with all the sparrows and finches that frequent the feeder outside my window, I rarely find eggshell fragments, much less see the noisy fledglings emerge. That life emerges from being broken is not part of my daily experience. So I have to take a lot on faith.

Tenderness towards all people, no matter how they define their faith, is one result of the divine encounter. I delight in the multiple meanings of tenderness, for a wound may be tender or we may feel tender love towards a newborn. It has connotations of healing, of caring for others and awareness. It reminds me to live lightly and to hold up the well-being of those around me. To be tender is to be humble as a child of a tender age. A tender spot may be sore and require gentle care. A tenderfoot is one who is inexperienced or naive. A tender is a boat supplying provisions to other ships, or a railcar carrying fuel and water. To tender something is to make an offer and repay obligations. Above all, being tender is to pay attention to one's conscience.

Turning Again

When the Light pushed me to be public about my failings and about the openings I have had (I don't know which prospect terrified me more), I found myself stepping forth blindly. The great mystics say I must be willing to give up all I cherish. Yet I may never actually be asked to do this. All I can do is be prepared, live with an open heart and not be bound by fear. That is where hope lies.

Janeal Ravndal's, grandmother of eight, tells how in "A Very Good Week Behind Bars"[113] she spent a week in a maximum security federal prison for civil disobedience in protest of the U.S. invasion of Iraq. This was not something she did lightly – she considered the possibility carefully with others in her community, prayed, and had a clearness committee. I wonder if I ever will be called to such an action. Experience tells me that the community will help me ask right questions and stand with me, or even prod me when fear gets in the way.

Among Quakers I have found something life-renewing. While neither my experience nor specifics of the Quaker way are unique, the particular take on the Gospel that I am learning from early Friends echoes what I know in my being. I have found that seeking, while life-long, is not aimless. I have encountered the Seed, the divine reality which can guide my life.

As I finish writing this book, I find myself in a place of transition. Much of my inner condition is one of waiting, not sure what is next. Outwardly, I am often speaking with an unexpected sense of confidence and authority. There no longer seems to be space to continually agonize. To apologize because I've always been shy and have had few words seems inappropriate – it is time to stand where I am now.

It seems like this transition point snuck up on me and is more visible looking back than in a great "aha" moment. It is a queer place where simultaneously I am conscious of how broken I am – how many my missteps are, written or spoken – and am hearing others say how right my words, or just my presence is in various situations.

So once again I wait attentively as I complete my responsibilities as clerk of Friends Committee of National Legislation and finish writing, unsure of what comes next and hoping to remain tender to the movement of Love's hand in mine.

And, in case of erring from him, or sinning grievously against him, be not discouraged; ... What tender mother can be more ready to forgive and embrace the child, that appears broken and afflicted with her sore displeasure? Yea, He gives brokenness, He melteth the heart, that he may tender towards, and embrace it in his arms of reconciliation, and in the peace of his Spirit.
—Isaac Penington (n.d.)[114]

As a father has compassion for his children,
so The Lord has compassion for those who fear him.
For he knows how we were made;
he remembers that we are dust. – Psalm 103. 8-14

"SOMETHING BROKEN GOT FIXED"

In early 2008, *Friends Bulletin*, the publication (now known as *Western Friend*) for unprogrammed Friends in the West, featured an article titled "Coming Out for Christ."[115] In this article, Joe Franko, former American Friends Service Committee regional director from California, confessed he was a Christian and had been for many years. This public coming out with his love for Jesus felt harder to him than when he came out as a gay man. This article made me wonder about how the simple fact of its existence says something has been broken among liberal Friends. If we profess to be open to and value all faiths, when did it become so traumatic to be Christian?

Belief is possibly emerging from its long status as a dirty word among liberal Friends. A decade ago, it was not unusual for me to have a liberal Friend confide in me that they loved to attend communion at other churches and then push me to make sure I would never tell anyone. As I am writing this, I have just led two classes at Multnomah Meeting on what Friends believe, requested by the young adults in the Meeting. These classes each drew 35-40 people, high attendance for us. The first session was pretty straightforward for me: what did early Friends believe? Isaac Penington's "An Exhortation to True Christianity" and

Margaret Fell's "True Testimony" are among the documents showing how they proclaimed a Christianity that is inwardly known and totally transforming. The second session was more of a challenge as I began with offering about my own faith before asking others to share in small groups about what they believe.

In that second session I was nervously aware of times in the Meeting when people have resigned their membership because others were "too Christian" or told others who have spoken in worship about Jesus that their words were hurtful. There have also been people who resigned or left the Meeting because it was not Christian enough, but all this too often happened quietly behind the scene, leaving raw, unresolved feelings.

The atmosphere has changed within the Meeting. Of that I am sure. How completely I do not know. Being clear about one's own belief and respecting others whose beliefs are different is an act of spiritual maturity. The hurts of encounters with the harsh, judgmental dimension of belief are real, yet too many people get stuck nursing that harm. Unprogrammed Friends have taken the route of gentleness (and sometimes, fear) in not speaking of belief for the past half century or more. The challenge for us is to find the Life in the words spoken and see if we can recognize it even when the words are quite different: something we have long professed is possible.

The other day I mentioned the title of this book to an evangelical Quaker pastor. She immediately heard the word "broken" as being about our hopelessly broken selves – the state of sin that we are immersed in. In this conversation, I found myself once again advocating change within the community of evangelical Friends as well as my own tradition. In this, I hope to affirm the important differences between the theology of early Quakers and that of the modern generic evangelical church along with the hope that we all might be able to avoid a fundamentalism that condemns others.

Early Friends taught about the potential to be free of sin despite our human frailties if we make space for the Seed to grow within and railed against the frequent any who taught that humanity is hopelessly trapped in sin in this lifetime despite Grace. I hear this teaching with both an awareness of sin as separation from God and a consciousness of how the barriers keeping us apart from all that is holy can be gone in an instant. My pastor friend was only aware of how broken we are and had not thought that it might be the walls between humanity and God that were broken or that the breaking of these walls is a salve to our broken selves.

It is hard for me to know how much of the change I am seeing is in others, how much in me. Something broken in me got fixed in 1991— the largeness of isolation and denial of my true self—and there have been regular minor repairs happening since them. Another significant broken part of me feels like it is in the shop right now being repaired. It is connected with having the confidence to stand and speak honestly of what is close to my soul and to hear others do the same without flinching because we do not agree.

Over the years, many repairs have been tested and sometimes remade by my Meeting community as a whole or by smaller Quaker groups. The Meetings' religious education classes have been a key repair shop for me. When I first led them I had to write out every word and could not bring my nose away from the paper as I read my words. Someone was always gently asking me to speak up. But these unknowing mechanics of the soul listened and they thanked me. How freeing to be able to stand and project my voice in a large group and speak directly to them of what I know. One next bit of repair is likely about being able to do this in a large group of people who do not know of my journey or what to expect from me.

Recovering Vibrant Language

My friend and sometimes co-author and co-teacher, Peggy Parsons, who comes out of the evangelical Christian tradition of Friends, has a knack for making theology accessible. Her take on Jesus' death caught my attention in a column titled "Geek Squad Jesus."

> I have previously stated that I think that the death of Christ had nothing to do with punishment. Even Pilate knew that this was a farce. So what did happen on that day outside of Jerusalem almost 2000 years ago?

> I think something broken got fixed. I see Jesus the redeemer, as Jesus the repairman, tech support if you will. See, there was this system called 'time and space' and running on this system was a program called 'humanity.' And it got all buggy. And the code called 'the law' just wasn't working. So the system designer had

to crack it all open. Get inside, wipe some stuff, patch other stuff, write some whole new stuff.[116]

This fits in just beautifully with my sense that faith is all about being broken and tender – in all the multiple senses of both those words. I can buy it that Jesus fixed something that was broken – or more accurately, is a name for the Infinite Force that is still fixing things now. Certainly humanity was – and is – broken in many ways. I don't know anyone who doesn't need some kind of repair or healing and while external laws help sustain a degree of orderly society, they don't really get at the heart of the matter – cleaning up the bugs on the hard drive in Peggy's computer metaphor.

Peggy is acutely aware of the resistance people cling on to – about religion, the church, certain language. She is one of those bi- or even multi-lingual folks who can one day preach a good sermon in a way which pleases elderly conservatives and the next day connect with a group of teenagers who find the Bible at best a curiosity but can relate to the idea of the Resurrection as "the reboot to end all reboots."

Having Friends like this pushes me hard. It is not enough to sit in my familiar silent worship no matter how nourishing that might be. It is not enough to know "this" has happened to me. I may not think of myself as a computer repair tech support, but that is a way of describing what I am called to do which gets me out of my rut.

Perfection

I have had numerous images which speak to me of the healing in my life. The Pacific Northwest Quaker Women's Theology Conferences have been bringing together evangelical and liberal Quaker women since 1995. At the first of these conferences, I spent a lot of time in tears and missed some of the sessions despite the fact that I had worked for years to make it a reality and had led the planning committee along with an evangelical pastor. For me, those few days were an intense confrontation with the darkness within, an old trauma which I was finally able to face.

The darkness came in a voice, and in a long-gone presence whose echo tormented me. Like a small bird, who when alone hops on the ground under an oak tree and gathers nourishment in its shelter, I could step cautiously into the open when I sensed the world was still. Then, at each passing shadow, or motion, the bird flits to a thorn bush grown and shaped by the years. The bush is riddled with small resting places filled with soft down. Some spaces are near the surface where the world can be seen, others set where little light can reach and sounds dimly reverberates. When I pulled away and withdrew, I could see, hear and respond at some level to what was happening, and I accomplished many tasks. Being thrown back to a time when I was much younger, speaking about this experience, did not seem possible in the moment.

At that stage of healing, seeing myself in the bird helped me to imagine becoming more extroverted and building relationships. But then and for months afterwards my self-definition was as someone who had been badly damaged — a victim. Making that next transition, from "surviving" to being complete is much slower and harder than the initial step from blindness to being given an eye to see the invisible world. We are called to be whole and complete, to love with the unconditional love of God and to know that we are so loved.

Another image of faith for me is of a pool of molten gold. This pool is slivered by the rotations of a sharp blade. Segments of this golden pie are offered without ceasing, yet it is always whole. Its weight and being are infinite in the thin space it occupies. This pool is light, reflecting and gleaming with rays splintered by its soft wealth. The molten circle absorbs all cuts and bitterness, melding all sharpness in its heat. Its never-ceasing source is beyond knowing.

This golden pool is one way of describing the unbounded love which flows into each heart and can be given without caution or measure. This love can be shared forever without waning and is renewed with each slice that is given to others, no matter how sharp and deep the cut. This love, my spiritual mentors affirm, sustains even in the face of death.

How great a Benefit do I enjoy, beyond many, I have such a large time of Preparation for Death, being daily dying, that I may live forever, with my God ... My outward man daily wastes and moulders down, and draws towards his Place and Center, but my Inward man Revives and Mounts upward – John Camm, 1656[117]

By the tender mercy of our God, the dawn from on high will break upon us, to give light to those who sit in darkness and in the shadow of death, to guide our feet into the way of peace. – Luke 1:78, 79

BREAKING THE FEAR OF DEATH

At the close of each yoga class, my teacher has us lie back in *savasana*, corpse pose. "In relaxation the body lies as still as a corpse and the mind is at peace. Once the posture is mastered, quietness can be called upon at will."[118] Quakers do not have a daily reminder of the finiteness of life such as lying in corpse pose, although considering one's death is part of the Christian contemplative tradition. Monastics such as Benedict counsel, "Keep your own death before your eyes each day." Neither Hindu nor Christian contemplatives mean this in a morbid way, but rather as a reminder that we are part of a whole and that death is not something to be feared.

The stillness sought in yoga practice is familiar. Our worship draws us to sit in a stillness which allows the mind as well as the body to find a peace settled in God. In that state of openness, it is possible to encounter ourselves – the ugliness we run from or ignore as well as the beauty. We can take time to explore what we find or look for new places to hide. But ultimately there is no place to hide from the piercing Light which connects us with the Infinite as well as with one another. In both Quaker and yoga practice, this state of stillness is a time of gaining the self-knowledge underpinning spiritual growth and freedom.

John Woolman died of smallpox in 1772 while traveling in the ministry in England, He was conscious to the very end of "how many are spending their time and money in vanity and superfluities, while thousands and tens of thousands want the necessities of life."[119] Near the end of his *Journal*, he expressed his relation to death, a statement which would sit easily with the yoga practitioner:

> In the course of a few weeks it pleased the Lord to visit me with a pleurisy; and after I had lain a few days and felt the disorder very grievous, I was thoughtful how it might end. I had of late, through various exercises, been much weaned from the pleasant things of life; and I now thought if it were the Lord's will to put an end to my labors and graciously to receive me into the arms of his mercy, death would be acceptable to me; but if it were his will further to refine me under afflictions, and to make me in any degree useful in his church, I desired not to die.[120]

This lack of attachment to the end – either living or dying was acceptable to Woolman – and the knowledge of death as a process of loving comfort are pretty amazing to my modern mind. He was certain that death is not to be feared.

Our communities can teach a spiritual discipline which allows detachment and speaks to a relationship with the Eternal which extends beyond death. Both these dimensions point to a state of being where death loses its capacity to terrify, and thus to control our lives. In a culture which shies away from death and expends huge amounts of money and energy to prevent it, this is a precious thing. It is doubly precious as it is a path which does not seek out or value death, but rather affirms life.

Discipline & Light

Part of me asks, how can I know if I have lost my fear of death if I have never come close to dying? It seems that only those who have experienced the extremes of illness or danger can really be free of this fear. But I also am aware of how often people in those situations become even more terrified and determined to do anything possible to avoid being in that position again. So my logical mind takes me in circles.

Friends don't have a systematic discipline with specific steps to follow that has been laid out in the way of the yoga sutras or the Benedictine rule, although modern Friends such as Douglas Steere, Mary Morrison, Diana Lampen and Rex Ambler have offered written guidance. Friends do have a pattern which we learn largely by an odd osmosis from the expectant silence, the practice of posing queries, and association with others we respect. *Quaker Faith and Practice* of Britain Yearly Meeting (1994) advises:

> Approach old age with courage and hope. As far as possible, make arrangements for your care in good time, so that an undue burden does not fall on others. Although old age may bring increasing disability and loneliness, it can also bring serenity, detachment and wisdom. Pray that in your final years you may be enabled to find new ways of receiving and reflecting God's love.[121]

Are you able to contemplate your death and the death of those closest to you? Accepting the fact of death, we are freed to live more fully. In bereavement, give yourself time to grieve. When others mourn, let your love embrace them.

This willingness to reflect upon the end of life is a long-standing tradition. In fact, for over two centuries, beginning in the 17th century, a series of volumes called *Piety Promoted: A collection of Dying sayings of many of the people called Quakers* was published to be used for meditation and teaching, for children as well as adults.[122] Each volume contained a brief biography of a Friend – sometimes an older, respected Friend, but also sometimes children were included as many people died in childhood in that time. A significant part of each biography was the last weeks, days and hours of that person's life. Edward Burrough, for instance, directed his words to God when he was taken ill after being imprisoned for his faith:

> Lord rip open my heart, and see if it be not Right before thee.... There lies no iniquity at my door; the Presence of the Lord is with me, and his Life I feel Justifies me.[123]

Often Friends recorded the last words, including those of young people, such as those of Springette Penn, the son of William Penn, who died at age 21. As he neared death, Springette said to his father: "My eye looks another way, where the truest pleasure is.... All is mercy, dear father; everything is mercy."[124]

From these words we see a twin clarity, clarity that the individual has examined their own life and made amends for any wrong-doing and absolute assurance of God's loving embrace. With such assurance, death holds no terror.

Living Without Fear

Not being afraid of death is incredibly appealing. Yet even the concept seems alien. We have glimpses of what such a community might look like when we read of Tom Fox making his decision to join with the Christian Peacemaker Team in Iraq. Friends in Langley Hill Meeting in Virginia, and many others, supported him as he journeyed to Iraq out of concern for the people whose lives American military forces disrupted with the 2003 invasion. His willingness to listen and to act humanely to meet the needs of local people threatened the terrorists' attempts to vilify Americans. The result was his capture and physical death. Friends such as Tom Fox undoubtedly experienced fear, but did not let it govern their decisions or their hearts. So this state of being can free us for action which might seem impossible.

Decisions need not be so momentous. I am aware of more than one Meeting where a few people knew about a sexual predator and declined to tell the whole community, perhaps out of fear of causing upset or making a false accusation. I'm sure this silence seemed easier, but the fear of controversy too often hides ugly secrets which can only fester. Bringing the painful into the Light does take courage and can open many wounds. Careful thought and prayer, and strong clerking to set boundaries of discussion can open a group to healing and reconciliation – and at times put a stop to destructive behavior. Transformation happens in community as well as in individuals. This can occur on many levels, in actions large or small. When fear is not in charge, life may not follow a neat, predictable pattern, but Mercy and forgiveness are present, the community and its members can grow in the Light.

For me, and I am sure for many others, the physical death we face– be it our own end or that of someone we love – our Quaker heritage brings us to a place at odds with our culture. From ads for anti-wrinkle facial creams to news reports about lawsuits against manufacturers which do not protect us adequately from our own stupidity, the world presses on us the lesson that we must do everything possible to deny the fact of aging and avoid danger.

Statistics tell us that the largest portion of our medical expenses are spent in the last days or months preceding death. American hospitals have elaborate machines designed to cure or at least ameliorate disease, which I am grateful for as I spend time with a friend who has leukemia. But, having accompanied another friend who in her nineties was firm that she did not want extra tests and procedures and having to constantly ask doctors "why do you want to do this?", I am certain we have much to learn about when not to use all these expensive tools. How do I make choices about when to stop? Will the people around me listen? Each time I accompany someone facing a health crisis or reaching the end of life, I am more acutely aware of the strength of inertia impelling ongoing, invasive efforts to keep a person alive, when it is time to let go. Having medical personnel, friends, and/or family who are sensitive to these questions helps make room for choice. Room to acknowledge the sacredness of this time of life. Space for living with grace up to the very end rather than being buried under the pressure and near panic of mechanical systems.

When my time comes, I want someone who will sit by my bed at the end and help remind me not to be afraid and perhaps help me reach an ease with my life and with God. Will I be able to say "I am clear, I am fully clear," as George Fox is reported to have said? How many regrets will I have? How many unresolved, bitter relationships will be there? I cannot know when my time will come, so I cherish those who push me to do this "death work" now.

Is my trust in the Infinite Power enough to put myself in harm's way if need arises? Is there something my conscience tells me is worth dying for? Having friends and acquaintances who live in Afghanistan, in Jerusalem, in Burundi, in other places where there is no guarantee of safety, makes me conscious that I might be called to such work. I would be surprised to find myself called to a witness dangerous to my health and life, but it is not totally outside the realm of possibilities. Even in this country, we are not immune from such decisions.

Friends' history of teaching through sharing life stories gives us a way to imagine what it takes to be in a place of witness which arises out of love rather than fear – a witness that is sometimes a call to take up the cross literally. A call to drink the bitter cup of total obedience. Not many of us know this call – or at least very few are willing to hear it when it comes. But the readiness to hear is part of a life immersed in God. In our communities we can teach one another to recognize when fear has hold and controls everyday actions and words, then encourage each other to step into that way of being whereby fear takes its proper place.

... For he brings a sword and war, and not peace to that nature they lived in, ... before they received the Prince of peace, ... and the peace of all fellowships must be broken, before they come into the fellowship of the spirit, and unity therein, which is the bond of peace; and the peace of all earthly teachers must be broken, who are made of men by natural tongues, before they come to the heavenly teacher, and the tongue of the learned indeed. – George Fox, 1673[125]

Do not think that I have come to bring peace to the earth; I have not come to bring peace, but a sword. – Matthew 10:34

THAT WHICH MUST BE BROKEN
BEFORE FINDING PEACE

I've never spent much time with Buddhist koans — those self-contradictory sayings meant to break down our reliance on analysis – but I find similar concepts almost everywhere I look. In Matthew, Jesus' juxtaposition of peace and conflict is certainly one of these. This paradox comes in various forms; the sword he brings to rend people from their comfortable way of life defined by family connections is one of Jesus' better known sayings. George Fox expanded on this to make clear how many ties and how many old ways of seeing the world need to be broken as a person becomes spiritually mature and knows the bond of peace.

I find it easy to joke about how Friends tend to be heavily conflict-avoidant. Along with being opposed to war, we don't like raised voices or outward signs of serious disagreement. We slip into the appearance of cooperation and congeniality with ease. Too often we are afraid to engage one another with respect and empathy when our opinions conflict.

Conflict Maturing

Elise Boulding, the Quaker sociologist who has written extensively about peaceful resolution of conflict, believes that we can best practice becoming peacemakers in our everyday relationships, particularly within the family. She does not mean that we are to smooth over hostility, or even become mediators, although the latter is a useful skill. She rather wants us to be individuals able to recognize conflict and not shy away from it. In conflict, she sees the creative spark and way to transformation. By neither hiding conflict nor allowing it to escalate into verbal or physical violence, we are pushed to change and grow, a process she calls "conflict maturing," a process grounded in the Spirit and in respect for that divine spark in each person:

> The more we are faithful to our togetherness and our separateness, which is what the inherent contradictions of the family Tao ensure, the more pain we may feel. Pain can either be seen as something to be avoided, which is what our society generally teaches, or it can be seen as a signal of growth. It is seeing pain as a signal of growth that makes the conflict-maturing process possible. Each element of the conflict can be allowed to take its own shape, and then, by stepping back, this impossible, warring configuration can be seen as an embodiment of Creation. What stands there is in the hand of God. The letting be of the other is crucial. In the facing of contradiction is growth. In fleeing it – though there are times when we do flee, and perhaps should flee – we shrink at least a little.[126]

I know I have sometimes seen the tension between the willingness to engage and the desire to flee in Meeting for Worship for Business. Despite the many things my Meeting did wrong when a man just released from five years in prison for child sexual abuse came to worship with us, I saw moments when we did engage in this process of conflict-maturing. We did engage all the adults in the Meeting from the start, holding a public gathering with this man (a member of another Meeting) soon after he arrived in Portland. We quickly discovered that the dimensions of our response had to be much broader than any of us expected and tempers often flared in this tension.

The three years we dealt with this situation, however, did not lead to a clean solution. Some members of the community stopped attending business Meeting to avoid the pain or left the Meeting altogether. The man left our community before we were in full agreement. At times we ignored the people who had the most to offer. Emotions were close to the surface and not easily controlled. Pain and fear flavored the agenda even as we sought holy guidance, strength, and the spaciousness which allows divine love to act.

We did develop new ways to care for our children, and came to acknowledge the potential for unknown abusers among us whom we did not recognize as such. At least one adult stood and thanked us for talking about abuse directly and not hiding it in some committee. She had felt shame at having been abused. The open consideration started to lift that shame and fear from her and she was able to get the counseling she needed. Other small stories indicated the moments when we acted with grace.

This time provided glimpses of the strength and patience which allow Boulding's "conflict maturing" – or perhaps are a consequence of facing conflict rather than running from it. As someone with a life-long pattern of avoiding conflict, I have to keep telling myself that the world doesn't end just because I let someone them know I disagree with him. Relationships don't necessarily shatter, although both the personality of the other person and my specific words and body language can have crucial effects. I know I can take a lot of flak from others and I want to respect the strength that others have to rebound.

Coming Back into a Different Peace

It still surprises me when I recognize that I am angry. I used to stuff any anger so deep that I couldn't see it. The moment when God broke down my inner walls opened me to the spiritual, mystical realm. It also opened me to myself – to more awareness of my own feelings, to recognition that ignoring them warped my relationships with others, and to the energy I put into pretending they don't exist.

I had always prided myself on my calmness and steadiness. Breaking the walls around my heart forced me to see how much of that calm was sustained by avoidance and keeping myself apart from engagement with issues or even with people. Thus, my apparent calm too often was a way to hide fear. One of the problems of figuring this out so late in life is that I have so many years of habits to change. Such change does not come easily.

At times now, my calm is more grounded. Tenderness is reaching out in empathy with others rather than self-protective awareness of my own sores. Some of this grounding comes from being able to say I have been hurt and I have come through. I can laugh about some of these hurts, others are scars which will always be with me, and yet other hurts are ones which I've inflicted or initiated. These latter press on me to make atonement for my actions. Some of the change in me — as when I learned I could clerk a Meeting with many angry, hurt people without being drawn into their pain – comes from gaining perspective that this kind of encounter is part of the human condition, not something peculiar to any group. Most important, I started to learn I did not have to solve every problem for everyone else. My role as clerk was to help hold the space open, space where there would be a container for all the thrashing, a container which would neither break nor leak as it was part of the Infinite Presence, not something generated by my self-will.

In being broken by the Eternal, we are held in God's arms. We do not have to hold ourselves; we are sustained. As Jesus said in Matthew 11:28-29:

> Come to me, all you that are weary and are carrying heavy burdens, and I will give you rest. Take my yoke upon you, and learn from me; for I am gentle and humble in heart, and you will find rest for your souls. For my yoke is easy and my burden light.

Knowing God at work in me directly is my experience – I can literally feel the tension drop from my shoulders when I pray — but I see and feel the same process at work in the letting go and self-emptying of Buddhism, Hinduism or Taoism and in practices of other traditions.

This process of practicing peace is tempered and shaped in community. When we are with others we can experience being present to the suffering which so permeates the world but not weighted down into depression, inaction, fear, anger or any of the other morasses which await. A community that seeks to engage the Spirit reminds us that there is a place where we can set our feet on solid rock rather than the mire of unknown depth. Such a community can show us that there is a place where the calm can be both an inward and an outward state: a place where we find a rich vocabulary for speaking of the work of the Water of Life flowing in each of us; and a place of new freedom of action where we can be a strength to others, so that they might hear each other and see the movement of the Spirit through whatever situation is before us.

… For saith Christ, which is the Word of God, My sheep, hear my voice, and they follow me; and I the Word will give them eternal life, and none can pull them out of his hand, which is that living Word, from whence this testimony of mine proceedeth. Oh how my bowels [heart] yernes in that living Word! Yes, that ye may not fall short, but be crowned with Immortality and glory.
– Sarah Jones, 1650[127]

Thomas said to him, "Lord, we do not know where you are going. How can we know the way?" Jesus said to him, "I am the way, and the truth, and the life."
– John 14:5, 6

GOD'S WAY AND HUMAN WILL

I am quite clear that theological reflection is invaluable in learning to live as a Friend, and I believe that we, in unprogrammed Friends Meetings, do have an implied common theology. We have found something deep, rich and life renewing. Our seeking, while lifelong, is not aimless, but is driven by the need to live closer to that inward fire which warms, refines and draws us to the heart of Life.

We know something of the Unity of all beings and all creation in God. The mystery of God has a reality whereby we cannot limit God to any one religious path or definition. Divine wisdom, holy actions, and the names by which we speak of the Eternal are varied and beyond what any one person can grasp. No matter what name we call the source of Love and Truth in the universe, we leave room for other understandings and experience. Some of us know a close, personal, loving, guiding Spirit; some know Jesus as our brother or as a prophet or as God embodied in human flesh; some find a river of Love flowing through the universe and dip into its waters; others may find a mother, strong and wise; others are not sure "God" exists, but experience a compelling desire drawing them to justice, mercy and humility. This entity/force/mystery known as God has dimensions beyond measure.

I have met individuals who come to Friends from other Christian churches, loving the words and message of Jesus and seeking a community which lives as Jesus lived. They find this in Friends Meetings – whether because of or despite the fact that we place a low value on formal teachings about what we have to *believe about* Jesus, but rather seek to *live in* the same Spirit as Jesus. Rather than recognizing other fellow travelers by the name they call God or the way they define Jesus, we believe the work of the Spirit is known by its fruits.

The Way to the City of God

I offer the following description of liberal Quaker belief as a path (for simplicity, I call it the Way). This Way is rooted in the Christian story yet open to other expressions which share the commitment to living in the place of truth, simplicity justice and peace.

There is a Way of Love, Truth and Unity which we can tap into, and which can guide our lives. This Way is what many call God's way or God's will and is the creative energy of the universe and all that is.

The Way can be described as to "love mercy, act justly and walk humbly with God." It can be described in terms of the Sermon on the Mount. The Way is "content with the low places that people disdain," so that "when you are content to be simply yourself and don't compare or compete, everybody will respect you," as expressed in the Tao Te Ching.[128] The Way can be expressed in the teaching of Buddha as well as of Jesus. It is the way of peace.

All people have access to the Way. The Way beckons every child, woman and man. The choice is ours to respond and seek or to close our inner ears and stay bound in the ways of the world, caught in the lure of personal self-gratification.

We are all wounded in some way, by life, by circumstances, by deliberate actions, by random events. Some of us actively turn away from the Spirit for a time and do conscious damage. We all regularly make mistakes and harm others even while attempting to be helpful or do what is right.

Asking for forgiveness for the wrongs we have participated in and forgiving others is an integral part of the Way. Divine forgiveness is complete when we ask for it out of a contrite heart. Knowing forgiveness is healing and transforming. Offering forgiveness to others releases us from the snares of bitterness and revenge.

Healing of our lives and spirits is possible; wholeness is possible. In this healing, we will become full persons whose heart, mind, body and soul come to unity as our lives become more attuned to the Way. In this holiness, neither our egos nor the pulls of the world will be our guide, but rather the Spirit.

Those who walk in God's Way will know the fruit of the Spirit and their lives will show patience, love, peace, joy, gentleness, self-control, kindness, generosity and faithfulness in contrast to jealousy, anger, quarrels, dissensions, factions, enmities, strife, licentiousness, conceit and competition. The Way has strong ethical and moral dimensions which are not easily captured in rules.

The encounter with the Spirit is an inward one which can be painful and difficult when it shows us our limitations and how we fall short of what we might be. The process of growth and change is before us as long as we live, although some few might achieve completion as Jesus did. Cycles of small inward deaths and births are one way to see this process.

Thus, we are called to right relationship with one another and with all that exists. This is an active process grounded in humility and leavened with humor — an individual process as well as a group dynamic. Both will be reflected in the institutions and communities we create.

It is possible to visualize the City of God: what the world might be like if all people would abide in God's Way. This City is an ideal, yet it is realized in part among us today on earth insofar as individuals and communities seek to live in accord with the Spirit.

Much is wrong in the world. Defining this wrongness in terms of pain and suffering as the Buddhists do, or through psychological explanations, takes away the human tendency to act as judge. It leaves whatever judgment is to be made in the hands of the Holy, where it belongs. Our place is to do what we can to right what is wrong and help mend what is broken. We can stand clear and strong for justice. We can create the space and hope for healing and coming right, but ultimately, that work is the work of the Spirit. For us to think we are the healers rather than vehicles for the healing of the Spirit is to be caught up in the traps of the ego and conceit.

Jesus fully embodies the Way and thus can be seen as both human and divine.

Jesus, Buddha, and all those 'saints' of all faith and no faith whose lives define compassion, even to the point of death, embody the Way and are our true guides. Life is more than the limits of the physical body. But both heaven and hell can be experienced in this earthly lifetime. They embody hope, forgiveness, and the means by which we might "hit the mark" and be free of "sin."

This Way is part of all of us and thus we are each both human and divine; but the divine is a Seed which can be nourished or ignored, watered or allowed to wilt and be stunted.

The Way can be found in waiting and listening, even in the midst of energetic action or outward lively sound. As we learn to use and trust our inward eyes and ears, we become more in tune with the Way.

Oh, his tender dealings can never be raced out of our remembrance, he hath printed them in our hearts, and his engaging love constraineth us to speak well of him.
–Katharine Whitton, 1681[129]

The Lord is near to the brokenhearted, and saves the crushed in spirit.
–Psalm 34:18.

BEING A  FRIEND

As I finish this book about what I know of God and the implications for how I live, I want to share a few final thoughts on what it is to claim friendship with all that is holy.

Seeking is a lovely place to be. Seeking feels purposeful. Seeking feels safe. It asks me to keep looking, but puts little demand on me, especially when I don't really know what I am after. Even so, there are those quirks of dissatisfaction and those hints of absence which don't make much sense. The first hint fuels the continued hunt. The second bemuses.

Then it all crashes apart. Nothing holds and everything is wonderful. The presumption that my worth is nil evaporates. The close-held secret that I can't be loved is held up in the air and folded in invisible loving arms which tell another truth.

So *this* is what it means to be a friend of God. A lifetime's worth of assumptions about the world is dumped in an instant, overwhelmed by the power of unconditional love. I experience a gut comprehension that this is what I am called to be.

I guess you could say there are strings attached—the tethers of a hot air balloon rather than the bindings of a captive. I am told to stop being such a prickly jerk and sulking in a corner. Mend the relationships you've strained. Find words to speak of this!—to say what it is you've found as well as the need to remake your life.

Speak what it means to be a friend of God! That's the primary doing which arises from this core. Carry in your being and beneath all your words the pain of wandering lost and frightened. Share out of the isolation that was and the brokenness of being each in our worldly pursuits, hiding what we know in our hearts.

Walk in the shoes of those you used to mock and deride, accompanied by the other. Find out what it is to be friends with those you could not see as friends of God.

Stand in the knowledge that abundance is present in every heart, each linked to the next. Affirm the truth of the paradox that is at the core of each dichotomy that blinds us to the Seed. Know that there is a fullness that is more than minds can conceive. Know that we are asked to be present at the conception of a fresh way, where strength is to be found in our weaknesses, and in the mire of the swamp, our feet may be set on a rock.

Speaking of Friendship

I stood in the midst of a circle of twenty or more Friends at the Way of Ministry program (TWM) with the instruction that I was to tell them about the Source, about that which is at the heart of my faith — the story I told earlier in this volume. Just talking didn't seem enough and there seemed to be a fresh way to frame this story which might break our easy assumptions about worship and how God speaks to us. Thus, I asked them to imagine themselves as part of a popcorn meeting. I motioned someone to rise to represent a speaker from that time in 1991. Then I motioned to another to represent the woman who offered "O Come Emanuel" as a rich solo. Yet another and another stood, then sat again. I ended with an old man who had rambled on and on, probably as he had done week after week.

Then I went and sat in my place in the circle, telling these TWM Friends how I had been enveloped in tears in the midst of worship overstuffed with apparently superficial messages. Retelling this story to TWM, tears rose and I felt again the arms which embraced me that day so many years before. In what had seemed to others present to be a popcorn meeting, I had experienced being held by God in unconditional love. Each message, no matter how trite, had something to say to me, about care and attention, about moving into a new way of being despite any fumbling and discomfort. And in acting out this story, that same Love was again holding me and carrying me forward.

In my attempts over the years to be faithful to this call, it has become apparent that more was being asked of me. The expanse of the call grew with each step I took, even though it often felt as if I were walking in a fog where only a small space of ground is visible at any time. It took time to realize that the u-turns were really switchbacks lifting me steady up the hillside.

The gentle nudges on the heart are my surest, most frequent Guide. Only rarely do vivid images arise to grant me new language and new concepts for expressing my faith and articulating the transformation of my heart. All of this has happened within community and I cannot conceive how it could have happened if I had tried to respond in isolation. Learning to speak of God present was one of the hardest things I have ever done and I am thankful for the friends willing to sit with me in patience so the words could at last form. And I am grateful for the other friends who listened as I read my first efforts to share this in a wider circle at a time when I was so tender the only way I could speak was to write it first. Yet this too turned out to be a gift, and my writing became central to my ministry.

What I had first named as a call to "vocal ministry" on Sunday mornings, had a meaning similar to that which 17th century Friends gave to "conversation": Both involve not only speaking but all our actions in the world. My experience of this call to ministry is but one example of the myriad ways open to each of us to befriend the world as God has befriended us.

Study Guide

This section is designed to encourage readers to explore their own relationship with the Holy and how they understand their faith. This can be done alone or in conversation with others. To facilitate this process, I've provided expanded versions of the quotations presented at the beginning of each chapter along with some queries.

A group may elect to share with each other using worship sharing out of the silence – a time when each person speaks out of their own experience and does not respond directly to what others have said. Time is left between speakers so that each person might fully listen to what is being said. In all cases, response is optional so that no one is pressured to speak beyond their measure and all that is heard is held in confidence.

Alternatively, a group may choose to share there responses in a freer back-and-forth discussion. Whichever format is used should be made clear to participants in advance and care taken by the leader to ensure no one person dominates and that all who wish to speak are given space to respond. An hour or ninety minutes are often good lengths of time for a group to meet. The group should feel free to choose the quotations and queries which seem most alive to them.

Here are the primary individuals I cite: George Fox (1624 -1691), who is pointed to as "the founder" and whose vision on Pendle Hill in northern England in 1652 identifies the start of Quakerism, is most frequently quoted. Margaret Fell (1614—1702) is probably a close second. She provided much organizational structure for early Friends and, as someone of relative wealth, her home became a place of hospitality and a base of stability in the early years. William Penn (1644—1718) is probably best known as the founder of Pennsylvania. He also wrote several books on faith as well as issues of governance. Robert Barclay (1648—1690) was a well-educated Scottish Friend who wrote the first systematic Quaker theology. Isaac Penington, (1616 -1679) one of the wealthier, better educated Friends, became both a spiritual guide for many individuals and an apologist for the faith who wrote many letters, pamphlets and books. A few other individuals are also quoted. Each was recognized by Friends of their day to have a gift in the ministry and to speak for Friends.

Languages of Salvation

Many languages exist to express our faith in the deepest matters of the soul. Some use the language of judgment and punishment and draw up images in me of police, jail and the legal process so that we might "saved from" something. Alternatively, words can draw from music so we speak of attunement to the divine and our actions as in or out of harmony with the Spirit. Other words, like alignment, contrast with disorientation or being at cross purposes with the Inward Teacher.

The language of the natural world and of cultivation is rich with possibilities. The preparation of the ground, planting the seed, the slow growth, weeding, ripening, and maturation all have meaning in our relationship with God, who is both Seed and Planter. The processes of growth are infinite for plants as well as humans. Some require human help, others do not. Some seeds only germinate after forest fires, others are tender and require well-tilled soil, fertilizer and careful weeding.

WAITING, ATTENDING

1. WAITING AND ATTENDING

I wait for the Lord, my soul waits,
and in his word I hope;
my soul waits for the Lord
more than those who watch for the morning,
more than those who watch for the morning.

Psalm 130:5, 6

Mind and watch to that which quickens and enlivens the soul towards God, and watch against that which flats and deadens it; for they are both near, and they both seek after you, the one for your good, the other for your hurt.

Isaac Penington, 1671[130]

Likewise the Spirit helps us in our weakness; for we do not know how to pray as we ought, but that the very Spirit intercedes with sighs too deep for words. And God, who searches the heart, knows what is the mind of the Spirit, because the Spirit intercedes for the saints according to the will of God.

Romans 8:26, 27

QUERIES

When was there a time in your life when you were aware of an absence, a dull ache, a longing, or something missing close to your soul? What was that time like? What was your response at the time? How does that seem to you now?

Can you sense when there have been conflicting pulls on your life and energies? Can you sense what kinds of activities and choices deadened your spirit and what gave/gives life? What choices did you make that enriched your life?

What helps you pay attention to your emotions and to the deeper movement within that is the action of the Spirit? How do you sort out/discern the pressures of your own ego, your desire to please or get back at others, and the motion of the Spirit?

2. THE CONSUMING FIRE

I stood up in my pew, and wondered at his doctrine; for I had never heard such before. Then he went on, and opened the Scriptures, and said: "The Scriptures were the prophet's words, and Christ's and the apostle's words. What, as they spoke, they enjoyed and possessed, and had it from the Lord.' He said, 'Then what had any to do with the Scriptures, but as they came to the spirit that gave them forth. You will say Christ saith this, and the apostles say this; but what canst thou say? Art thou a child of light, and hast walked in the light; and what thou speakest, is it inwardly from God?"

This opened me so, that it cut me to the heart. Then I saw clearly we were all wrong. So I sat down in my pew again, and cried bitterly. I cried in my spirit to the Lord: 'We are all thieves; we have taken the Scriptures in words, and know nothing of them in ourselves.' So that served me, that I cannot well tell what he spoke afterwards…

Margaret Fell, 1652[132]

From this time forward I make you hear new things, hidden things that you have not known.

Isaiah 48:6

God is our refuge and strength,
a very present help in trouble.
Therefore we will not fear, though the earth should change,
though the mountains shake in the heart of the sea;
though its waters roar and foam,
though the mountains tremble with its tumult.

Psalm 46:1-3

QUERIES

Have you ever experienced a time when your heart and your understanding were opened to God/the Universe in a new way? What was that like? How has that changed your life?

How has delight grown in you as a result of this opening? Has fear shrunk as a force in your life? Has a new passion for caring for the world (or a tiny part of it) grown in you?

3. SIFTING THROUGH FEARS

And so, Dear Friends, there is an enemy near, against whom it is greatly needful to watch continually, that so the mind may be kept Single, Pure and Clean; and so that you may feel more and more these things, and to enjoy the Comfort and Consolation in your selves, when the mind is kept single and clean of all Incumbrances, and Reasonings, and Consultations about things which you cannot discern nor under stand, and leave it to the Lord who is onely Wise, and knows every ones Condition, State and Capacity; who watcheth over his own, as a Father doth over his Children, teaching and instructing every one according to their growth and ability, of those things that are his Will concerning them. And Friends, Take heed of that Spirit that still will seek to excuse himself, and to diminish and hide that which is not well, ... this is the Spirit of the world, and is out of Truth, ...

Elizabeth Hendricks, 1672[133]

[Jesus said] "Do not judge, so that you may not be judged. For with the judgment you make you will be judged, and the measure you give will be the measure you will get. Why do you see the speck in your neighbor's eye, but do not notice the log in your own eye? Or how can you say to your neighbor, 'Let me take the speck out of your eye,' while the log is in your own eye? You hypocrite, first take the log out of your own eye, and then you will see clearly to take the speck out of your neighbor's eye."

Matthew 7:1-5

QUERIES

What triggers distress within you? Are you someone, like Isaac Penington, who worries when your heart is at odds with what your rational mind tells you and thus constantly prone to doubts, or is there something else which causes you to ignore the promptings of the Spirit?

When have you ignored the sense that you have acted in a hurtful way and tried to blame it on someone else? What made you do this? What was the result? What steps did you take to right the situation?

4. Salvation

Now in Jerusalem by the Sheep Gate there is a pool, called in Hebrew Beth-zatha, which has five porticos. In these lay many invalids – blind, lame, and paralyzed. One man was there who had been ill for thirty-eight years. When Jesus saw him lying there and knew that he had been there a long time, he said to him, "Do you want to be made well?" The sick man answered him, "Sir, I have no one to put me into the pool when the water is stirred up; and while I am making my way, someone else steps down ahead of me." Jesus said to him, "Stand up, take your mat and walk." At once the man was made well, and he took up his mat and began to walk.

John 5:2-9

I [William Penn] close this Scripture doctrine of waiting, with that passage in John about the pool of Bethesda:

> *There is at Jerusalem, a pool ... which is called Bethesda, having five porches. In these lay a great multitude of invalids, of blind, lame and paralyzed, waiting for the moving of the water. For an angel went down at a certain time into the pool, and troubled the water. Whoever then first stepped in was made whole of whatever disease he had. (John 5:2-4)*

This represents exactly the subject of waiting. For, as there was then an outward and legal Jerusalem, so there is now a gospel and spiritual Jerusalem. This is the church of God, consisting of the faithful. The pool in that old

Jerusalem represented that fountain which is now set open in this new Jerusalem. That pool was for those that were under infirmities of body. This new fountain is for all that are invalid in soul. There was an angel then that moved the water, to make it beneficial. It is the angel of God's presence now that blesses this fountain with success. They that went in before and did not watch the angel found no benefit in stepping in. Those that now do not wait for the moving of God's angel, but rush before God, as the horse to battle, are sure to miscarry in their expectation.

William Penn, 1669[134]

QUERIES

In what ways do you wait, hoping someone or something will heal your hurts? Do you find yourself feeling resentful of others who move ahead of you and are made well? What might change this?

How might you sort out Penn's definition of waiting based on alertness for the "moving of God's angel" from a waiting which leaves you feeling passed by and helpless? Can you imagine yourself open to the words "stand up, take your mat and walk?"

ENCOUNTERING THE SEED

5. Breaking Down the Walls

So by this faith you come to know the partition wall broken down, that hath been betwixt you and God.

George Fox, 1676[135]

For [Christ Jesus] is our peace; in his flesh he has made both groups into one and has broken down the dividing wall, that is, the hostility between us. He has abolished the law with its commandments and ordinances, that he might create in himself one new humanity in place of the two, thus making peace, and might reconcile both groups to God in one body through the cross, thus putting to death that hostility through it.

Ephesians 2:14-16

QUERIES

Is there a dividing wall between you and God? What does it look like? Does it have openings in it or is it solid?

Ephesians is referring to the hostility between Gentiles and Jews as to what it means to be a follower of Jesus. What might be the hostilities in your life and your community which are a barrier to peace and to right relationship between one another and with God? Can you envision "one new humanity" which is grounded in reconciliation and imagine ways this might come to be?

6. The Nature of God

Doth the kingdom of God consist in righteousness, peace, and joy in God's Spirit? This is all in this seed, and is partaken of and enjoyed, as this seed springs up, and gains authority and dominion in the heart. Yea, the horn of God's anointed, the righteous and peaceable sceptre of the Savior is known and exalted in this seed, as it springs up, and spreads abroad in the life and virtue of the Father.

Secondly, the divine nature of God Almighty is hid and wrapped up in it. It is the seed of God, and it is the very nature of God; and he in whom it springs, and who is gathered into it, born of it, and one with it, partakes of the divine nature.

Isaac Penington (n.d.)[136]

This is the message we have heard from him and proclaim to you, that God is light and in him there is no darkness at all.

I John 1:5

QUERIES

Have you felt something of the divine within your own heart? What is that like? How might you describe it to others?

What causes that holy seed within you to grow? Do you take time to nourish it?

7. THE LIGHT OF CHRIST

But in this free spirit of the Lord Jesus was I sent forth to declare the word of life and reconciliation freely, that all might come up to Christ, who gives freely, and who renews up into the image of God which man and woman were in before they fell, that they might sit down in heavenly places in Christ Jesus....

Jesus Christ that died for them, and had enlightened them, that with his light they might see their evil deeds and their sins, and with the same light they might see their saviour...

George Fox, 1649, 1658[137]

Those who have been born of God do not sin, because God's seed abides in them; they cannot sin, because they have been born of God. The children of

God, and the children of the devil are revealed in this way: all who do not do
what is right are not from God, nor are those who do not love their brothers
and sisters.

I John 3:9, 10

QUERIES

What role does Jesus play in your life and faith? In what way does
Jesus give an image of what God is like? If Jesus is not central to
your life, what person/image/concept most inspires you and speaks
to you of all that is holy and right in the universe?

How do you explain or reconcile within yourself the existence of
evil in the world?

8. THAT OF GOD IN EVERYONE

Friends,

*And this is the word of the Lord God to you all, and a charge to you all in the
presence of the living God, be patterns, be examples in all countries, places,
islands, nations, wherever you come; that your carriage and life may preach
among all sorts of people, and to them. Then you will come to walk cheerfully
over the world, answering that of God in every one; whereby in them ye may
be a blessing, and make the witness of God in them to bless you. Then to the
Lord God you will be a sweet savour and a blessing.*

*Spare no deceit. Lay the sword upon it; go over it; keep yourselves clear of the
blood of all men, either by word, or writing, or speaking. And keep yourselves
clean, . . .that nothing may rule nor reign but power and life itself, and that in
the wisdom of God ye may be preserved in it.*

George Fox , 1656[138]

*"... And who is my neighbor?" Jesus replied, "A man was going down from
Jerusalem to Jericho, and fell into the hands of robbers, who stripped him,
beat him, and went away, leaving him half dead. Now by chance a priest was
going down that road; and when he saw him, he passed by on the other side.*

So likewise a Levite, when he came to that place and saw him, passed by on the other side. But a Samaritan while traveling came near him; and when he saw him, he was moved with pity. He went to him and bandaged his wounds, having poured oil and wine on them. Then he put him on his own animal, brought him to an inn, and took care of him.

Luke 10:29

QUERIES

When you consider "that of God in every person," how do you see this bit of God inside you? In what way is your life a pattern and example to others? What actions has this led you to that you might not have taken otherwise?

What tells you when you are acting out of "that of God"? What might Fox have meant about keeping oneself clean as well as keeping clear of spilling the blood of others? The priest and the Levite were faithful to the old rules of cleanliness which kept them from touching the man by the side of the road: what rules in your life keep you from acting out of compassion?

9. THE LIGHT THAT IS IN US ALL

In the beginning was the Word, and the Word was with God, and the Word was God. He was in the beginning with God. All things came into being through him, and without him not one thing came into being. What has come into being in him was life, and the life was the light of all people. The light shines in the darkness, and the darkness did not overcome it.

John 1:1-5

The Lord created me [wisdom/Sophia] at the beginning of his work, the first of his acts long ago.... and I was daily his delight, rejoicing before him always, rejoicing in his inhabited world and delighting in the human race.

Proverbs 8:22-31

Whereupon, after I had plunged [the priest] about his proof, I had a fit opportunity to open unto [the priests and lawyers] the right and proper use, service, and excellency of the Scriptures; and also to show that the spirit of God, which was given to every one to profit withal, and the grace of God, which bringeth salvation, and which hath appeared unto all men, and teacheth them that obey it to deny ungodliness and worldly lusts, and to live soberly, righteously, and godly in this present world: that this is the most fit, proper, and universal rule, which God hath given to all mankind to rule, direct, govern, and order their lives by.

George Fox, 1674[139]

QUERIES

What is eternal in your theology? How would you describe this force/person/energy/Light?

Where do you find your primary written source of inspiration and moral teaching?

10. Spiritual Maturity

Love never ends. But as for prophecies, they will come to an end; as for tongues, they will cease; as for knowledge, it will come to an end. For we know only in part, and we prophesy only in part; but when the complete comes, the partial will come to an end. When I was a child, I spoke like a child, I thought like a child, I reasoned like a child; when I became an adult, I put an end to childish ways. For now we see in a mirror, dimly, but then we will see face to face. Now I know only in part; then I will know fully, even as I have been fully known. And now faith, hope, and love abide, these three; and the greatest of these is love.

I Corinthians 13:8-13

And how do we grow up in Christ, but by the growing up in this seed, and feeling this seed grow up in us? And here, in truth and demonstration of God's Spirit, we are formed in Christ, and Christ formed in us, as this seed groweth up into a form and shape in us, and we into a form and shape in it. Now we cannot receive this seed, but as we part with and deny our own wisdom and fleshly confidence; and denying that, and crying to God for wisdom, God brings up the wisdom of the seed in us, and makes Christ become unto us wisdom therein.

Isaac Penington (n.d.)[140]

QUERIES

How do you imagine "spiritual maturity"? Can you see this in yourself and in others around you? What helps you "grow up in Christ"? What might the "wisdom of the seed" be?

What kind of growth have you seen in yourself over the years? What part does community play in your spiritual growth?

11. BEING PRESENT TO OTHERS

Deare Brethren James & Francis, prisoners of the Lord [Eph.4:1] … you have peace, you have joy, you have boldness and you stand over all the world's standing, over it in the particular, stand over it all in the general, in purity, in love, glory, in righteousness; and there is a pure discerning springing which is refreshed by you. I do see the secret work of God going on in people's minds, look not at the work, nor look not at briars nor look not at all the thorns, nor at the mountains, nor the coldness; for well it may be so for there hath been no vinedresser nor no plough man there; none to dress the ground, no seeds man to sow the seed, and therefore the Lord hath set you forth to do his work, and the plough man shall not plough in vain nor the seeds man shall not sow in vain … so thou son of man understand, the Lord give thee an understanding in all things [2 Tim. 2:7], and the glorious God keep thee in his glory…

Margaret Fell to James Nayler and Francis Howgill, 1653[141]

And [Jesus] told them many things in parables, saying: "Listen! A sower went out to sow. And as he sowed, some seeds fell on the path, and the birds came and ate them up. Other seeds fell on rocky ground, where they did not have much soil, and they sprang up quickly, since they had no depth of soil. But when the sun rose, they were scorched; and since they had no root, they withered away. Other seeds fell among thorns, and the thorns grew up and choked them. Other seeds fell on good soil and brought forth grain, some a hundredfold, some sixty, some thirty. Let anyone with ears listen!"

Matthew 13: 4-9

QUERIES

What is the sowing and the ploughing that Matthew and Margaret Fell speak of all about? If you do not have any experience to draw upon, what might you imagine this to mean? What role do we play in accompanying one another, encouraging one another and bringing each other's attention to the Eternal Love that is at the heart of the universe?

Does your Meeting seek to attract new people and introduce them to Quakerism? If does, how does it explain what Quakers are all about? If it doesn't, do you feel it should? What is your role in all this?

TAKING UP THE CROSS

12. TAKING UP THE CROSS DAILY

*And he that would ... hear the voice of God in his true ministry, must first
take up the cross to that part of him which is not of God, and receive from
God the eye which sees, and the ear which hears.*

Isaac Penington, 1680[142]

*The obedience of the light of Christ Jesus is the obedience to the cross of
Christ... The light, the power of God, the cross of Christ, the apostle did not
preach with the wisdom of words, lest the cross of Christ should become of no
effect, which is unto all that are saved, the power of God. He says, "for since, in
the wisdom of God, the world did not know God through wisdom, it pleased
God through the folly of what we preach to save those who believe." (I Cor.
1.21). This is the wisdom of God, the way of God, not to teach people by that
which man's wisdom teaches, that which man's dark heart invents, imagines,
and studies out of his brain, but by that which the Holy Ghost teaches in this
His day in which He is risen in His eternal Spirit.*

Margaret Fell, 1660[143]

... but [God] *said to me, "My grace is sufficient for you, for power is made
perfect in weakness." So, I will boast all the more gladly of my weaknesses,
so that the power of Christ may dwell in me. Therefore I am content with
weaknesses, insults, hardships, persecutions, and calamities for the sake of
Christ; for whenever I am weak, then I am strong.*

2 Corinthians 12:9-10

QUERIES

What is your sense of the contrast between the wisdom of God and
the wisdom of words? What do you think she means when she tells
us not to teach what "man's dark heart invents"? Does her warning

hold any validity in your life?

What is your concept of the Cross? What might the wisdom of the Cross look like? Does "obedience to the Cross" have any meaning in your life?

13. ATONEMENT

And it was called the light in man and woman, which was the true light which had enlightened every man that came into the world, which was a heavenly and divine light which let them see all their evil words and deeds and their sins, and the same light would let them see Christ their saviour, from whence it came to save them from their sin and to blot it out.
George Fox, 1657[144]

Have mercy on me, O God,
according to your steadfast love;
according to your abundant mercy
blot out my transgressions.
Wash me thoroughly from my iniquity,
and cleanse me from my sin.
Psalm 51:1, 2

And you, that were sometime alienated and enemies in your mind by wicked works, yet now hath he reconciled in the body of his flesh through death, to present you holy and unblameable and unreprovable in his sight...
Colossians 1:21, 22 (KJV)

QUERIES

What blocks do you have around Christian theology? Does it cause you to cringe, to reject anyone who uses this language, or to label them in some way? If so, what might it take to allow you to drop your defensiveness and to be more at ease with and/or respectful towards those whose theology seems at odds with yours?

All of us make mistakes and do harm, even inadvertently. How do you address the tension between the wrong you have done and the desire to be right with the world? What allows you to forgive yourself? To ask others for forgiveness? What part does God play in forgiveness?

14. FLEEING THE CROSS

Consider whether ye did not flee from the cross, in your transplanting into New England, and so let us that part in you there, which should have been kept down by the cross here, and gave advantage to that spirit to get ground in you, which you outwardly fled from. The safety is in standing in God's counsel, in bearing the cross, in suffering for the testimony of his truth; but if at any time there be a fleeing of the cross (whether the inward or the outward) without God's direction, the evil spirit is thereby let in, his part strengthened, and the life weakened. That spirit that would save itself from the cross, is the same with that which would persecute that which will not save itself.

Isaac Penington, 1660[145]

Then he said to them, "I am deeply grieved, even to death; remain here, and stay awake with me." And going a little farther, he threw himself on the ground and prayed, "My Father, if it is possible, let this cup pass from me; yet not what I want but what you want." Then he came to the disciples and found them sleeping…

Matthew 26:38-40

QUERIES

Think about a time when you were upset about someone else's actions, then found yourself treating other people similarly or behaving in the same way. What helped you to recognize the behavior in yourself? How does settling into the silence, or otherwise being aware of the Spirit, help you change your response to wrong-doing, either in yourself or in someone else?

What causes you to flee from the cross – from doing something you know is yours to do or from letting go of actions which satisfy your personal desires but damage relationships or are in some way unjust?

15. SUFFERING

So then I went to Dublin, where I spake in the High-Court of Justice amongst the Judges; and then they put me in Prison, where I lay upon Straw, on the Ground and when it Rained, the Water and Filth of the House-of-Office ran in under my back: And they Arraigned me at the Bar, and bid me plead Guilty, or Not Guilty: And I answered, that there was no guilt upon any ones Conscience for what they did in Obedience unto the Lord God.

Barbara Blaugdone, 1691[146]

Here is my servant, whom I uphold,
my chosen, in whom my soul delights;
I have put my spirit upon him;
he will bring forth justice to the nations.
He will not cry or lift up his voice,
or make it heard in the street;
a bruised reed he will not break,
and a dimly burning wick he will not quench;
he will faithfully bring forth justice.
He will not grow faint or be crushed
until he has established justice in the earth;
and the coastlands wait for his teaching.
Isaiah 42: 1-4

QUERIES

How do you understand suffering? Have you ever suffered as a result of your faith? How do you stand with others who are suffering?

When you experience something painful, or hear others tell of their pain, how do you respond? Or when someone hurts you, how do you react? What does the Light tell you about how you might respond?

THE NEW CREATION

16. THE CITY OF GOD

[The angel] showed me the holy city Jerusalem coming down out of heaven from God. It has the glory of God and a radiance like a very rare jewel, like jasper, clear as crystal... I saw no temple in the city, for its temple is the Lord God the Almighty and the Lamb. And the city has no need of sun or moon to shine on it, for the glory of God is its light, and its lamp is the Lamb. The nations will walk by its light, and the kings of the earth will bring their glory into it. Its gates will never by shut by day – and there will be no night there. People will bring into it the glory and the honor of the nations. But nothing unclean will enter it, nor anyone who practices abomination or falsehood, but only those who are written in the Lamb's book of life.

Then the angel showed me the river of the water of life, bright as crystal, flowing from the throne of God and of the Lamb through the middle of the street of the city. On either side of the river is the tree of life with its twelve kinds of fruit, producing its fruit each month; and the leaves of the tree are for the healing of the nations. Nothing accursed will be found there any more.

Revelation 21:10, 11, 22-27, 22:1-3

...for the Vine shall yield its increase, and the blessing of the Lord shall multiply upon the works of his hands, his new creation; ... And all must feel the overcoming Life of Love to overcome; that is that which must remain Love to the Brethren; and this must convince the World that we are of God, because we love the Brethren...

Dorothy White, 1662[147]

Therefore, for us to be clear of your blood, and not to be guilty of innocent blood, we lay these things upon you, that if any be prisoned to death, as very many have been in these Nations, by Priests and impropriators, that we shall be clear in the sight of God and have forewarned you, and let their blood be upon you, who are in the place to do Justice, and to take off oppression which you may do while you have time, if you live in the power of God; and let not the Nation be ruined, and people prisoned to death, and the blood of the innocent be drunken, as abundance of it hath been within these few years, which lies upon the heads of some; Therefore keep it clear off your own heads, we warn you which to you is the word of the Lord God.

7000 Handmaidens of the Lord, 1659.[148]

QUERIES

Early Friends knew both the City of God and the Lamb's War as inward states and as evidence of Christ formed within the human heart. How does your experience of that which is Eternal shape your life?

What is your image of a world made right? Is there a metaphor that sums up your hopes about how humanity will live at peace in the world? If so, what is it and why does it speak to you?

The epistle of James articulates one understanding of how we might live in the City of God? Does this speak to you? How do you recognize the New Creation being formed and lived out in your life?

17. JUSTICE

When I had staid the firstday's Meeting there, which was very large and precious, there being a ship ready, and the wind serving, we took our leave of Friends; parting in much tenderness and brokenness, in the sense of the heavenly life and power, that was manifested amongst us… .

A good, weighty, and true people there is in that nation, sensible of the power of the Lord God, and tender of his truth, and very good order they have in their Meetings; for they stand up for righteousness and holiness, which dams up the way of wickedness. A precious visitation they had, and there is an excellent spirit in them, worthy to be visited. Many things more I could write of that nation, and of my travels in it, which would be large to mention particularly; but thus much I thought good to signify, that the righteous may rejoice in the prosperity of truth.

George Fox, 1669[149]

*When the ear heard, it commended me, and when the eye saw, it approved;
because I delivered the poor who cried, and the orphan who had no helper.
The blessing of the wretched came upon me, and I caused the widow's heart
to sing for joy. I put on righteousness, and it clothed me; my justice was like a
robe and a turban. I was eyes to the blind, and feet to the lame. I was a father
to the needy, and I championed the cause of the stranger. I broke the fangs of
the unrighteous, and made them drop their prey from their teeth…. If I have
withheld anything that the poor desired, or have caused the eyes of the widow
to fail, … then let my shoulder blade fall from my shoulder, and let my arm be
broken in its socket.*

Job 29:11-17, 31: 16, 22

QUERIES

What is the relationship between compassion and justice? How do
you experience that connection?

What tells you when you have acted justly? What did that feel like?
What was the response of those around you?

When have you witnessed oppression? What was your response?
Was there something different you wished you had done? What
might help you respond in the way you wished?

18. RESPONDING TO VIOLENCE

*So when they came to anchor, they went to trim and dress themselves as usual;
this took up some time. I was under a weight of trouble; and when they were
ready to go on shore, a marshal came aboard, with orders from the governor,
that none should come ashore, … The governor sent for the master of the vessel,
who was no Friend, and bound him in a bond of one thousand pounds sterling,
to carry us back to Antigua. But there came on board us one Col. Stapleton,
who was governor of Montserrat, and several men of account with him.*

*I told them, it was very hard usage, that we being Englishmen, and coming
so far as we had done to visit our countrymen, could not be admitted to come
on shore, to refresh ourselves, within King Charles' dominions after such a
long voyage: Colonel Stapleton said, it was true, but, said he, we hear that*

since your coming to the Caribbean islands, there are seven hundred of our militia turned Quakers; and the Quakers will not fight, and we have need of men to fight, being surrounded with enemies, and that is the very reason, why Governor Wheeler will not suffer you to come ashore.

William Edmondson, 1672[150]

Blessed are those who hunger and thirst for righteousness, for they will be filled. Blessed are the merciful, for they will receive mercy. Blessed are the pure in heart, for they will see God. Blessed are the peacemakers, for they will be called children of God.

Matthew 5: 6-9

We do therefore declare (to take off all jealousies, fears and suspicions of our truth and fidelity to the King and these present governors) that our intentions and endeavors are and shall be good, true, honest, and peaceable towards them; that we do love, own, and honor the King, and these present governors, so far as they do rule for God, and His truth…

Margaret Fell, 1660[151]

When they had brought them, they had them stand before the council. The high priest questioned them, saying, "We gave you strict orders not to teach in this name, yet here you have filled Jerusalem with your teaching and you are determine to bring this man's blood on us." But Peter and the apostles answered, "We must obey God rather than any human authority."

Acts 5: 27-29

QUERIES

What is the inward state which allows you to act peacefully even when things are chaotic around you? Has listening to the inward Guide changed your life in a way which opens you to non-violent responses to difficult situations? Where are the struggles or the cutting edge for you as you seek to live without doing violence to yourself, to others and to the world?

Is it ever right to disobey civil law? If so, under what circumstances might that happen? Are there limits to such action or provisions as to how such disobedience should be undertaken? How do you distinguish between the need for separation of church and state and the call to bring all your actions under divine guidance?

How would you (have you) discern when and how it was right to break the law? What guidelines might help you in this process? How might you speak of this to someone who objected to your decision?

19. THE WHOLENESS OF THE EARTH

God is in the life of every creature, though few there be that know it.

James Nayler, 1656[152]

... And wait all in the light for the wisdom by which all things were made, and with it to use all the Lord's creatures to his glory (and none to stumble one another about the creatures, for that is not from the light), for which end they were created, and with the wisdom by which they were made, ye may be kept out of the misuse of them, in the image of God, that ye may come to see, that the 'earth is the Lord's and the fulness thereof,' and the earth may come to yield her increase, and to enjoy her sabbaths.

George Fox, 1653[153]

And God said, "Let the earth bring forth living creatures of every kind: cattle and creeping things and wild animals of the earth of every kind." And it was so. God made the wild animals of the earth of every kind, and the cattle of every kind, and everything that creeps upon the ground of every kind. And God saw that it was good.

Then God said, "Let us make humankind in our image, according to our own likeness; and let them have dominion over the fish of the sea, and over the birds of the air, and over the cattle, and over all the wild animals of the earth, and over every creeping thing that creeps upon the earth." So God created humankind in his image ... And there was evening and there was morning, the sixth day.

Genesis 1:24-27, 31

QUERIES

How do you articulate your own experience of right relationship with the earth, with one another and with God? How does the potential for significant change in worldwide ecosystems change your sense of the wholeness of the earth?

Do Friends bring a distinctive perspective to care for the globe we live on? If so, how would you describe the key features of that perspective?

Humanity has developed great capacity to change the world, from generation of power to manipulation of the human gene. Are there limits to the use of our scientific and technological knowledge? Is it right to act just because we can? How might we define such limits and on what basis?

RETIREMENT

20. Solitude

Not that I would be thought to slight a true retirement, for I do not only acknowledge but admire solitude. Christ himself was an example of it; he loved and chose to frequent mountains, gardens, seasides.... I have long thought it an error among all sorts that use not monastic lives, that they have no retreats for the afflicted, the tempted, the solitary and the devout, where they might undisturbedly wait upon God, pass through their religious exercises, and being thereby strengthened, might with more power over their own spirits enter into the world again. For divine pleasures are found in free solitude.

William Penn, 1669[154]

In the morning, while it was still very dark, [Jesus] got up and went out to a deserted place, and there he prayed.

Mark 1:35

QUERIES

In what ways do you wait upon God? Are there certain settings which make this more possible for you?

What is your experience of prayer? What place does prayer have in your life?

How easy is it for you to set time aside during each day to listen inwardly? Do you have reminders which make you more aware that it would be helpful to stop – stop talking, acting busily, fuming angrily, etc – so that you might become more centered in the Spirit?

21. COMMUNION

Be still and cool in thy own mind and spirit from thy own thoughts, and then thou wilt feel the principle of God to turn thy mind to the Lord God, whereby thou wilt receive his strength and power from whence life comes, to allay all tempests, against blusterings and storms. That is it which moulds up into patience, into innocency, into soberness, into stillness, into stayedness, into quietness, up to God, with his power.

George Fox, 1658[155]

Come, behold the works of the Lord;
see what desolations he has brought on the earth.
He makes wars cease to end of the earth;
he breaks the bow, and shatters the spear;
he burns the shields with fire.
"Be still, and know that I am God! . . ."

Psalm 46: 8-10

QUERIES

Have you ever been aware of God present in your life, or of being a part of the unity of all humanity, or of angels on your shoulder? What was that like for you? How did it change you?

Do you desire awareness of God in your life but feel it missing? Are you open to the possibility that this may already be true, but in a form you were not expecting? Can you imagine how the Spirit might be present in surprising ways?

22. THE HARD WORK OF RETIREMENT

The enemy kindles a great distress in the mind, by stirring up an earnest desire, and a sense of a seeming necessity, to know. When a motion ariseth, "how shall I do, to know whether it be of God or no? — for if it be of God, it ought to be obeyed; and if it be not of God, it ought to be resisted; but what shall I do, who cannot tell what it is? I must of necessity fall either into disobedience to God's Spirit, or into the snares of the enemy"—Thus the enemy raiseth up a strength in the reasoning part, even unanswerable there. But what if it be better for thee at present to be darkened about these things, than as yet to know? "Can that possibly be?" will the strong reason readily say. Yes, that it may, in many respects.

Therefore, retire out of all necessities, according to the apprehension of the reasoning mind; and judge that only necessary which God, in his eternal wisdom and love, proportions out unto us. And when thou comest hither, thou wilt come to thy rest; and as thou abidest here, thou wilt abide in thy soul's true rest, and know the preciousness of that lesson, and of whom thou art to learn it, even in every state to be content.

Isaac Penington (n.d.)[156]

Then Jesus was led up by the Spirit into the wilderness to be tempted by the devil. He fasted forty days and forty nights, and afterwards he was famished. The tempter came and said to him, "If you are the Son of God, command these stones to become loaves of bread." But he answered, "It is written, 'One does not live by bread alone, but by every word that comes from the mouth of God.'" … Then the devil left him, and suddenly angels came and waited on him."

Matthew 4:1, 5, 11

QUERIES

Many people find solitude difficult, whether it be physical isolation, or simply being quiet within oneself. Is this true for you? What sense do you have of the reasons why solitude is difficult? What might make it more possible for you?

What community do you turn to when you are facing inner darkness? How do its members help you? How do you wish they might help you? How might you help make that more possible?

23. BE GENTLE WITH YOURSELF

And you, young convinced ones, … Look not out but within; let not another's liberty be your snare: neither act by imitation, but sense and feeling of God's power in yourselves: crush not the tender buddings of it in your souls, nor overrun in your desires and your warmness of affections the holy and gentle motions of it. Remember it is a still voice that speaks to us in this day, and that it is not to be heard in the noises and hurries of the mind, but is distinctly understood in a retired frame. Jesus loved and chose out solitudes, often going to mountains, to gardens, and sea-sides, to avoid crowds and hurries, to show his disciples it was good to be solitary and sit loose to the world.

Two enemies lie near your state, Imagination and Liberty; but the plain, practical, living, holy truth, that has convinced you, will preserve you, if you mind it in yourselves, and bring all thoughts, imaginations, and affections to the test of it, to see if they are wrought in God, or of the enemy, or your own selves: so will a true taste, discerning, and judgment be preserved to you, of what you should do and leave undone; and in your diligence and faithfulness in this way you will come to inherit substance, and Christ, the eternal wisdom, will fill your treasury.

William Penn, 1691[157]

Some wandered in desert wastes,
finding no way to an inhabited town;
hungry and thirsty,
their soul fainted within them
Then they cried to the Lord in their trouble,
and he delivered them from their distress;
he led them by a straight way,
until they reached an inhabited town.
Let them thank the Lord for his steadfast love,
for his wonderful works to humankind.
For he satisfies the thirsty,
and the hungry he fills with good things.

Psalm 107:4-9

QUERIES

In the silence, do fears and self-doubt or shame arise? What allows you to let these go? Have you ever tried to invite the "demons" into your cave as the hermit did in the ancient story? What was that like?

In the silence can you experience that you are loved? Can you imagine God's tenderness towards you? How might you be more tender towards yourself?

How have times of solitude satisfied your thirst for God and awareness of all that is holy? What gives your soul rest and refreshment?

TO BE BROKEN AND TENDER

24. Brokenness and Tenderness

This was on a seventhday, and he offering his house for a Meeting, we had the next day a pretty large one; for most of the town were at it. Here had never been a Meeting before, nor any within a great way; but this was a very precious one, many were tender, and confessed to the truth, and some received it; blessed be the Lord for ever.

George Fox, 1672[158]

He called the crowd with his disciples, and said to them, "If any want to become my followers, let them deny themselves and take up their cross and follow me. For those who want to save their life will lose it, and those who lose their life for my sake, and for the sake of the gospel, will save it... "

Mark 8:34, 35

QUERIES

How would you describe a Meeting which meets your deepest needs?

Does the concept of denying the self and taking up the cross hold any meaning for you? If so, how would you articulate that meaning? If not, how would you describe the experience of letting go of the ego and willingness to be faithful to the Light?

25. "Something Broken Got Fixed"

O my Friends and brethren in the pure life! be faithful to the Lord in returning him all the incomes of his Spirit; follow on in every drawing of his love, while any of the virtue of it lasts upon your spirits. Walk with him all the day long, and wait for him all the night season. And, in case of erring from

*him, or sinning grievously against him, be not discouraged; for he is a God
of mercies, and delighteth in pardoning and forgiving much and very often.
What tender mother can be more ready to forgive and embrace the child,
that appears broken and afflicted with her sore displeasure? Yea, He gives
brokenness, He melteth the heart, that he may tender towards, and embrace it
in his arms of reconciliation, and in the peace of his Spirit.*

*That ye may pass smoothly along from out of darkness and from under the
shadow of death, know this with me.*

Isaac Penington (n.d.)[159]

*The Lord is merciful and gracious,
slow to anger and abounding in steadfast love.
He will not always accuse,
nor will he keep his anger forever.
He does not deal with us according to our sins,
nor repay us according to our iniquities.
For as the heavens are high above the earth,
so great is his steadfast love toward those who fear him;
as far as the east is from the west,
so far he removes our transgressions from us.
As a father has compassion for his children,
so The Lord has compassion for those who fear him.
For he knows how we were made;
he remembers that we are dust.*

Psalm 103. 8-14

QUERIES

How have you experienced being broken? In what ways has that
been a healing experience? Has this been a path to forgiveness, of
yourself? Of others?

What allows you to stay open to the possibility of transformation
within yourself? Within others? Are you willing to speak of your
own beliefs and experiences? How do you support and encourage
others? Are you willing to be helped and challenged?

26. BREAKING THE FEAR OF DEATH

How great a Benefit do I enjoy, beyond many, I have such a large time of Preparation for Death, being daily dying, that I may live forever, with my God… My outward man daily wastes and moulders down, and draws towards his Place and Center, but my Inward man Revives and Mounts upward.

John Camm, 1656[160]

[Zechariah said] *By the tender mercy of our God, the dawn from on high will break upon us, to give light to those who sit in darkness and in the shadow of death, to guide our feet into the way of peace.*

Luke 1:78, 79

QUERIES

Have you thought about preparing yourself for death? What has that been like for you? If not, what do you imagine such work to be?

What fears arise when you consider dying? What might break those fears?

27. THAT WHICH MUST BE BROKEN BEFORE FINDING PEACE

And so we may see, when people are convinced, what variance it maketh in a family. This hath been seen and fulfilled, when a husband is convinced, or a wife is convinced, or son or daughter in a family is convinced. And this must be fulfilled, and interprets itself in the filling; for he brings a sword and war, and not peace to that nature they lived in, and had in old Adam, before they received the Prince of peace, and the sword of the spirit from him to war against the other peace which they had; and so the peace of all religions must be broken, before they come to the true religion from above; … and the peace of all fellowships must be broken, before they come into the fellowship of the spirit, and unity therein, which is the bond of peace; and the peace of all earthly teachers must be broken, who are made of men by natural tongues, before they come to the heavenly teacher, and the tongue of the learned indeed;

... And so the Lord preserve you in his fear, and give you wisdom from above, that you may be preserved in the unity of the spirit, which (as I said before) is the bond of peace, which is your duty to keep the peace of the Prince of princes.

George Fox, 1673[161]

Do not think that I have come to bring peace to the earth; I have not come to bring peace, but a sword ...

Matthew 10:34

QUERIES

What might Fox mean by his assertion that "the peace of all fellowships must be broken before they come into the fellowship of the spirit"? Does this resonate at all with your own experience?

Has your faith in any way alienated you from family or friends, or impelled you to act in ways that they disagree with? What has that experience been like for you? Have you found ways to reconcile with those individuals without compromising your faith?

28. GOD'S WAY AND HUMAN WILL

... for saith Christ, which is the Word of God, My sheep, hear my voice, and they follow me; and I the Word will give them eternal life, and none can pull them out of his hand, which is that living Word, from whence this testimony of mine proceedeth. Oh how my bowels [heart] *yernes in that living Word! Yea, that ye may not fall short, but be crowned with Immortality and glory.*

Sarah Jones, 1650[162]

Thomas said to him, "Lord, we do not know where you are going. How can we know the way?" Jesus said to him, "I am the way, and the truth, and the life."

John 14:5, 6

QUERIES

How do you understand faithfulness to the leadings of the Spirit? Do the words of Jesus, "I am the way, the truth and the life" hold meaning for you? Could you speak to this?

How would you describe the Way that you seek to follow? What is the role of Divine Guidance in that path?

29. BEING A FRIEND

...Yea the Winter is now through mercy, with many far spent, and the storms in measure over, and the spring time come, and the singing of Birds, and the voice of the Turtle is heard in our land. O! The glorious day that is dawned upon us, where the morning Stars do sing together, and all the Sons of God do shout for joy. Oh! The wonderful works of our God, and the noble Acts that he hath done; he hath made us see his wonders in the deep, and as Israel of old, to sing his praises: Oh, his tender dealings can never be raced out of our remembrance, he hath printed them in our hearts, and his engaging love constraineth us to speak well of him and make mention of his Name, and speak of his loving kindness and tender mercies which endureth forever!

Katharine Whitton, 1681[163]

When the righteous cry for help, the Lord hears, and rescues them in their troubles. The Lord is near to the brokenhearted, and saves the crushed in spirit.

Psalm 34:17, 18

QUERIES

What is at the core of your faith? Where do you find tenderness when your spirit feels broken?

How might anything which stands between you and God be broken? How might your heart become more tender?

GLOSSARY

AFSC. American Friends Service Committee (AFSC) was founded in 1917 to support alternative service for consciencious objectors in World War I and to offer food and other help to victims of war. AFSC was awarded the Nobel Peace Prize in 1947 on behalf of all Friends in recognition of Quakers' extensive relief work. AFSC continues to be a Quaker witness in the world against injustice.

BUSINESS MEETING. Friends conduct the business of the community as a meeting for worship with attention to business. All members, and in many meetings, attenders as well, are encouraged to participate in the monthly meetings for business where all major decisions are made. The intent of Friends business meetings is to determine where the Spirit is leading the group in this time and time place.

CALL TO MINISTRY. Many Friends experience a divine call to service, sometimes clearly and unmistakeable, more often through a gentle inward leading or nudge to take up a particular work. This may be in the form of work within the community such as pastoral care or teaching,or it may be a call to an outward witness which may lead a Friend to go to Iraq to work with the victims of war or devote themselves to ending the death penalty or any of an infinite other ways they might witness to God's love and mercy in the world.

CHURCH. Friends believe that the people are the church, not the building, thus many Friends speak of their worship space as the meetinghouse. Many Evangelical Friends speak of themselves as the Friends Church.

CLERK. The clerk of a meeting is the individual who presides at business meeting. The task of the clerk is to lay out the agenda, to listen for the sense of the meeting, then to name the decision that the community has come to. An individual may also clerk a committee, or be clerk of the governing board of a large organization.

EPISTLE. Yearly meetings, and at times other Quaker bodies, write epistles addressed to Friends around the world reporting on their annual sessions and noting how God is at work among them. Historically, individual Friends, such as George Fox would write epistles following the example of Paul and others in the Christian Testament.

EVANGELICAL FRIENDS. A term used to refer to Friends who belong to yearly meetings which profess belief in Jesus Christ and where Friends largely worship in programmed meetings. Often such Friends call themselves part of the Friends Church rather than the Religious Society of Friends.

FCNL. Friends Committee on National Legislation (FCNL) is the national Quaker lobbying organization on Capital Hill. FCNL staff lobbies directly on peace and justice issues and also provides information and training to aid Friends and supporters around the nation to lobby Congress. The FCNL Board, made up of Friends from all traditions around the nation, sets the policies and priorities for the organization.

FIRST DAY. Early Friends objected to the use of pagan names for the days and months and spoke only of "first day" instead of Sunday and "first month" instead of January.

LEADINGS. Movement of the Spirit guiding an individual to particular words or actions. A person may be led to speak during unprogrammed worship, or lead to undertake a concern, such as care for the homeless or witness against war.

LIBERAL FRIENDS. A term used to refer to Friends who are open to a range of theological belief and who are generally liberal on political and social issues. Most liberal Friends worship in unprogrammed meetings.

LIGHT. Friends initially called themselves "Children of the Light" referring to the Light of Christ which they believe is available to every person (see the first chapter of the Gospel of John), whether they know of Jesus or not. The Light is both a guide and a monitor and its transforming work is central

MEETING. The word "meeting" is used to refer to the time of worship on First Day mornings and to the community which worships together.

MEETINGHOUSE. The building where Friends worship is known as the meetinghouse and may be a home, an old factory building or a specially built structure, but is not held to be a consecrated space. Groups of Friends will worship in any space available.

MONTHLY MEETING. The basic worshipping community of Friends and the body in which membership is held. Members of a monthly meeting meet weekly for worship and monthly to conduct the business of the meeting.

PROGRAMMED. The majority of Friends worldwide today worship in a form similar to Protestant church services with hymn singing, Bible readings and a planned message (sermon) offered by the pastor. Since many of these churches, particularly in the U.S. hand out printed programs, the moniker "programmed" has become attached to this form of worship. Quaker pastors, however, will at times find they have no message to give and offer a longer period of "open" or "unprogrammed" worship where anyone may speak out of the silence as lead.

SACRAMENTS. Friends believe that the sacraments are an inward and spiritual experience. While the outward sacraments such as baptism and communion are not wrong, Friends have always held that the focus on the external bread and wine or water can get in the way of knowing the direct baptism of the Holy Spirit and the communion which is at the heart of every gathered meeting for worship.

TESTIMONIES. How one lives is central to Friends' faith and often Friends will use the term "testimonies" to refer to how their lives are a witness to the Light and Truth. In the late twentieth century, many Friends began to name the central testimonies as simplicity, peace, integrity, community, and equality (SPICE), concepts which underlie all dimensions of life.

UNPROGRAMMED. Friends' belief that God is available to all people without the need of a priest, or even the Bible, to mediate, lead to their unusual form of worship where individuals gather in expectant silence. In the silence, Friends listen for the movement of the Spirit and at times, an individual will feel words rising which he or she is led to offer to the gathered group as vocal ministry. A gathered or covered meeting is a time when many present are aware of the divine presence among them and a sense of communion. This may occur even if no words are spoken.

YEARLY MEETING. All the monthly meetings and worship groups in a region jointly form the yearly meeting. This body normally holds an annual meeting where Friends gather to worship together and conduct business of mutual interest. The yearly meeting has responsibility for creating the book of Faith and Practice used in that region. The yearly meeting normally has several Quarterly Meetings which meet three times a year for worship and fellowship in its geographic sub-regions.

ENDNOTES

1. Isaac Penington, "To Friends in Truth, In Chalfont, and thereabouts" (Letter, 1671), *Works of Isaac Penington, Vol. IV* (Glenside, PA: Quaker Heritage Press, 1997), p. 410.

2. Isaac Penington, "The Seed of God and of His Kingdom . . ." (n.d.), *Works of Isaac Penington, Vol. IV* (Glenside, PA: Quaker Heritage Press, 1997), p. 337.

3. Publications included: *On Visiting and Being Visited* (1984), *Handbook for Worship Groups* (1985) and *Survival Sourcebook* (1989).
4. *World Gathering of Young Friends, Epistle*, 1985. *http://www.quakersong.org/ wgyf_epistle/ Accessed 3/1/2010.*

5. Margaret Fell, *The Life of Margaret Fox, wife of George Fox, compiled from her own narrative, and other sources* (Philadelphia: The Association of Friends for the Diffusion of Religious and Useful Knowledge, 1859), p. 8. Another helpful quotations is in Margaret Fell "An Epistle to Friends" (1654) in Mary Garman, et al, eds., *Hidden in Plain Sight: Quaker Women's Writings 1650-1700* (Wallingford, PA: Pendle Hill Press, 1996), pp. 457-8.

6. Fell, *The Life of Margaret Fox, wife of George Fox*, p. 8.

7. Margaret Fell "An Epistle to Friends" (1654) in Garman, *Hidden in Plain Sight*, pp. 457-8.

8. John L. Nickalls, *Journal of George Fox* (Philadelphia: Religious Society of Friends, 1985), pp. 283, 367.

9. Nickalls, *Journal of George Fox*, p. 21.

10. Elizabeth Hendricks, "An Epistle to Friends in England," in Mary Garman, et al, eds., *Hidden in Plain Sight: Quaker Women's Writings 1650-1700* (Wallingford, PA: Pendle Hill Publications, 1996) p. 472.

11. Snell, *A Month with Isaac Penington*, Day Eight.

12. William Penn, *No Cross, No Crown*, Ronald Selleck, ed. (Richmond, IN: Friends United Press, 1981), pp. 45, 46.

13. According to dictionary definitions, enlightenment can be the process of shedding the light of truth and knowledge or freeing from ignorance; of being filled with spiritual light and insight; or it can refer to a philosophic movement of the 18th century "characterized by a lively questioning of authority, much theorizing in the sphere of politic, and emphasis on the empirical method in science."

14. "Even in the New Testament salvation can be physical and this-worldly." (Mark 5.34ff, Mark 10. 52ff) "... [here] Jesus proclaims that their faith has "saved" them; most recent translations correctly render the Greek verb *sozo* 'has made you well.' ... But the majority of occurrences in the New Testament of the Greek verb *sozo* ('to save') and its derivatives, especially the noun *soteria* ('salvation') have to do with the ultimate salvation of believers in Christ Jesus. The same phrase used in the stories of healing is also used of forgiveness of sin ... forgiveness of sin is a spiritual kind of healing concomitant with the physical restoration of health. For the one forgiven this spiritual healing is thus 'salvation' in the sense of admission into the kingdom of God understood as both a present and future reality. " Bruce M. Metzger and Michael D. Coogan, eds., *The Oxford Companion to the Bible* (New York: Oxford University Press, 1993), pp. 669, 670..

15. Patricia Loring, *Listening Spirituality, Vol. 1: Corporate Spiritual Practice Among Friends* (Washington, DC: Openings Press, 1999), p. 51.

16. John Calvi, *The Dance Between Hope and Fear: Healing From Trauma*, (Tallahassee, FL: Southeastern Yearly Meeting, 1995), p. 3.

17. Douglas V. Steere, "On Listening to One Another," in *Gleanings: A Random Harvest: Selected Writings by Douglas V. Steere* (Nashville, TN: The Upper Room, 1986), pp. 93, 94.

18. George Fox, Epistle, 1676, "Collection Of Many Select And Christian Epistles, Letters And Testimonies," in *Works of George Fox, Vol. 7 & 8, Earlham School of Religion, Digital Quaker Collection, http://dqc.esr.earlham.edu:8080/ xmlmm/search accessed 3/1/201.*

19. Nickalls, *Journal of George Fox*, p. 27.

20. Isaac Penington, "The Seed of God and of His Kingdom ," p. 341.

21. I recognize that Friends believe in and stress the centrality of the direct experience of God. However, starting in the 17th century, Friends also have articulated a particular understanding of the gospel message that underpins all the testimonies we hold dear. A definite theology flows through Fox's *Journal*. Robert Barclay wrote the most important, but not the only systematic theology. However, for the most part, our theology has been transmitted through story – through the journals of individual Quaker ministers – rather than through academic argumentation.

22. Elizabeth Bathurst, *Truth's Vindication* ... (London: T. Sowle, 1695), p. 120. Also published in part in Garman, *Hidden in Plain Sight*, p. 400.

23. Bathurst, *Truth's Vindication* ... pp. 400, 401.

24. These images come respectively from Deuteronomy 32:11 "As an eagle stirs up its nest, and hovers over its young; as it spreads its wings, takes them up, and bears them aloft on its pinions;" Matthew 23:37 "even as a hen gathers her brood under her wings;" Psalm 131 "But I have calmed and quieted my soul, like a weaned child with its mother."

25. Northwest Yearly Meeting of Friends Church, *Faith and Practice: A Book of Christian Discipline* (Newberg, OR: The Barclay Press, 1987), paraphrase from pp. 9-10.

26. The way I know, and thus the way I describe God, is in many ways closer to the biblical terminology used by the majority of Friends worldwide than to the words used by many of the individuals in my own Meeting. Yet I am uneasy speaking of God using the biblical language of kingship, priests, and a distinctly masculine hierarchy. Specific language aside, Friends' understanding of God is distinctly a New Testament one. I hope we can apply the Jewish tradition of lively argument about what some of those Old Testament stories really are about instead of dismissing them as so many of us in unprogrammed Meetings do. My attitude about stories such as that of Sodom and Gomorrah shifted when I was pushed to consider what it actually said about the importance of hospitality to strangers and wrongness of forced sex and let go my old impression that it was it was all about condemnation of homosexuality. See also, Catherine Griffith, "The Bible and Same-Sex Relationships," *Friends Journal*, Vol. 51, No. 1, January 2005, p. 12.

27. Nickalls, *Journal of George Fox*, pp. 39, 326-7.

28. The box on this page "The Light" is drawn from T. Canby Jones' and Henry Cadbury's compilation in *Annual Catalogue of George Fox's Papers*, No. 23 (Boston: Cambridge University Press, 1940), 51A, p. 47.

29. A version of this story was published by the Wider Quaker Fellowship (Philadelphia, 1999) as "What Does It Mean to Call Oneself A "Friend'?".

30. See Hugh Barbour, *Quakers in Puritan England* (Richmond, IN: Friends United Press, 1964), pp. 110-111. "Friends spoke of the Light, the Spirit, and Christ within so interchangeably that no uniform distinction can be made clear. Friends were not 'Christ-mystics' any more than they were seekers of mystical union with the Godhead. Their 'unity in the Eternal being' was their bond with other Friends . . The sense of a personal presence, of the inward fellowship of Christ's personality, was quite rare among early Friends. They called the Spirit 'it' more often than 'he.' . . The leading, which Friends obeyed, came as a personal voice, yet one without distinct personality: they reported that 'it was said to me,' hardly ever that 'Christ spoke.'"

31. Isaac Penington, *The Works of the Long-Mournful and Sorely-Distressed Isaac Penington, whom the Lord, in his tender Mercy, at length Visited and Relieved by the Ministry of that despised People called Quakers*, Vol II, (2nd Edition: London: Printed by Samuel Clark, for John and Thomas Kendall, Booksellers, 1761), pp. 268-270.

32. Nickalls. *Journal of George Fox*, p. 263.

33. All quotations from the 1656 letter of Fox are taken from Nickalls, *Journal of George Fox*, p. 263.

34. Nickalls, *Journal of George Fox*, p. 263.

35. As quoted in Hugh Barbour, *The Quakers in Puritan England* (Richmond, IN: Friends United Press, 1985), p. 166.

36. Nickalls, *Journal of George Fox*, p. 687.

37. Rufus Jones, *The Trail of Life in the Middle Years*, as quoted in David Hinshaw, *Rufus Jones: Master Quaker* (New York: G.P. Putnam's Sons, 1951), p. 220.

38. Tom Harpur, *The Pagan Christ: Recovering the Lost Light* (Toronto: Thomas Allen Publishers, 2004), pp. 24, 25.

39. *Nickalls, Journal* of George Fox, p. 65.

40. Isaac Penington, "The Seed of God and of His Kingdom . . ." (N.d.), p. 347.

41. Margaret Hope Bacon, *Wilt Thou Go on My Errand? Three 18th Century Journals of Quaker Women Ministers* (Wallingford, PA: Pendle Hill Publications, 1994), p. 198.

42. I take use of "spiritual maturity" from Dean Freiday's chapter on Perfection in *Barclay's Apology in Modern English*. (Manasquan, NJ, 1967). Also, in its biblical usage, "The word *perfect (teleios)* comes from *telos*, which means 'end,' 'goal,' or, 'limit.' Usually, it signifies 'attaining to the end – complete maturity.' Here, however, the comparison is made between God and his children; hence, the meaning must be expanded to include more than 'maturity.' This perfection must be a God-like quality of love and kindness even for those who do not deserve it, a quality that is possible for us to attain . . . ." Harold Lindsell, *New Revised Standard Version: Harper Study Bible expanded and updated* (Grand Rapids, MI: Zondervan Publishing House, 1991) footnote to Matthew 5:48.

43. Margaret Fell to James Nayler and Francis Howgill, 1653, in Elsa F. Glines, ed, *Undaunted Zeal: The Letters of Margaret Fell* (Richmond, IN: Friends United Press, 2003), pp. 23-24.

44. Isaac Penington, "A Further Testimony to the Truth . . ." (1680) *Works of*

Isaac Penington, Vol. IV (Glenside, PA: Quaker Heritage Press, 1997), p. 9.

45. Margaret Fell, "True Testimony" in Terry S. Wallace, *A Sincere and Constant Love* (Richmond, IN: Friends United Press, 1992). pp. 34-35.

46. Ibid.

47. Starhawk, *Truth or Dare: Encounters with Power, Authority and Mystery* (San Francisco: HarperSanFrancisco, 1987), p. 9 ff.

48. William Barclay, *New Testament Words: English New Testament Words Indexed with References to The Daily Study Bible* (Philadelphia: Westminster Press, 1974), pp. 178-188.

49. Stephen Mitchell, *Tao Te Ching: A new English translation* (New York: HarperPerennial, 1991). Another translation of Chapter 16, by Stephen Addiss and Stanley Lombardo, *Lao-Tzu, Tao Te Ching* (Cambridge, MA: Hackett, 1993) which sounds very different, reads:

Tao Te Ching (16)
Attain complete emptiness,
Hold fast to stillness.
The ten thousand things stir about;
I only watch for their going back.
Things grow and grow,
But each goes back to its root.
Going back to the root is stillness,
This means returning to what is.
Returning to what is
Means going back to the ordinary.
Understanding the ordinary:
Enlightenment.
Not understanding the ordinary:
Blindness creates evil.
Understanding the ordinary:
Mind opens.
Mind opening leads to compassion,
Compassion to nobility,
Nobility to heavenliness,
Heavenliness to Tao.
Tao endures.
Your body dies.
There is no danger.

50. Penn. *No Cross, No Crown*, p.19.

51. Nickalls, *Journal of George Fox*, p. 303.

52. Van A. Harvey, *A Handbook of Theological Terms: Their meaning and background exposed in over 300 articles* (New York: Collier Books, 1964), p. 33.

53. I draw on Eugene Teselle, "Atonement" in *A New Handbook of Christian Theology*, Donald W. Musser and Joseph L. Price, eds. (Nashville: Abingdon Press, 1992), p. 41ff; Van A. Harvey, *A Handbook of Theological Terms* (New York: Collier Books, 1964), pp. 33-35; and Wilmer A. Cooper, *A Living Faith* (Richmond, IN: Friends United Press, 1990), p. 38.

54. John Bowker, *The Oxford Dictionary of World Religions* (Oxford: Oxford University Press, 1997), pp. 107, 108.

55. Bowker, *Oxford Dictionary*, p. 107.

56. Wilmer A. Cooper, "Atonement" in *The Historical Dictionary of the Friends (Quakers)*, Margery Post Abbott, Mary Ellen Chijioke, Pink Dandelion, and John Oliver, eds. (Lanham, MD: The Scarecrow Press, 2003), p. 13, and Wilmer A. Cooper, *A Living Faith* (Richmond, IN: Friends United Press, 1990), p. 38, 43.

57. Isaac Penington, "Some Observations concerning the Priesthood of Christ," in *Works of Isaac Penington, Vol. 4* (Glenside, PA: Quaker Heritage Press, 1996), p. 104.

58. See Jeremiah 31:31 ff and Hebrews 8:8 ff.

59. George Fox, Epistle 10, 1652, "Collection Of Many Select And Christian Epistles, Letters And Testimonies," in *Works of George Fox, Vols. 7 & 8, ESR Digital Quaker Collection, http://dqc.esr.earlham.edu:8080/xmlmm/search,* accessed 3/1/2010.

60. Joseph Pickvance, *A Reader's Companion to George Fox's Journal* (Kelso, England: Curlew Productions, 1989), p. 97.

61. Penn, *No Cross, No Crown*, p. 120.

62. Penn, *No Cross, No Crown*, p. 128.

63. Isaac Penington, "An Examination of the Grounds or Causes Which are said to induce the Court of Boston in New England to make that order or law of banishment, upon pain of death, against the Quakers . . ." (1660) *Works of Isaac Penington, Vol. I* (Glenside, PA: Quaker Heritage Press, 1997), p. 348.

64. Rachel Hicks, *Memoire of Rachel Hicks* (New York: G.P. Putnam's Sons, 1880), pp. 7, 8.

65. Nickalls, *Journal of George Fox*, p. 18.

66. Penington, "Examination," p. 349.

67. Barbara Blaugdone, "An Account of the Travels, Sufferings & Persecutions of Barbara Blaugdone" in Garmen, *Hidden in Plain Sight*, p. 282.

68. Michael L. Birkel, *A Near Sympathy: The Timeless Quaker Wisdom of John Woolman* (Richmond, IN: Friends United Press, 2004), pp. 34, 35 and 57.

69. Birkel, *A Near Sympathy*, p. 60.

70. Birkel, *A Near Sympathy*, p.66.

71. Nickalls, *Journal of George Fox*, p. 19.

72. Robert Barclay, *A Catechism and Confession of Faith*, Dean Freiday and Arthur O. Roberts, eds. (Newberg, OR: The Barclay Press, 2001), p. 33.

73. Barclay, *Catechism*, p. 119.

74. 7000 Handmaidens of the Lord, "To the Parliament of England, who are set in place to do justice, to take off oppression and to stop the oppressors" in Garman, *Hidden in Plain Sight*, p. 62.

75. Dorothy White, "A Trumpet Sounded Out of the Holy City, . . .," in Garman, *Hidden in Plain Sight*, p. 148.

76. I often use the phrase "City of God" rather than the more prevalent "Kingdom of God" for a number of reasons. The primary one is that in the United States, as in much of the world, we no longer live in kingdoms. Thus I have chosen to focus on a place where people congregate and bump elbows with each other in numerous ways rather than use either the archaic "king" model or try to wade through the nuances of modern terminology of leadership. The City of God, the New Jerusalem, is a strong biblical image, particularly in Revelation.

77. Revelation has been a mystery over the centuries and used in many ways. Many scholars interpret Revelation as a vision of destruction of the Roman empire. Calvinists have used parts of this vision to determine that only 144,000 will be saved and everyone else will be damned, and yet others have developed into an elaborate allegory of how the earth will end with the Rapture—the bodily lifting of true believers into heaven and eventual, bloody destruction of everyone who has not accepted Christ Jesus.

78. Isaac Penington, *Way of Life and Death Made Manifest and Set Before Men* (Lodowick Lloyd, 1658), 1.17, as quoted in R. Melvin Keiser and Rosemary Moore, *Knowing the Mystery of Life Within* (London: Quaker Books, 2005), p. 214.

79. George Fox, "Journal Or Historical Account Of The Life, Travels, Sufferings,

Of George Fox," in *Works of George Fox, Volume 1 & 2, 1831, p.90. http://dqc.esr. earlham.edu:8080/xmlmm/search,* accessed 3/1/2010.

80. Nickalls, *Journal of George Fox,* p. 26.

81. Walter C. Smith (words), "Immortal, Invisible, God Only Wise," *Hymns of Christ and the Christian Life* (1876).

82. In this section I am indebted to the retreat described in Carol Luebering, *Job & Julian of Norwich: Trusting that all will be well* (Cincinnati, Ohio: St. Anthony Messenger Press, 1977).

83. George Fox, Epistle 200 "The Line of Righteousness . . ." in *The Power of the Lord is Over All*, T. Canby Jones, ed. (Richmond, IN: Friends United Press, 1989), p. 153-156.

84. William Edmondson, *The Journal {Abridged} of Wm. Edmondson:, Quaker Apostle to Ireland & the Americas, 1627-1712*, Caroline N. Jacob, ed. (Philadelphia: Philadelphia Yearly Meeting, 1968), p. 47. William Edmondson was born in England in 1627, served in the army and was convinced after moving to Ireland. This quotation describes the way he was treated, as a pacifist, during his travel in the ministry to the American colonies.

85. Larry Ingle, *First Among Friends*, as quoted by John Spears in "How would George Fox respond to terrorism?" *Friends Journal*, January 2005, p. 5.

86. Vernie Davis, "John Woolman and Structural Violence: Model for Analysis and Social Change" in Mike Heller, ed., *The Tendering Presence: Essays on John Woolman* (Wallingford, PA: Pendle Hill Publications, 2003), pp. 243-260.

87. Adam Curle, *True Justice: Peace Makers and Peace Making* (London: Quaker Home Service, 1981), p. 56ff.

88. Curle, *True Justice* p. 57.

89. Marcus Borg and John Dominic Crossan, *The Last Week: A Day by Day Account of Jesus' Final Week in Jerusalem* (New York: HarperCollins, 2006).

90. Gil Skidmore, "A History of the Quaker Testimonies," *The Friends Quarterly*, Vol 26, No. 5, January 1991, pp. 197-209.

91. Martin Luther King, *Letter from Birmingham Jail* (April 16, 1963) as cited in Jane E. Calvert, "Political Obligation and Civil Dissent," *Quaker Religious Thought*, nos. 106-107, November 2006, pp. 75-76.

92. Based on a statement attributed to Richard Baxter, a 17th century opponent of Friends.

93. James Nayler, "Concerning the fall of man and concerning light and life."

in *Love To The Lost,* (1656, A collection of sundry books, epistles and papers), (London. J. Sowle, 1715), pp. 260-61.

94. George Fox, *Works of George Fox, Vol VII. Epistles, Vol. I. 1653,* (New Foundation, 1990), Epistle 33, 40, as quoted in Anne Adams, ed. *The Creation Was Open To Me: An anthology of Friends' writings on that of God in all creation,* (Wilmslow, England: Quaker Green Concern, 1996), pp. 86, 87.

95. *Webster's New Universal Unabridged Dictionary* (New York: Barnes & Noble, 1996), p. 1917.

96. Science & Environmental Health Network, "Precautionary Principle", posted 2008, accessed 4/7/2008, http://www.sehn.org/precaution.html. The January 1998 Wingspread Statement on the Precautionary Principle reads: "When an activity raises threats of harm to human health or the environment, precautionary measures should be taken even if some cause and effect relationships are not fully established scientifically. In this context the proponent of an activity, rather than the public, should bear the burden of proof. The process of applying the precautionary principle must be open, informed and democratic and must include potentially affected parties. It must also involve an examination of the full range of alternatives, including no action."

97. William Penn, "No Cross, No Crown," in *Collection of the works of William Penn, Vol. 1 (1726)* p. 296, *http://dqc.esr.earlham.edu:8080/xmlmm/search,* accessed 3/1/201.

98. Margaret Fell, *Works of Margaret Fell,* pp. 95, 136; quoted in Hugh Barbour, *The Quakers in Puritan England* (New Haven: Yale University Press, 1964), p. 98.

99. William Penn, *No Cross, No Crown,* in Collection *of the works of William Penn (Volume 1)* (1726), page 296. Earlham School of Religion Digital Quaker Collection http://dqc.esr.earlham.edu:8080/xmlmm/search, accessed 2/24/2010.

100. Mary Penington, *Experiences in the life of Mary Penington (written by herself),* (London: Friends Historical Society, 1992 reprint), p. 22.

101. Nickalls, *Journal of George Fox,* p.346.

102. Steve Smith *A Quaker in the Zendo* (Wallingford, PA, Pendle Hill Pamphlet # 370, 2004), p.13.

103. Smith, *Zendo,* p 14.

104. Douglas Gwyn, *The Covenant Crucified: Quakers and the Rise of Capitalism,* (Wallingford, PA: Pendle Hill Publications, 1995), p. 373, 102-6; Gwyn, *Seekers*

Found: Atonement in Early Quaker Experience (Wallingford, PA: Pendle Hill Publications, 2000), p. 249; Gwyn, *The Covenant Crucified*, p 105.

105. George Fox, Epistle # 10, 1652, in T. Canby Jones, ed., *"The Power of the Lord is Over All:" The Pastoral Letters of George Fox* (Richmond, IN: Friends United Press, 1989), p. 7.

106. Isaac Penington, undated, unaddressed letter, in Snell, *A Month With Isaac Penington,* Day Eight.

107. Jennifer Elam, *Dancing With God* (Wallingford, PA: Pendle Hill Pamphlet # 344, 1999), pp. 38, 39.

108. William Penn, *The Rise and Progress of the People Called Quakers* (Richmond, IN: Friends United Press, 1976) pp. 74, 75.

109. Hannah Whitall Smith, *The Christian's Secret of a Happy Life* (Chicago: The Christian Witness Company, 1885), Chapter 12.

110. Jelalludin Rumi, *Unseen Rain,* translated by Kieran Kavanaugh, OCD, and Otilio Rodriquez, OCD (New York: Paulist Press, 1979) Chap. II, no. 8. p. 42. as cited in Maria Jaoudi, *Christian and Islamic Spirituality* (New York: Paulist Press, 1993), p. 35.

111. Hannah Whitall Smith, *The Christian's Secret of a Happy Life* (Chicago: The Christian Witness Company, 1885) chapter 12.

112. George Fox, "Journal or Historical Account of The Life, Travels, Sufferings, of George Fox," in *Works of George Fox, Vol. 1 & 2 (1831), p. 131. http://dqc.esr. earlham.edu:8080/xmlmm/search, accessed 3/1/2101.*

113. Janeal Turnbull Ravndal, *A Very Good Week Behind Bars* (Wallingford, PA: Pendle Hill Pamphlet # 380, 2005).

114. Isaac Penington, from a general, undated letter to Friends, Snell, *A Month with Isaac Penington,* p. 10.

115. Joe Franko, "Coming Out for Christ," *Friends Bulletin,* March 2008, pp. 3-7.

116. Peggy Senger Parsons, "Geek Squad Jesus," *UPI Religion and Spirituality Website,* 3/4/08. http://www.religionandspirituality.com/.

117. John Camm, expressions shared during a considerable time of illness, as recorded in John Tompkins & John Fields, eds., *Piety Promoted* (Dublin, 1721), p. 22.

118. Silva, Mira and Shyam Mehta, *Yoga the Inengar Way* (New York: Alfred A. Knopf, 1997), p. 150.

119. Reginald Reynolds, *The Wisdom of John Woolman* (London: Quaker Home

Service, 1988), p. 39.

120. John Woolman, *The Journal of John Woolman and A Plea for the Poor, The John Greenleaf Whittier Edition Text* (New York: Corinth Books, 1961), p. 184.

121. Britain Yearly Meeting, *Quaker Faith and Practice* (London: Friends Home Service, 1994), Advices and queries 1.02.29.

122. Lucy Screechfield McIver, *A Song of Death, Our Spiritual Birth: A Quaker Way of Dying,* (Wallingford, PA: Pendle Hill Pamphlet No. 340, 1998).

123. Dying testimony of Edward Burroughs, from Tompkins and Fields, *Piety Promoted*, pp. 29-32, as quoted in McIver, *A Song of Death*, p. 15.

124. William Penn, *The Death-bed of a young Quaker* (Boston: Pierce and Parker, 1833), p. 17.

125. George Fox, "Collection of Many Select and Christian Epistles, Letters and Testimonies," in *Works of George Fox, Vol. 7 & 8 (1831)*, p. 50. *http://dqc.esr. earlham.edu:8080/xmlmm/search*, accessed 3/1/2010.

126. Elise Boulding "The Family as a Way into the Future" in *One Small Plot of Heaven* (Wallingford, PA: Pendle Hill Publications, 1989), pp. 211, 212.

127. Garman, *Hidden in Plain Sight*, p. 36, 37.

128. Stephen Mitchell, Tao Te Ching (New York: HarperPerennial, 1988).

129. Katharine Whitton, "An Epistle to Friends Everywhere" in Garman, *Hidden in Plain Sight*, p. 505.

130. Isaac Penington, "To Friends in Truth, In Chalfont, and Thereabouts," (Letter, 1671) *Works of Isaac Penington, Vol. IV* (Glenside, PA: Quaker Heritage Press, 1997), p. 410.

131. Isaac Penington, "The Seed of God and of His Kingdom . . .," page 337.

132. Margaret Fell, *The Life of Margaret Fox*, p. 8. Another helpful quotation is in Margaret Fell's "An Epistle to Friends" (1654) in Garman, *Hidden in Plain Sight* pp. 457-8.

133. Elizabeth Hendricks, "An Epistle to Friends in England," in Garman, *Hidden in Plain Sight*, pp. 471-472.

134. Penn, *No Cross, No Crown*, pp. 45, 46.

135. George Fox, Epistle, 1676, "Collection Of Many Select And Christian Epistles, Letters And Testimonies," in *Works of George Fox, Vol. 7 & 8, Earlham School of Religion, Digital Quaker Collection, http://dqc.esr.earlham.edu:8080/ xmlmm/search* accessed 3/1/2010.

136. Isaac Penington, "The Seed of God and of His Kingdom . . ," p. 341.

137. Nickalls, *Journal of George Fox*, p. 39, p. 326-7.

138. Nickalls. *Journal of George Fox*, p. 263.

139. Nickalls, *Journal of George Fox*, p. 687.

140. Isaac Penington, "The Seed of God and of His Kingdom . . ." (N.d.) *Works of Isaac Penington, Vol. IV* (Glenside, PA: Quaker Heritage Press, 1997), p. 347.

141. Margaret Fell to James Nayler and Francis Howgill, 1653, in Elsa F. Glines, Undaunted Zeal, pp. 23, 24

142. Isaac Penington, "Testimony," page 9.

143. Fell, "True Testimony," in Wallace, *A Sincere and Constant Love*, pp. 34, 35.

144. Nickalls, *Journal of George Fox*, p. 303.

145. Isaac Penington, "An Examination," p. 348.

146. Barbara Blaugdone, "An Account of the Travels, Sufferings & Persecutions of Barbara Blaugdone" in Garman, *Hidden in Plain Sight*, p. 282.

147. Dorothy White, "A Trumpet Sounded Out of the Holy City," in Garman, *Hidden in Plain Sight*, p. 148.

148. 7000 Handmaidens of the Lord, "To the Parliament of England, who are set in place to do justice, to take off oppression and to stop the oppressors," in Garman, *Hidden in Plain Sight*, p. 62.

149. George Fox, "Journal Or Historical Account Of The Life, Travels, Sufferings, Of George Fox," in *Works of George Fox, Volume 1 & 2, 1831, p.90*. *http://dqc.esr.earlham.edu:8080/xmlmm/search, accessed 3/1/2010.*

150. William Edmondson, *The Journal (Abridged) of Wm. Edmondson: Quaker Apostle to Ireland & the Americas, 1627-1712*, Caroline N. Jacob, ed. (Philadelphia: Philadelphia Yearly Meeting, 1968), p. 47.

151. Margaret Fell, "A Declaration and an Information from Us, The People Called Quakers," in Wallace, *A Sincere and Constant Love*, p.51.

152. James Nayler, "Concerning the fall of man and concerning light and life" in *Love To The Lost* [1656] (London. J. Sowle, 1715), pp. 260-261.

153. George Fox, *Works of George Fox, Vol VII. Epistles, Vol. I. 1653* (New Foundation, 1990) Epistle 33, 40 as quoted in Anne Adams, ed. *The Creation Was Open To Me: An anthology of Friends' writings on that of God in all creation* (Wilmslow, England: Quaker Green Concern, 1996), p. 86, 87.

154. William Penn, "No Cross, No Crown," in *Collection of the works of William*

Penn, Vol. 1(1726) p. 296, http://dqc.esr.earlham.edu:8080/xmlmm/search, accessed 3/1/201.

155. Nickalls, *Journal of George Fox,* p.346.

156. Isaac Penington, undated, unaddressed letter, in Snell, *A Month with Isaac Penington,* Day Eight.

157. William Penn, *The Rise and Progress of the People Called Quakers,* (Richmond, IN: Friends United Press, 1976) pp. 74, 75.

158. George Fox, "Journal or Historical Account of The Life, Travels, Sufferings, of George Fox," in *Works of George Fox, Vol. 1 & 2 (1831), p. 131. http://dqc.esr. earlham.edu:8080/xmlmm/search,* accessed 3/1/2101.

159. Isaac Penington, from a general, undated letter to Friends in Snell, *A Month with Isaac Penington,* p. 10.

160. John Camm, expressions shared during a considerable time of illness, as recorded in Tompkins & Fields, *Piety Promoted,* p. 22.

161. George Fox, "Collection of Many Select and Christian Epistles, Letters and Testimonies," in *Works of George Fox, Vol. 7 & 8 (1831), p. 50. http://dqc.esr. earlham.edu:8080/xmlmm/search,* accessed 3/1/2010.

162. Garman, *Hidden in Plain Sight,* pp. 36, 37.

163. Katharine Whitton, "An Epistle to Friends Everywhere" in Garman, *Hidden in Plain Sight,* p. 505.

Author Margery Post Abbott is a released Friend from Multnomah Monthly Meeting in Portland, Oregon. She has traveled among Friends in Intermountain Yearly Meeting as the Brinton Visitor and taught at Pendle Hill and Woodbrooke, among other venues. Marge has written several books and pamphlets, including *Walk Worthy of Your Calling* (with Peggy Senger Parsons), *A Certain Kind of Perfection,* and *Christianity and the Inner Life* (Pendle Hill pamphlet # 402). She has also edited and co-edited numerous books, including the *Historical Dictionary of the Friends (Quakers)*. After completing service as clerk of Friends Committee on National Legislation, she is now clerk for the Friends World Committee for Consultation Steering Committee, organizing a worldwide consultation on global change.

Order these other titles from us online at WesternFriend.org

Enlivened by the Mystery: Quakers and God

edited by Kathy Hyzy

"How have you experienced God or the Divine?"
With this query, Western Friend invited Quakers across the Western US to share their stories through art, poetry, fiction and essays. The contributions of over fifty Friends are gathered in this testament to the breadth of spiritual experience in the Religious Society of Friends.

Compassionate Listening
and Other Writings by Gene Knudsen Hoffman

edited by Anthony Manousos

Quaker Gene Knudsen Hoffman dedicated much of her life to seeking out the deep, psychological causes of violence and to helping bring about healing and reconciliation through a process she calls "Compassionate Listening." Her work inspired Leah Green to begin The Compassionate Listening Project, whose workshops have taught hundreds of people how to listen with their hearts and well as minds. This collection of writings sheds light on Hoffman's life and inspiration.

EarthLight: Spiritual Wisdom for an Ecological Age

edited by Cindy Spring and Anthony Manousos

Founded and inspired by Quakers, *EarthLight* magazine featured articles by the world's seminal figures in secular and religious thought about the place and participation of humankind in creation. This anthology embodies the best of *EarthLight* and of Quaker writers on spirituality and ecology during the past twenty years. Contributors include Maya Angelou, Thomas Berry, Jim Corbett, Joanna Macy, Terry Tempest Williams and many others.

Western Quaker Reader: Writings by and About Independent Quakers in the Western US, 1929-1999

edited by Anthony Manousos

This collection provides vivid, first-person testimonies by Friends involved in the "reinvention" of Quakerism in the Western USA from the 1930's to the present. This is the first historical work about Western Quakerism written from the viewpoint of Independent Friends, and the only one that describes the development of Intermountain and North Pacific Yearly Meetings—some of the most vital, lively Yearly Meetings in the USA today.

nigsville, PA USA
une 2010
711BV00001B/4/P